8856

915.2
E64s

Epton, Nina Consuelo.
Seaweed for breakfast; a picture of Japanese life today.
New York, Dodd, Mead ₁1964, °1963₁

xiii, 268 p. illus., ports., map. 22 cm.

1. Japan—Soc. life & cust.   ɪ. Title.

DS821.E65   1964   915.2   64–14331

Library of Congress   ₁5₁

Seaweed
For
Breakfast

Seaweed For Breakfast

A PICTURE OF
JAPANESE LIFE TODAY

Nina Epton

Illustrated with photographs

DODD, MEAD & COMPANY

NEW YORK

First published in the United States February 1964

Library of Congress Catalog Card Number: 64-14331
Printed in the United States of America

To

Rachel and

Reginald Cudlipp

in friendship

Acknowledgments

$\mathcal{I}$ wish to express my grateful thanks to: Mr T. Wada, Chief of the Cultural and Information service of the Japanese Foreign Office in Tokyo, who invited me to Japan, and to Mr Kei Miyakawa, the Cultural Attaché of the Japanese Embassy in London, through whose good offices the invitation was extended to me and who, both before and after my journey to Japan, supplied me with so much valuable background material.

In Tokyo, my stay was made possible by the invitations of Mrs Hazue Matsuo, President of the Japan Women's International Association and various members of the latter. I must also thank Miss Yoko Matsuoka, the indefatigable, efficient and helpful Secretary of the Japan P.E.N., who introduced me to so many interesting people, Mr Hideto Mori, without whose assistance I could never have seen the slums of Tokyo, and our interpreter Mr Noboru Kojima of the Kyodo News Service; Miss Kikuko Harada, the tireless Secretary of the Housewives' Federation, Mr Hessell Tiltman, the correspondent of the *Guardian* who so generously spared time to talk to me about his vast experience of the country and its people, my Foreign Office guide Miss Kazuko Iino, who accompanied me throughout the fortnight of my official visit, and Mr Koichi Tsutsumi, of the Cultural and Information department, who went to great trouble to arrange interviews for me with a large number of people.

In Kyoto, the assistant Mayor, Mr Shoichiro Yoshimura, kindly showed me round his beautiful city. Mr Francis King, the Director of the British Council, acted as friend, counsellor, host and letter-box, as he does to the far too many visitors who take advantage of his kindness; Miss Dorothy Dessau, the devoted American social worker, found time to help me *and* some of my Japanese friends in need of her professional advice; the Kyoto City government officials, Mr Hisao Morita, Chief of the Foreign Affairs section and Mr Masuo Yamaguchi, sub-chief of the Foreign Affairs section, kindly introduced me to sociologist Hidetoshi Kato and anthropologist Toshinao Yoneyama and others who were of invaluable assistance to me.

My hosts and friends in Dazaifu, Kumamoto, Niigata, Kahoku and Yamagata are mentioned in the course of this book. I can never thank them enough for their hospitality, generosity and unfailing friendliness.

Mr Frank H. Agui, Director, Foreign Department, and Mr Shotei Saito, Assistant Manager, Foreign Department, of the Japan Tourist Association, were of the greatest help in arranging my itineraries, with the generous co-operation of the Japanese National Railways.

Contents

Illustrations

Following page 144

Introduction

*W*hen I received an invitation to visit Japan from the Japanese Foreign Office in Tokyo, through their London Embassy, I was delighted at the prospect of seeing a country which had attracted me for so long. Since the invitation was for a fortnight only, I made private arrangements to stay on in Japan in order to collect material for a book.

Excellent travel books are published almost every year by people who know Japan intimately and have had the good fortune to live in that country for some time, but it seemed to me that very few of them give an unbiased picture of contemporary Japanese life and people.

In Great Britain, despite Press reports about Japan's amazing post-war industrial achievements, many people tend to look upon the Japanese either as ruthless business men or as rather quaint *objets d'art*; both views are tinged by wartime prejudices and memories. What are the Japanese like today, seventeen years after the war and Hiroshima? That is what I wanted to find out and I believed that the only way to do so was to live in Japanese style, with Japanese families.

I sent a letter to the editor of the English-language *Asahi Evening News* asking whether any Japanese families would accept me as a guest in return for English conversation lessons. I had read that the Japanese are eager to learn English—just how eager they are will become transparent in the following account of my experiences. My story begins after my fortnight's official tour, when I began to keep a sporadic journal to which afterthoughts were added later, on my first night in a private Japanese home. . . .

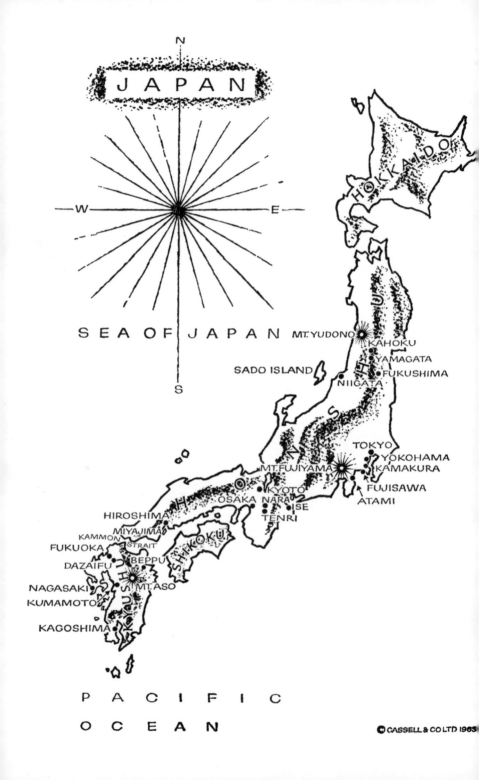

PART I

Ten

Million Japanese:

Tokyo

Kokoshi doll

Reflections
in a Japanese
bedroom

March 20th   *This* is my first night in a Japanese home, away from palatial hotels, American tourists sparing a week for Japan on a world tour, carefully appraising western business men and their cautiously taciturn Japanese guide-interpreters; away from what passes for western food served with trepidation by diminutive waiters and fluttering waitresses in kimono to whom our sharp cutlery appears to gleam as ferociously as weapons.

Wooden chopsticks have a gentler feel and are more harmonious, slender twins to be manipulated in close proximity with one hand, presented side by side in a narrow envelope inscribed with characters that look like a talisman to ward off the evil spirits capable of causing indigestion; moreover, chopsticks are personal. Once you have used them in a restaurant, nobody else will, they become your exclusive property. I am not yet mistress of my chopsticks; they still tend to elude me, to slip from my awkward fingers and wander off on their own among the grains of rice in my bowl, at times throwing them up disdainfully in an unelegant and unJapanese manner as if to imply: 'See how this barbarian mismanages us! We who are so delicate and feminine and need firm, guiding fingers to play us.' I shall learn. The day will come when I too shall be able to pick up peas, daintily, one by one, with my mastered, docile chopsticks, as children are taught to do under their devoted mother's observant eye.

I am in a Japanese home, secure from the reckless avalanche of Tokyo's traffic and the wild taxi-drivers, all potential *kamikaze* pilots in a war which nobody here wants or anticipates, for the accent is on peace. It is because of an article on peace in a Japanese magazine that I am in this house. The article, written by my present hostess, Mrs Hazue Matsuo, President of the Japan Women's International Association, induced me to ask her whether she would accept a foreigner in her home. Her assent came almost by return, signed in Japanese, because Mrs Matsuo does not know English.

It is brave of her to have me. The only other people in the household who speak a few words of English are her young daughter-in-law, Michiko, who learned the language at college and is therefore better equipped to translate Shakespeare into Japanese than to carry on an everyday conversation, and the gardener, a university graduate, who cannot find a job commensurate with his diploma and has been befriended by the Matsuos.

One finds university graduates filling all kinds of unlikely jobs in Japan where competition is keen and life is so earnest; there are seventy-two universities where quality of tuition varies. Tokyo university has the highest prestige value and the strain to pass the entrance examination takes its toll of young people's mental health. It has been estimated that four per cent of the incoming students suffer from mental disorders requiring medical treatment.

It is a curious sensation to be in a Japanese house, with a Japanese family, where no conversation is possible; it is like being invited to take part in an Eastern 'Method' play in which I have been cast in the role of a mute foreigner while the rest of the cast unravel the plot.

I caught a brief glimpse of Mr Matsuo tonight. He disappeared soon after dinner, which I ate in the company of my hosts, served by their daughter-in-law and a rosy-cheeked servant girl in pigtails who comes from the country and occasionally utters a few words in English—she has been to high school where English is taught for five hours a week—and giggles uncontrollably every time she comes into the room as if my presence were a great joke. In a way, I suppose it is. I have not yet become moulded to the decor; I feel that I am the wrong shape for a Japanese home.

In their youth, Mr and Mrs Matsuo were actors. The theatre united them and although they are as undemonstrative as all other Japanese couples—who never kiss each other in public or in front of the family—one senses that a deep affection binds them; I am sure they had no need of a *nakodo* or go-between to arrange their marriage, except as a pure face-saving formality.

Nowadays, however, Mr Matsuo is a successful impresario and theatre owner. He travels abroad and brings back troupes of exotic artistes: Mexican dancers, Red Indians and American cowboys who, after being met at Haneda airport by the entire Matsuo family down to their exquisite two-year-old granddaughter Emmi-san, clad in miniature, doll-like kimono, perform in the Matsuo theatres of Tokyo, Osaka and 'Dreamland'—a Disney fantasy created by Mr Matsuo in the vicinity of historical Nara.

Mr Matsuo is a self-made man; he has had little education. Although this lack does not appear to have hampered him, he is nevertheless anxious to assist poor students to attain the eagerly sought objective of a university education and he finances thirty of them at Tokyo University.

Perhaps it is because of their theatrical background that Mr and Mrs Matsuo are so unlike the cliché-image of the formal, reserved, middle-aged Japanese couple. Mr Matsuo is tall, sixtyish, still slim and handsome; he wears a benevolent expression and he smiles easily, which is unusual for a middle-aged Japanese. Most Japanese men of his age look harassed or dispirited until they are roused by a few thimblefuls of *sake* or the adolescent playfulness of hard-working geishas. I am sorry that I am unable to talk to him. He looks fatherly and he encourages confidences. Few Japanese men look fatherly when they approach middle age; they are too withdrawn and self-centred. Young men with infants look more paternal although their wives do most of the carrying on their round, fragile backs.

Mrs Matsuo must be in her late fifties, her hair is greying, she is a grandmother and wears kimonos in subdued shades of lavender and old gold; any woman in Japan past the age of forty—indeed, even before—is considered to be old and expected to behave accordingly, but Mrs Matsuo's movements and gestures are gracefully youthful. It is a pleasure to watch her lowering herself on to a cushion on the *tatami* (rice straw mat) like a butterfly condescending to be momentarily earthborne, or tripping eagerly along the corridor to answer the telephone in small, slippered feet, hands half-raised, fingers curled delicately as chrysanthemum petals.

Japan is a damp country and there must be many sufferers from rheumatism, but I have never seen anybody deformed by that complaint. All the Japanese grandmothers I have met are surprisingly agile, sometimes more so than younger people who go in for western gymnastics and look so stiff in western clothes which accentuate their flat chests and thin shoulders.

A woman's figure is transformed by the kimono and the posture appropriate to the wearing of it into an inverted S. To be sure, one sees old ladies in the countryside bent almost double after years of bearing loads on backs which nature intended for nothing heavier than a few bamboo sticks but, with this exception, no Japanese woman walks stiffly or crabwise like the arthritics of the West.

The Japanese have an inferiority complex about their small stature and the women fall for any foreigner who is a few inches taller than their own men. The old Japanese court costumes for men, now only worn by priests in Shinto shrines or Kabuki actors, built up the masculine figure through layers of shimmering silks and brocades. Shorn of these, the average Japanese man looks inconspicuous, unless he happens to be a sumo wrestler, gorged like a *pâté de foie*-producing French goose, on vast quantities of meat and rice.

If flowers could walk, they would no doubt walk like Japanese ladies in kimono, who give the impression that they have been plucked off a stalk and are still a little unsure how to advance. One would expect men to be for ever rushing forward to assist them. In fact, however, Japanese men avert their eyes and keep their hands to their sides. They never help anybody.

If they do (some of them have read western books on etiquette) they are likely to cause embarrassment. Japanese women are not used to being pampered. It is the westerner who treats them like fragile flowers, not the Japanese.

Mrs Matsuo, in addition to being an expert dancer and hostess, is as warm-hearted as her husband and she finds time to impart the secrets of her willowy grace to a little band of widows who, in the privacy of a Japanese inn, meet once a week to learn dancing from her. Although Japanese widows have never been expected to per-form *suttee*, society believes that they should live in semi-mourning; it is considered improper to remarry (only widowers are encouraged to) and it is considered very proper to visit temples and shrines as the elderly 'incense guests' used to do in pre-revolutionary China. Religion and old age are bracketed. Young or middle-aged women whom I question on religious topics often reply, half-reproach-fully, as if my query implied a veiled insult, 'We are not old enough to take an interest in these things.'

Behind the sliding-door of the room in which I am sleeping is a superb, highly gilded Buddhist altar, concealed behind a fitted cupboard. Michiko, the daughter-in-law, opened it for me this afternoon and showed me the image of the seated Buddha, the memorial tablets, the lacquered offering table with its minute bowls of rice and vases of flowers before which the devout are supposed to bow and recite prayers every morning. Above the altar are suspended photographs of the Matsuo's parents and of Michiko's grandparents. Every religion that enters Japan sooner or later falls under the influence of Shinto, ancestor-worship, and Buddhism is no exception. Ancestors, one feels, are more important than Buddha.

The Japanese like to tell you, with a gleam of pride in their malicious eyes, followed by a meaningful expression which conjures up memories of bloody western crusades and religious wars, that they are a religiously tolerant people. It would probably be nearer the truth to say that they are indifferent and non-metaphysical. As a Japanese daily wrote a little while ago, referring to a controversial Japanese film depicting the life of Buddha, which offended so many of their more orthodox fellow-Asians, 'Indifference and laxity can easily creep into the Japanese types of Buddhism, and the Japanese tend to forget that many Buddhists in other Asian countries are living an admirable religious life and following the precepts of Buddhism faithfully.'

The President of the motion picture company responsible for this film was said to be a devout Buddhist, but 'the production of the film represented an ambitious venture to outstrip Cecil B. De Mille' and was considered altogether too lush. Protests were made by six chiefs of diplomatic missions in Tokyo representing Ceylon, Burma, Thailand, Laos, India and Pakistan. The Japanese daily concluded: 'It would have been better, however, if the Japanese Buddhists had made the first move.'

Religion here has always been centred in the family with its long lineage reaching back to a mythical past. This is not unknown in the West. An English family, the Pilkingtons of Windle, preserve a lineage going back to the Saxon goddess of the waning moon, which its present-day representatives are prepared to accept as valid, but this is an exceptional case.

Many Japanese are still in the animistic stage which we abandoned long ago and for which I have a sneaking, irrational sympathy. I like their custom of praying once a year for the souls of the

departed salmon which have been canned by modern methods; I
think it is a charming idea to hold an annual festival in honour of
used and broken needles which have rendered good service
throughout the year, and a touching gesture on the part of a private
railway company to allow an old locomotive to have a last run and
to thank it for services rendered before dispatching it to the scrap
heap.

Michiko is the perfect Japanese wife, mother, and daughter-in-
law: gentle, submissive, dutifully playing second fiddle to her
mother-in-law, patient with her two small children who crawl over
everything and everybody, affectionate with her husband, the
Matsuo's son, a well-built, serious young man whom I have hardly
seen, for he helps his father and belongs to the 'life is earnest'
brigade who leave for work early and return home late. The young
couple take their meals together. They are fortunate that the house
is large and there are several servants, so that mother-in-law
trouble—marital problem number one in Japan—does not arise; it
is difficult to imagine that it would ever arise, even under different
circumstances, with such a good-natured and pliable person as Mrs
Matsuo.

Emmi-san, Mrs Matsuo's two-year-old granddaughter, and I,
have something in common, which draws us together: neither of
us can speak Japanese. Emmi-san, however, has the advantage of
understanding a good deal of that language. As she has already met
a number of foreigners, she did not open her eyes in astonishment
and stare at me fixedly as less worldly Japanese infants are liable to
do when they first see me. She is a budding dancer; to see her tiny
bottom wriggling in imitation of the Twist she sees on television
sends us into peals of laughter. This evening I taught her some of
the steps of the Highland fling, which are quite different from anything she has seen before. Emmi-san watched me, fascinated,
carefully observed the foot and leg-lifting movements, clapped her
little hands, chirruped with glee, and then began to imitate me—
not at all unsuccessfully. When I gave up, exhausted from the
unaccustomed effort, she ran up to the chair in which I had
thrown myself and drew me up again with an emphatic tug of her
small but forceful hands. (A further example of Japanese imitative
genius is the Japanese girl worker in a Limerick factory who
recently ran off with most of the prizes in a National Irish Dance
Contest.)

Japanese infants generally look more mature than western ones but our children catch them up and by the time both reach their teens there is a marked difference: our adolescents are much more sophisticated. Teenage Japanese girls look as sexless and innocent as Eve before the Fall and it is difficult to determine their age. Their lack of bosoms emphasizes their sexlessness, which adults help to overcome by means of falsies. The bosomy stars of western films have made Japanese women self-conscious about their deficiencies which they attribute to under-nourishment and tight *obis*. It was recently announced, however, by official collectors of odd statistics, that the Japanese woman's bust is expanding. From an average of 30·1 a decade ago it has now reached 31·5. It is expected that figures will continue to improve now that people are eating more and better food. (Girls with heavy busts and light morals are in great demand for 'art photography' in the dubious studios of Tokyo that cater for passing foreign tourists who wish to photograph them in the nude. Colour photographs, they advertise, are processed in one day.)

The house I am living in is situated in the residential area of Minato-ku. It is surrounded by a fairly high wall (the Japanese, like the English, keep their home life private whenever they can, although few people can afford to) and divided into a traditional, Japanese style of dwelling with a western-style annexe. In this annexe, where the ladies of the International Association meet over sandwiches and coffee, everybody sits on chairs at a high table. In the other part of the house, where I am sleeping, we sit on cushions at a table approximately ten inches high under which, when I grow tired of adopting a Japanese posture, i.e. sitting on my heels, I stretch my legs. (For the time being I cannot kneel longer than five minutes at a time. An excruciating pain darts down the upper part of my thighs, while another jabs at my ankles and ends by making my feet go numb. We must be made differently from the Japanese. How is it, for instance, that they can eat rice three times a day and remain slim whereas I immediately begin to put on weight?)

In Japan, one's degree of foreignness is measured by the replies given to the following stock questions:

Can you sit on *tatami*? (i.e. in Japanese posture)
What do you think of Japanese toilets?
Do you like raw fish?

For the moment, my answer to the first question is unsatisfactory, since I cannot honestly say that I am able to sit on the *tatami* and feel happy for longer than five minutes. As regards the second question, I obviously prefer a flush toilet to the oblong hole in the floor guarded by a porcelain shield which constitutes a Japanese toilet. (I like the vase of flowers which invariably decorates these toilets but I cannot for the life of me understand how, as one of my Zen friends has assured me, one can practise *zazen* or deep meditation, in a Japanese toilet. In a western toilet, yes. . . .)

My answer to the third question amazes the Japanese, because it is definitely in the affirmative and they find this unusual. I not only like, I *love* raw fish and it is one of the delicacies I miss at home. I am sure that if an enterprising Japanese were to open a *sushi* bar in London, Paris or New York (playing down the fact that *sushi* refers to slivers of raw fish spread on small oblongs of vinegared rice until people got used to the idea) he would earn a fortune as well as the gratitude of many a western *gourmet*. To those who have not tasted raw fish and make a grimace at any reference to it, I can only say that it is not unlike smoked salmon in consistency although some varieties, like raw squid, are tougher, and others, like raw tunny fish, more tender; the flavours vary to a surprising degree. Sea-urchin has a strong maritime tang, baby eel a smoky flavour that reminds one of certain brands of Chinese tea, tunny fish (my favourite) melts in one's mouth, halibut is far more interesting than when it is cooked, while 'dancing prawns' pulsate with vitamins and not quite extinguished life.

It is all very well to state that I am in Minato-ku, which is a large ward, but I do not really know where I am. Even the taxi-drivers do not know, so Michiko has drawn a map which takes up a page of my notebook and this I brandish silently but purposefully under drivers' noses, watching intently to see whether they are going to nod their head and say '*hai*' or shake their head and look bewildered. The small, 70-yen taxis are usually hopeless. Their drivers come from the country, have not yet learned how to cope with the admittedly almost insuperable problem of locating Tokyo addresses, and blandly expect their customers to guide them.

The drivers of the larger 80-yen taxis are more sophisticated. They tune in to western music on their radios for your benefit (unless there is a baseball or a sumo wrestling match on) and when one arrives at a station they actually help to find a porter.

There are bound to be accidents when everyone drives so madly and competitively but the figures of the deaths that have occurred at main cross-roads, though constantly kept up to date and marked on huge signs, do not deter the living. The other day a lorry drove into the back of my taxi as we were speeding towards the main station. Without turning a hair, my driver jumped out nimbly, opened the door for me to get out, hailed a passing colleague, explained where I was going and waved me off. Then, only then, did he turn to the lorry driver, who was waiting for him on the pavement, and begin to argue.

As everybody knows by now, Tokyo was rebuilt after the war but the houses have not been numbered, building went on haphazardly and few streets have been given names. It always astonishes me when people turn up on time for appointments. Foreigners nearly always arrive very late and in an emotional state verging on nervous collapse. Diplomats occasionally have advertisements inserted in the Press asking for 'chauffeurs who know where the main embassies are situated'. The Japanese tell you patiently that all you have to do if you get lost is to go and ask the police attached to a given ward or *ku* but I, for one, can never find a police-box and most taxi-drivers would rather die than lose face by asking their way from a policeman.

How is it that letters are ever delivered? The answer is that postmen are usually assigned to the same *ku* for life. They are obviously the people to ask if you get lost, but one rarely sees them exercising their functions. They operate invisibly and mysteriously.

Japanese characters look beautiful, but it is unnerving not to be able to read them. One feels unlettered and this in a country which boasts 0·2 per cent illiteracy. But it is impossible to absorb all those Chinese or *kanji* characters in a few days or weeks. You can, of course, attempt to learn a few colloquial phrases, but there are pitfalls. I bought a slim volume of *Colloquial Japanese* one month before I left London which I enjoyed reading ostentatiously in buses and trains, deriving a great deal of childish satisfaction from the looks of mingled awe and respect bestowed upon me by fellow-passengers, but when I came to utter the phrases before Japanese acquaintances, I realised that the book had not been written for me—it had been written by a man for men. 'Ssh!' exclaimed my Japanese friends, 'that word must never be used by a woman!' So I gave up.

In addition to the sex difference, there are the many differences in rank to be observed whenever one opens one's mouth to speak Japanese. When foreigners complain, as I often did, that many Japanese are taciturn, the answer probably is that they are not accustomed to expressing themselves spontaneously without having to worry about rank and age.

Old-timers in Japan informed me that it is much better to be a hundred per cent foreigner in Japan and not attempt to speak imperfect or even fairly good Japanese. The Japanese help foreigners to a remarkable extent, especially those with fair skins and hair. Fellow Asiatics do not receive the same treatment, I was assured by a young Indian Professor of Economics whom I met in Tokyo. (He was labouring under the additional difficulty of his age. No Japanese would take him seriously, he said, because they thought he was too young.)

How long will this friendly attitude towards fair-skinned foreigners last? Until the Japanese have absorbed all our technical know-how and closed down the American bases? At times I feel that I am still in an occupied country. Westerners are still occasionally fawned upon as conquerors and they receive preferential treatment, but there are also certain bars, certain inns, where foreigners are *not* admitted; they are turned away politely, without resentment, for reasons much deeper than a difference in skin colour. A foreigner in Japan is more alien than he is anywhere else, except perhaps China, because the cultural heritage is so different. The Japanese who studies western culture still remains Japanese; but in nine cases out of ten the foreigner who tries to absorb Japanese culture ends by becoming more Japanese than foreign— he cannot strike a balance. He lacks the Japanese knack of dividing his life and thoughts into water-tight compartments.

I do not know where I am, and I am staying in a house in which nobody speaks my language. I am the perfect stranger. All the objects in the room are alien to me, even the architecture. I am parted from my shoes, since they are not allowed on the sacred *tatami*, and this makes me feel like a prisoner—I am lost, nostalgic, without them. I do not even know where they are, because Japanese servants have a way of whisking shoes out of sight and producing them only when you are ready to leave the house and stand pausing uncertainly on the threshold, the step beyond which the wearing of shoes is permissible.

The Japanese threshold is a boundary line, a frontier separating private life from the jostling, bustling, competitive, monstrous world outside. It *is* monstrous in its hardness and rigidity. There should be two guardian images outside every private house, as there are before temples and shrines, to ward off evil spirits; but perhaps that is not necessary since the site of the house will probably have undergone a purification ceremony before construction began which is also intended to console the displaced land spirits. This Shinto custom is observed by Buddhists, the two religions often being almost interchangeable in this land of tolerance. When the frame of a new building is completed a symbol of the presence of the *kami* or spirits is placed at the centre of a pole and rice cakes, sweets and *sake* are distributed among the workers and neighbours. This is called 'the Ceremony of Placing the Ridge Pole'.

There is no furniture in my room. I lie upon a couple of *futons* or thin mattresses under numerous blankets and a quilt in the centre of a vast *tatami* space and try to come to terms with my surroundings. There is a bedside lamp beside me, and an electric heater, because the central heating system (rare in a Japanese house) has gone wrong and it is still very cold in the month of March.

The room is not as simple as it appeared at first sight; the dado is made of a rich-coloured wood and is delicately carved. There are three recesses on my left of varying shapes and sizes. One is filled with minute shelves and tiny drawers into which only dolls' clothes could fit (my own clothes are lying upon the floor—there is no wardrobe or cupboard). The second, larger recess is occupied by a painting of dove-grey birds and a low table while the third is half-filled by a china cabinet in which, seated upon four tiers, solemnly aligned in hierarchical splendour, is a superb collection of the traditional dolls displayed on March 3rd, the Little Girls' Festival. On the highest shelf the Emperor and Empress dolls glitter in the finery of their court clothes and stare, with fatuous vacuity, above the heads of the courtiers, attendants and musicians below them. Every doll in the china cabinet is in its appointed place, like ninety-nine out of every hundred Japanese in the world outside.

There is a screen behind me to ward off draughts; most Japanese houses are as airy as English houses and sleeping on the floor is not the best position to avoid the currents which creep under the sliding paper doors. These sliding-doors are intriguing; you never know from which side people are going to enter or leave a room and this gives a pleasant sense of mobility which is absent from western-style rooms. Come to think of it—the thought never occurred to me before—why should there be only one fixed entrance to a room?

Sliding doors are provided with at least four metal finger-clasps to enable you to choose your entry or your exit. Children love to play peep-bo with them and the smooth, gentle sound is kinder to the nerves than the abrupt staccato of a western door being opened or closed. This sound, and the subdued shush-shush of slippered feet, make Japanese homes restful to live in. In addition, Japanese adults rarely raise their voices. Women are expected to speak quietly; girls in department stores, coach-tour guides and the like are trained to coo like doves in a soft, low voice which is at times unbearably coy and affected and is no doubt supposed to reflect 'feminine modesty' which with virginity is still considered to be the Japanese woman's most precious possession. Both these virtues, however, are in danger of being lost in the modern, urban world of post-war Japan.

There is also a low dressing-table in my room, surmounted by a tall, narrow mirror, with a thin cushion before it upon which I shall have to kneel to do my hair and apply my make-up; the *tatami*-posture again, the constant kneeling position which westerners interpret as grovelling and which is characteristic of the Orient. (I found the Indonesian *dodok* posture even more difficult, as this entails *walking* upon your heels whenever you pass seated people. The Japanese don't go as far, or as low, as that.)

Before coming to Japan I thought that it would be uncomfortable to sleep upon a *futon*. The only one I had ever seen was in a film and it looked uncommonly narrow and very thin to a soft-bed lover like myself with an out-of-date liking for *feather* mattresses! I am therefore pleasantly surprised to discover that I like a *futon* and that it is thicker than I expected. My back feels straight and well supported—by the *tatami*-covered floor.

The pillows in this house are soft and therefore unJapanese; my hostess must have heard that westerners believe Japanese pillows are filled with stones (they are intended as a neck-rest; the Japanese sleep in the posture of a victim at the block).

A mild spiritual satisfaction is derived from sleeping on the floor, as ascetics have found out; one awakes feeling more refreshed and *alive* than after a night on a raised bed, maybe because one has been closer to the earth and strengthened by chthonic

kami. I shall conclude my notes and push them under the pillow.
All is still except for an occasional splash in the garden pool outside my window where the goldfish must be having a midnight
party.

Clay kings
and self-made
mummies

⊖his morning I had seaweed for breakfast. I am told that this is
a typical feature of a Japanese breakfast, as common to them as
cereals are to us. I did not realize it *was* seaweed, for it appears on
the breakfast table cleverly disguised as wafer-thin dark green
oblongs which one is supposed to wrap round a ball of rice in one's
bowl. This is one of the more delicate chopstick operations which
will take time to perfect. Mr Matsuo initiated me with great
patience. An even more delicate operation consists in the pre-
liminary dipping of the seaweed wafer in a tiny dish of soy sauce
before wrapping it round the rice. It is very difficult to pluck it out
without losing one's grip and splashing sauce around.

Breakfast, like so many activities in Japan today, is a blend of
East and West; whether my stomach is going to be able to accept
them both without protest is still a matter of conjecture. At home
I am satisfied with two cups of tea and two rounds of buttered
toast for breakfast; here I am confronted by a complicated set of
dishes, each one filled to the brim. Uncovering Japanese dishes is a
jolly little parlour game but one soon discovers that most of the
contents are tasteless. Japanese food is the most deceptive in the
world and must have been devised by crafty Zen priests determined
to make a *koan* or riddle out of it: how can it look so good and taste
like nothing? Answer: because it is intended to reflect the illusory
nature of all human desires.

So, we had seaweed and rice and bean soup for breakfast, and a
bowl of a dark brown granular substance with a bitter taste which
one spreads on one's rice. This was the eastern portion of the meal,
but eggs and bacon, toast and marmalade were also served in

abundance. At first I thought that the banquet was in my honour and I protested but as equally colossal breakfasts were served up in other Japanese homes and consumed by my hosts with relish it was evident that they had not been arranged for my sole benefit.

Mr Matsuo and his son rushed out immediately after breakfast, Michiko, in jeans and the knee-length frilly cotton overall that seems to be the Japanese Housewives' badge, disappeared into the kitchen, Mrs Matsuo prepared to receive an elderly man who had come with a petition for funds, one of many who plague families known to be well off, and I took a taxi to the National Museum in Ueno Park on the other side of Tokyo, where I had an appointment with the International Relations Officer, a knowledgeable gentleman who has studied in the States and can discourse in perfect English upon the fascinating objects with which the museum is filled.

What a good idea to have an International Relations Officer in a museum! European museums are either too big or too small to employ them. They either supply you with catalogues and leave you to wander in your own good time or you are plagued by voluble guides, who take you round at a gallop, and make you feel like a barbarian.

Mr Shigetaka may privately think that you are a barbarian, and he could be right, because most westerners' knowledge of Japanese art is limited, but never for a moment does he allow you to suspect so. He is grave and dignified without being ultra-formal, and he observes visitors with the acumen of an intuitive doctor, dwelling at some length upon the objects which have aroused their interest, hurrying past those which they cannot appreciate, unless it has some particular significance, in which case he pauses politely and presents the object like an urbane host introducing a *distrait* outsider to a distinguished guest. He does this unobtrusively but in a manner which rivets one's attention. Of course, how is it that one did not notice before? That celadon vase has a perfect shape, this bowl is undoubtedly original.

Mr Shigetaka pauses in the room devoted to the Haniwa clay figures which belong to Japan's remote past, to the 'Period of the Great Tombs' in the fifth century, before Chinese art penetrated into the island and caused the Japanese to lose interest in their early, primitive origins.

These striking terracotta figures are about three feet high and they were placed either singly or in groups on top of burial mounds of important persons. The mounds, like the imperial palaces of later centuries, were surrounded by moats and covered by clay houses, figures of warriors, dancers, musicians and other court figures, besides mounted horses, ducks, geese, dogs and monkeys. The clay houses no doubt represented 'spirit-houses' for the souls of the deceased to dwell in; memories of this custom survive in some Japanese funeral ceremonies to this day. The clay figures on the mounds were apparently preceded by clay cylinders which ultimately developed arms and legs but kept their drainpipe bodies. (The word *haniwa* means 'clay circle'.)

An apocryphal story relates their origin. When the emperor Suinin was returning from the funeral of his brother he was pursued by the agonizing screams of the household of the dead man who, in accordance with the then prevailing custom, had been buried alive up to their necks in the barrow built over him. The cries lasted for three days and three nights and so disturbed the emperor that he consulted with one of his ministers to discuss a possible means of putting an end to such a barbarous ritual. The minister, who may have had a potter and a future rake-off in mind, suggested that the clay workers might fashion clay replacements of noble households that could be placed on the funeral mounds instead of live ones. This story does not seem to have any solid archaeological foundation because to date no excavations have revealed any trace of burials in which the former custom prevailed, even though the Japanese have never been a squeamish race.

It is a pity that the museum authorities have not placed the Haniwa figures upon a reconstructed mound, as they were originally intended, instead of separating them and enclosing them in glass cabinets, for although the individual figures are striking in themselves, as a group they must have appeared even more so. Their positions corresponded to their various functions in and about the central Haniwa clay house: The soldiers guarded the outer rings of defences with their horses already caparisoned in the rear, ready to make a defensive *sortie* against the enemy; in front of them was a moat filled with boats and water-birds for the pleasure of the deceased king. Inside the house, court life proceeded much as it was to for hundreds of years until the present day: dancers and musicians amused the court, servants prepared their meals, nobles sat in magnificent costumes waiting upon the unseen regal presence within. On one mound alone ten thousand haniwa figures were set up in groups arranged with an already keen Japanese eye for

microscopic detail. One wonders whether they also planned the
gardens round the Haniwa house?

How impressive they must have been, these miniature cities of
the dead, how awe-inspiring for travellers coming upon them un-
awares by moonlight! Their ghostly realism is still capable of
inspiring terror, the vacant, slit eyes gouged out by their makers,
are full of expression, their bearing is unmistakably Japanese: the
warriors are as proud as Samurai and the womenfolk bow before
them in the lowly posture which has not yet disappeared from the
Japanese way of life.

A couple of miles away, also surrounded by a moat and the
slanting walls of large-sized stones characteristic of Japanese
palaces, the real-life descendants of the occupants of the great
tombs live in what may well be the last imperial palace and the last
imperial court of Japan, for who knows whether Crown Prince
Akihito will ever succeed his father and continue the two-
thousand-year-old dynasty, the oldest dynasty in the world?

The 'Emperor question' agitates a minority of die-hards who
would like to have him reinstated to his former position, which was
as mythical and ritualistic as the invisible presence in the centre of
Haniwa mounds, but on the whole the younger generation is not
interested. There is no mention of the Emperor in post-war school
textbooks and he is connected with Japan's defeat in the Second
World War—a blow from which Japanese pride has not yet
recovered. The Emperor, as is well known, was forced to make a
public pronouncement formally renouncing his claim to divinity
and his family's mythological link with the Sun Goddess, the great
Shinto ancestress Amaterasu. Shinto was separated from the State,
and the Grand Shrine of Ise, which had always included an
imperial prince among its priests, was shorn of its former prestige.

The present-day trend is against Emperors and Sun Goddesses
and yet. . . . Dr Sokyo Ono has written recently in *Shinto: the Kami
Way*, that one of the three fundamental principles of shrine Shinto
is to 'identify our minds with the Emperor's mind and, in loving
and being friendly with one another, to pray for the country's
prosperity and for peaceful co-existence and co-prosperity for the
people of the world'.

To identify our minds with the Emperor's mind. . . . What *is* the
Emperor's mind? From all accounts, it seems to be a sensible,
scientifically-inclined mind, absorbed by Japanese flora and marine
biology. His Majesty is more interested in his laboratory than in

his palace and from time to time he publishes learned tomes illustrated by the Empress.

The imperial entourage, especially the hide-bound court chamberlains, are said to be more attached to protocol and the old conventional palace ways than the Emperor himself. The court chamberlains wanted to find a bride for Crown Prince Akihito, but he foiled them and chose his own—the popular ex-commoner Michiko.

In July 1961, the Emperor and Empress broke all precedents by looking after their eldest daughter, Princess Shigeko Teru, and attending her subsequent funeral. They had never been allowed to do such a thing before. In 1953, when the Emperor's brother, Prince Chichibu, died, the Emperor did not pay him a visit or go to the funeral service. The principle behind this custom is said to be of ancient Chinese origin. The Emperor, the Son of Heaven, is without a family in the ordinary sense of the term. He has no human parents, no children. For a long time, however, the Emperor had quietly rebelled against this inhuman restriction and when his eldest daughter became ill he resolved to defy tradition and she was admitted to the Imperial Household Agency Hospital so that the Emperor and Empress could visit her whenever they wished to do so.

'Until Mrs Higashikuni (her husband was a commoner) breathed her last at 3.15 on Sunday,' reported the *Japan Times*, 'her parents had been by her bedside for more than seventeen continuous hours, without even a rest or a nap. A few minutes before death came to the patient, the Emperor and the Empress were able, like any other parents, to moisten her lips in conformity with the Japanese custom.

'All this was remarkable for the Imperial Household of Japan which is bound by millenia-old tradition. . . .'

The Imperial family live simply. They are not rich and they have modified their tastes to suit their income. It was only at the end of 1961 that the Emperor and Empress moved into a new two-storey house in the palace grounds, thus ending their sixteen-year residence in '*Obunko*', a wartime air-raid shelter. The Emperor had consistently refused to approve the Imperial Household Agency's plan to build a new residence until the general housing situation had eased in Japan.

The new imperial abode, designed by an architect of the Imperial Household Agency, is almost stark in its simplicity; the dining-room, with its small cherrywood table and chairs for two, would barely satisfy a lower middle-class English family. The only Japanese-style room in the building is the Empress's private room with its *tokonoma* and elegant woodwork in Japanese cypress. A modern Japanese touch is provided by the ivory-coloured tiles on the outer walls of the palace, which 'reflect the hues of the surroundings, and appear green, yellow and so forth, depending on the hour and season'. On the Emperor's birthday, the public are allowed to swarm into the imperial grounds. They also visit the palace on New Year's day to offer their greetings to the imperial family.

At all other times the entrance to the palace is heavily guarded but one can picture the rather pathetic figures imprisoned on the other side of the moat: the ageing couple seated at the small cherrywood table, the elderly Emperor poring over his specimens in his laboratory, the Empress playing with her grandson and wondering what the future holds for him; the younger, gayer couple, the Crown Prince and his Princess are the only people who leave the palace from time to time on state visits to foreign countries. The elderly couple, who have never conversed freely with foreigners, would no doubt be frightened out of their wits. So they live inside the moat, close to the core of old Japan, jealously preserved by archaic chamberlains and state musicians in gorgeous brocaded costumes who from time to time play *gakaku*— 'elegant music' which could have been composed by the Sun Goddess herself; the weird sounds seem to come from another world.

The white swan in the Imperial moat looks lonely. I guessed that he had had a tragedy in his life long before I was told that his mate had been killed the year before by Tokyo children who can be as cruel here as children elsewhere. But the lonely swan inspired a poor young man who worked in a printing shop and felt very bitter because all his friends were able to go to college; one day he saw the swan and was so struck by its beauty that he determined to make a study of the species. He saved money to visit all the places where the swans migrate to Japan and he found that many were being shot. He wrote letters to the authorities but nobody took any notice of him. There was only one solution: to be taken seriously he would have to study and become an official bird warden. He did so and now, at the age of twenty-one, Minoru Arao is Tokyo's youngest bird warden.

Dr Koga, the Curator of the Ueno Zoo, is the only person I met in Japan who professes to prefer animals to human beings. He deserves a statue for having preserved Japanese cranes from extinction. Cranes have always been considered sacred by the Japanese—they are the symbols of peace and longevity—but nobody was prepared to sacrifice rations and make an effort to keep them from dying out when, in the forties, so many children were suffering from malnutrition. Dr Koga looked after the last pair of cranes at the zoo with the solicitude of a scientific High Priest of Shinto. He made the important discovery that cranes, who usually only lay two eggs in a year, could be persuaded to lay six more if they were taken off the nests after every clutch was laid. He also devised a method of incubating and rearing the chicks hatched artificially. There is now a thriving colony of cranes at Ueno Zoo.

I am surprised that Dr Koga has not been declared a National Cultural property, a title which is bestowed in Japan on animate as well as inanimate objects worthy of preservation. From time to time, one reads in the papers that Mr X or Mr Y has been 'declared a national cultural property', as though he had been stuffed like a mummy, ready to be placed in a museum. How splendid it must be for the recipient of this honour! How ego-raising to be able to strut about and declare to the world at large: 'I am a National Cultural Property!'

Most people believe that mummy-making was a speciality of the ancient Egyptians but the Japanese made mummies, in a peculiar and individual way, from the tenth century to the twentieth, as Professor Kosei Ando of Waseda University, Tokyo, has recently proved.

Japanese and Chinese mummies are referred to in literature and this set the Professor wondering how mummification could be achieved in a country like Japan where humidity is so high, since aridity was considered to be an essential condition for the process of drying up the human body.

In 1960, the Professor examined some mummies found near Mount Yudono in Yamagata prefecture in northern Japan. A close examination revealed the astonishing fact that 'the person whose body was mummified took care of the major part of the mummification process by himself. This do-it-yourself method is peculiar to Japan and to China.'

This practice was started by Chinese Buddhists of the fourth century and copied by the Japanese, with a difference: whereas the

Chinese first dried the body and then coated it with lacquer and
hemp cloth, in the same way that they fashioned dry lacquer
statues, a method followed by Japanese artists, whose dry lacquer
Buddhas can be seen at the National Museum, Tokyo, the Japanese
mummy is not given any coating at all.

The idea behind mummification during one's lifetime is this:
the followers of the bodhisattva called Maitreya believe that he is
to come back to this world 5,670,000,000 years after the Buddha's
death. Human life expectancy will then be 84,000 years, all evil and
disease will have disappeared from the earth, treasures will spring
from the soil, and the peoples of the world will have become
united to the extent that they will all speak one language. Those
who believed in this Utopia wanted to wait for Maitreya's advent
but to do so, they had to have eternal life. The way in which to
attain it is called *nyujo*: it implies a perfectly stable frame of mind
which one can reach first by assuming the sitting posture of a Zen
priest in meditation and gradually ceasing to breathe. The Japanese
'mummy' is therefore supposed to retain his soul, unlike the
Egyptian mummies from whom the soul is believed to have
departed.

To attain the condition of a mummy, various prescribed pro-
cedures had to be followed over a long period of time. It was, in
brief a very slow 'fasting unto death', which had to be undergone
with the utmost care by the voluntary victim, since a too drastic
reduction in the intake of food would result in death before the
body was ready for dehydration and any traces of food left in the
body would bring about its decay. The fasting period lasted from
two or three thousand to ten thousand days.

In the case of a five and a half year's fasting period, the aspirant
mummy would abstain during the first three years from eating rice,
barley, millet and soy beans. Being a Buddhist he did not, of course,
eat any meat or fish, but only buckwheat, grass seeds, red soy
beans, green vegetables.

During the next two and a half years this meagre diet was reduced
to the point of total elimination. The aspirant's body was by now
free of fat and protein. As he drew closer to his ultimate goal he
merely drank water to cleanse his digestive tract. When he finally
died of self-inflicted starvation, his body was ready to become mummified *by itself*. There was no need to extract the viscera
as in the case of Egyptian corpses, for the body was completely
dried up.

A certain area round Mount Yudono, called hermits' valley, was placed at the disposal of fasting 'mummies to be'.

After his death, the mummy's body was arranged in a Zen posture with its hands clasped in front. Sometimes cords were used to fix the posture. Then the body was placed in a pinewood coffin and kept in an underground stone vault for three years. The mummification process was usually complete at the end of the three years but if it was not, or, to quote Professor Ando, 'should it prove to be yet somewhat raw, it was sometimes smoked by burning incense or leaves. Or sometimes it was heated by the flames of many thick candles while it was suspended from a temple beam.'

After the completion of the mummification process, the mummy was clothed in priestly vestments and headgear and worshipped 'as though it were a sacred statue'. The deceased priest was supposed to have attained the status of a Buddha.

The last Japanese to 'mummify' himself, according to Professor Ando, was a priest called Bukkai, who was attached to the Kannonji temple of Murakimi and who died in 1903. The professor excavated his grave in July, 1961. He found the coffin resting on four thick iron bars placed crosswise to keep the coffin free from moisture. 'The remains inside the coffin were covered with rice husks and although the body did contain a certain amount of moisture, it was completely mummified sixty years after the priest's death. Had it been extricated after the prescribed three years it would have been in a still better condition.'

The professor added that nobody was prepared to emulate those religious fanatics nowadays, but that many people still worship mummified Buddhas hoping to receive personal blessings from them.

On and off tatami

So much talk about fasting and asceticism had given me a hearty appetite and I did full justice to the very excellent supper served at the Matsuos, again by Michiko. Mr Matsuo was relaxing in his *tanzan* or house-kimono, as all Japanese gentlemen do at home, reading the papers. Supper consisted of a mixture of meat balls, chicken, fried oysters, a delicate kind of green vegetable which I was informed was 'spring chrysanthemum', radish sauce, soya cubes floating in boiling stock, followed by grilled salmon and rice with pickles, *sake*, tea, strawberries and cream. It is by now universally known that Japanese strawberries, like their carrots and turnips, are abnormally large. They also lack flavour. Under western influence, the Japanese, once the masters of the exquisitely small and refined, are now trying to produce the vulgarly large and ostentatious, from vegetables to hotels.

After supper, we retired to a western-style room to look at television. There are nine channels to choose from, with no great difference between them, except that station NHK serves more solid BBC-type fare. There are some good travelogues (Japan is an inexhaustible source of travelogue material), spontaneous street interviews, and masses of westerns efficiently dubbed into Japanese, which are extremely popular.

I am permitted to wear slippers in the western-style room; most households and all Japanese inns provide them for their guests. Worn with a kimono they pass unnoticed, but with western clothes it is a different matter; they ruin any attempt at elegance, because they are invariably at least two sizes too large, so that one is obliged to shuffle, often losing a slipper in one's progress from room to room; they seem to be mass-produced in only two colours, bright blue and bright green.

I occasionally forget that as soon as I reach a room covered by the sacred *tatami* I must leave my slippers at the door, but the horrified expression on my hosts' faces soon reminds me to repair this unforgivable breach of domestic etiquette. I feel rather cold in my stockinged feet in this weather; the Japanese ladies are better off—they wear thick, white socks called *tabi*, foot-mittens with an extra space for the big toe, which they wear in the street even when it is raining and manage to keep astonishingly clean, even when they wear sandals and not *geta*, the high wooden clogs which keep one four to six inches off the ground. I wish I could wear *geta* without falling on my face, as that is obviously the most sensible footgear for Japanese streets.

People are for ever urging me, 'tell us what you find wrong, or uncomfortable'; there is a morbid national urge for self-criticism, probably as a result of having been defeated in the war, which comes naturally to a race with masochistic tendencies. When you criticize them, the Japanese listen intently, almost with pleasure, as if they enjoyed this form of punishment and then—they do absolutely nothing about it. The actual words of criticism are sufficient and accepted as a form of absolution. One is forced to this conclusion on the vexed question of the state of their streets. So many foreigners have complained about Japanese roads and their potholes that are in such violent contrast with the ultra-modern buildings that there is no excuse for this unaccountable apathy.

The Japanese have a curious lack of urban sense which is tied up with their lack of civic sense. Tokyo is the largest, but also the ugliest city in the world (with Djakarta running a close second) a great uneven sprawl so bereft of trees that shopkeepers spend hours every year attaching paper cherry blossoms to artificial branches so as to give passers-by 'an illusion of spring'. There is no breathing space, and the one big park, Ueno, is being gradually filled with buildings: museums, a fine concert hall, a tea-house. . . . Where are the landscape architects? One would have thought that Japan would lead in this field, but no . . . the Japanese artist still works on 'the exquisitely small', the individual house, building, or garden; cities, with the exception of Nagoya and Hiroshima, are left to sprout untidily and passers-by splash through muddy, unpaved streets, fully absorbed by their personal problems.

This self-centredness prevents the Japanese from developing a civic sense. Not having had the commandment to love their neighbours as themselves, they have looked inward to their home and family. Public life, with its formalities and set patterns, has been a thing apart, on the other side of the *tatami*. As soon as he steps from the *tatami* on to the street the Japanese assumes a mask. He is no longer quite human.

Most Tokyoites begin the day, as one of my acquaintances put it, by meeting a big challenge—that of getting in and out of public conveyances. Many underground stations hire part-time students as an auxiliary force for 'the unique task of packing passengers into trains. Other students are employed to take surplus passengers off trains—young women protest when they are seized under the armpits . . '

Everybody is so intent on his or her own business that nobody has time to stop and lend a helping hand to those in distress. Heavily laden old women are never assisted (yet one is always told that the Japanese, like other Asiatics, look after their old people so much better than we do) and if you happen to fall and sprain your ankle, it is just too bad; you will have to struggle up by yourself. The wife of a university professor told me that she had seen a young girl fresh from the country being abducted by a gang of hoodlums in one of Tokyo's largest stations. The girl was struggling and protesting, but one of the youths put a hand over her mouth and two others helped to carry her out. Nobody stopped or raised a hand in protest. 'Why didn't you do something about it?' I asked the lady, in surprise. (She happens to be a Christian, incidentally.) 'What could I do?' she smiled at my suggestion. 'There was no policeman in sight. It was no use asking people to intervene—they would have refused—pretended not to notice.'

No Japanese denies this state of affairs. It is only too well known, but when one asks them why it should be so, they shake their head and look puzzled. 'We do not like to get involved,' is a frequent answer. 'By helping somebody, we assume an obligation. We are never anxious to do this when a stranger is concerned.'

When national honour is concerned, however, people react differently. While I was in Japan, an American woman tourist was assaulted and robbed in the spacious gardens of a large hotel near Hakone, a sightseeing resort near Mount Fuji. The incident was reported in the newspapers and public reaction was startling. Money poured in from all quarters, some very poor, to make up for the tourist's loss. An old Japanese peasant woman called on the American lady to take her a present and apologize for the misbehaviour of her countryman. The tourist ended by receiving more money than she had lost and she donated it to a local charity.

The usual practice, however, is to dissociate oneself from 'the others', a lack of communication which can very easily lead from a state of neutrality to an attitude of positive dislike and even hatred if 'the others' happen to be foreigners with whom one is at war. Ever since I have been in Japan I have pondered deeply over the seeming contradiction between their kindness as individuals and their coldness in the mass, relating it to Japanese wartime behaviour which has left such bitter memories in every country they occupied.

It is equally hard to explain the dichotomy in the German character. How was it possible for such a cultured, civilized people to undergo such a collective throwback to barbarism and send millions of fellow human beings to the gas chambers? Most of the German people protest, like the mass of Japanese: 'We did not know that it was going on.' The Japanese add: 'We heard rumours that our troops were behaving badly but we could not believe it. We thought it must be enemy propaganda. We had been told terrible stories about the enemy.'

There are moments in history when the powers of darkness possessed by certain individuals come to the fore and unite. This was the case in Hitler's Germany; it was the case in militarist Japan of the thirties. Life for a private in the Japanese army was no joke. Many people have told me that no European could have stood it. Several Japanese who were suspected of western sympathies nearly died from the treatment they received. If this was the treatment meted out to Japanese nationals it needs little effort of the imagination to realize what was reserved for the enemy. Moreover, the moral code was different. For a Japanese, it was a dishonour to be taken prisoner—they considered those who came into their hands as beneath contempt and treated them accordingly. This was the fanatical code that inspired the *kamikaze*, the famous suicide squads of Japan who hurled themselves against enemy submarines and literally threw themselves into the jaws of death.

One of the best anti-war films ever made in Japan is Daiei's 'Fires on the Plain', inspired by Kin Shohei Ooka's 1959 novel of that title which described with horrific Japanese realism how war can turn men into beasts; worse, into cannibals. In the film, as in the book, war is shown to be evil without any false trimmings of bogus glory, or sham excuse of 'duty done' or sense of camaraderie. But 'Fires on the Plain' was attacked by both Rightists and Leftists.

Japan is at the crossroads, or perhaps not yet quite at the crossroads when, after a long period of post-war defeatism and pandering to the foreign conqueror, she is beginning to want to regain her sense of national pride. The patient is slipping out of the doctor's hands: will he want to have his dangerous old playthings back again? There is a move afoot to instil a 'sense of patriotism' into the younger generation. Tomorrow there may be a plea to have Japan's armed forces, suppressed by the Peace Treaty of 1952, restored. Will they ever reach the tragically ironical point of manufacturing atomic weapons?

At the moment, there is great sensitivity about atomic tests but little resentment about Hiroshima. Young people came up to me when I was wandering through that city and asked me to talk to them in English. Nobody looked at me reproachfully when I visited the museum of horrors where relics of the devastation are preserved and seen by two million visitors a year. . . . When I told

Japanese acquaintances that I was going to Hiroshima 'by way of a pilgrimage', they looked uncomprehending.

Other Japanese put forward various theories to explain the attitude of their fellow-countrymen. One of them, a university professor, said: 'I think our people do not harbour resentment because they are imbued, consciously or unconsciously, with the Buddhist idea that nothing in life is permanent, everything is transient—evil as well as good—so they do not dwell on what is past. It is all over now.'

A Shinto priest thought that it was a reflection of Shinto traditions, in which 'moral judgments as to what is considered to be good or bad are not a fixed system of standards, but vary considerably depending on each specific situation. The Shinto manner of grasping truth takes into consideration the fact that values are constantly changing. For example, in Shinto ethics nothing—sex, wealth, killing, etc.—is regarded as unconditionally evil.'

A liberal-minded doctor in northern Japan shrugged his shoulders and said, a little sadly: 'Pearl Harbour came before Hiroshima. And the atrocities committed by our soldiers in China and Manchuria and elsewhere. . . . Now some of us feel we have atoned. Hiroshima wiped out all our faults.'

The argument that impressed me as being nearest the truth was the Shinto's priest explanation of Japanese moral opportunism: 'it depends entirely upon the specific situation'. . . . Do those Japanese who refuse to harbour any genuine resentment against the bombing of Hiroshima feel as they do because, deep down in their subconscious, they know that in the same 'specific circumstance', had they been in possession of the atom bomb, they would have acted as the enemy did? This is the least charitable of my suppositions, but it may be the nearest to the stark truth.

In a department store

*T*his morning I visited the large Mitsukoshi department store in the company of Kazuko, the interpreter loaned to me by the

Foreign Office. Kazuko is a university graduate, she works in the Economic section of the Ministry and specializes upon tariffs, a subject which is as foreign to me as the Japanese characters that dance so gaily upon the neon signs along the Ginza at nightfall.

Kazuko is a junior member of the 'life is earnest' brigade. She is in her twenties, works long hours and lives in a tiny one-room flat provided by the Ministry for its employees at a nominal cost. She does not earn very much but she has an extensive wardrobe of quiet clothes. She is far too modern to wear a kimono. Nobody wears kimono in the Ministries. Kimono is for the propaganda girls: air hostesses and geishas. Kazuko is a well brought-up Japanese young lady with a fair share of the Japanese feminine gifts of patience, devotion to duty, diligence, courtesy, flexibility. She constantly apologizes for her poor English which is actually quite good but inclined to be limited to economic questions and, since I am no expert on economics, there is little scope for the use of this technical vocabulary when she accompanies me.

There are times when I am not sure what Kazuko is thinking, because she is too polite to make any comments, to put herself forward and make a suggestion, but a cocktail can work wonders. The Japanese are very susceptible to the influence of alcohol. After one cocktail, the most demure Japanese girl flushes, puts her hand in front of her face (a national gesture denoting acute embarrassment—they are often embarrassed) and is ready to answer the most probing questions with disarming franchise. The mask of oriental inscrutability melts very quickly; it is a thin mask and the strength of the emotions behind it is apt to be startling.

Although Kazuko works with men, she is very shy. She blushed when we passed the underwear department at Mitsukoshi's and I insisted upon having the various under-kimono garments demonstrated to me, because a young man was in charge. I agreed that it was odd to have a young man in charge of ladies' underwear but at the same time there is nothing particularly suggestive—no panties, for instance—about the kind of lingerie worn under kimonos: just an under-skirt that looks like a narrow, old-fashioned petticoat, and an under-blouse; nevertheless, it was enough to make Kazuko cover her face with embarrassment while the young man amiably spread his wares out on the counter.

When one of the managers asked me how Mitsukoshi compared with our big London stores, I told him truthfully that it compared favourably with our more popular stores, but that it was not quite up to the standard of our more elegant ones, like Harrods or Liberty's. 'How is it different?' I hesitated before replying, 'Our climate is colder (this is dubious) so we have fitted carpets—they always give an elegant appearance; there is more space. . . .' I paused, then added brightly, 'but none of our department stores have a theatre as you have or playgrounds for children. They do not have a wedding room either.' The head of the store smiled happily, bowed with pleasure, presented me with a *furoshiki*, a silk square in which the Japanese carry a surprising number of parcels, and a plate of strawberries and cream.

The number of presents which one accumulates in Japan is staggering; I had to have three large boxes shipped to England by surface mail, but the selection is limited; *furoshikis* and dolls of various sizes, from six inches to eighteen, are the most popular. Cotton hand-towels with the donor's name printed on them are given to you with a handleless cup of tea when you pay a visit say to a dancing teacher or a small firm.

I asked the manager what kind of presents men bought for ladies. He squirmed uncomfortably on his plush chair, teased a strawberry and turned to his colleague with whom he exchanged a rapid dialogue in Japanese while Kazuko giggled half-apologetically for having to translate such an awkward query.

'It is not usual for Japanese husbands to buy their wives presents,' he said. 'They come here to buy what they want—with their husbands' money.' 'And they buy presents for their husbands?' 'Oh yes, of course.' (Japanese men abroad buy expensive presents for their girl-friends. The geishas know all about the latest Parisian perfumes and demand them from their patrons when they go on business trips.)

Christianity has not made much of an impact upon Japan, but Christmas has, because it appeals to the native blend of artistry and commercialism. It is an extra festival, and everybody loves festivals, especially one which makes people spend far more money than they do on Buddhist or Shinto feasts. Japanese shopkeepers are therefore as keen on Christmas as ours are and the department stores do good business at that time of the year.

I complimented the manager upon the current art exhibition held on the display floor. This was the most interesting feature of the store and indeed of all the big stores in Tokyo, who vie with one another in presenting first-rate exhibitions of modern and ancient art. These are the only places outside museums where national art treasures are allowed to be displayed, because the stores possess all the necessary safeguards against fire and theft. Against this it must be said that Tokyo does not possess as many museums or art galleries as other great capitals. One of the advantages of the exhibitions in department stores is that they appeal to a far wider clientele. I observed quite a few workmen in their everyday clothes pausing before the exhibits for quite a long time. There is no snobbishness about art in Japan.

The lift-girl in her green uniform wafted us out with a graceful gesture of her gloved hand and a low cooing sound which would surely help to increase sales if there were more male customers.

The lift- and sales-girls are all young and attractive. What would the customers think of our unsexy, terse male attendants at home? They told me what they thought of our sales ladies. 'They are so *old*,' they commented pityingly. Any woman over thirty in Japan is very *passée*.

The head of the store bowed me out downstairs in the main hall. 'That is another feature we have not got in our stores,' I said, pointing to the large figure of the Goddess of Sincerity, painted in luminous vestments of green and gold, who welcomes customers almost as soon as they walk inside. There is nothing incongruous about finding a Japanese deity in a place of commerce. The practical Japanese combine religion and business as shrewdly, but perhaps more blatantly, than our Puritans; it is part of the pleasant doctrine called *gense-riyaku*, literally: 'present life bliss', which is attached to the Kannon.

Close to the earth

The priest at the large Kannon Temple in Asakusa, the popular amusement quarter of Tokyo, was only too glad to provide me with figures which proved 'that the Japanese are not so irreligious as it is sometimes said'.

'You can see for yourself,' he said, 'that the temple is full of pilgrims.' I would have called most of them sightseers myself;

only a few people paused to bow before the image and clap their hands twice, a ritual observed by both Buddhists and Shintoists.

'Sometimes,' pursued the priest, 'we have as many as one hundred thousand people in a day. There are of course special days on which one visit has a special grace value. On July 9th and 10th, for instance, a visit to the temple has the merit, in Kannon's eyes, of 46,000 pilgrimages. New Year, too, is a special time. Offerings for the first three days of the New Year will give you an idea of our popularity.' He put on a thick pair of spectacles and read out: 'January 1st: twelve hundred pounds: January 2nd: eight hundred pounds. January 3rd: six hundred pounds. That is a fairly constant average for this time of the year.'

'And who are the main contributors?' I asked.

'We have a number of enrolled Kannon believers, then there are the occasional donations of wealthy visitors who wish to show their gratitude for favours received; a fairly regular source of income comes to us from the monthly dues paid by local business men who have shops in nearby Nakamise (shopping arcade) and from the sales of Kannon talismans and images. We cannot complain—the Kannon is still very popular with worshippers.'

'I presume that this popularity can be accounted for by the fact that Kannon is supposed to confer material benefits to those who petition her?'

'The Kannon,' the priest explained patiently, 'is the Bodhisattva whose chief sphere of action is the present world, and her great mission is to give all good things, spiritual and material'—he stressed the word 'spiritual'—'to any people who ask for her help, without any strings attached to the favour. In other words, charity is the Kannon's profession; her headquarters is in the world and she works day and night to make life easy and happy for everyone.' He looked at me fixedly and declared: 'You worship her too.'

'I was not aware of the fact,' I said. The priest smiled an esoteric smile. 'Probably not, but that makes no difference. It is part of Kannon's basic principle that whatever the religion or teaching calculated to promote the welfare of mankind, it is actually helping to forward Kannon's mission. Such religions are regarded as a manifestation of Kannon's mind and such teachers or prophets: the Messiah, Buddha, Bosatsu as an incarnation or reappearance of Kannon herself born in a different place and age and under a different name. So those who worship other gods are really worshipping Kannon without knowing it. Why then should she care if any of her professed devotees go to other deities or combine their worship of her with other gods? Is not her mercy universal, her benevolence unlimited, reaching to the ends of the earth, covering the entire world of living creatures, human, animal, and plant, even rocks?'

A modified form of stone-worship, in the guise of the artistic contemplation and placing of stones in gardens, is an importation from China which is gaining rather than losing popularity. Every summer there is a one-week exhibition and sale of stones in one of Tokyo's department stores and even Americans are to be found among the customers. The present Prime Minister has boosted the cult by declaring: 'Dwarf-tree culture is for women and children. Stones, that's the thing for me!'

An 'International Valuable Stone Club' has been founded by a restaurant owner, Mr Toshiharu Ito, who, it was recently reported, 'is so often away chasing stones that customers rarely get a chance to taste the owner's own delicious cooking'. Customers who know the restaurant well say that they can tell from the taste whether Mr Ito is out collecting or at home in his kitchen.

Mr Ito used to be a dwarf-tree fan until the smoke from passing trains killed his specimens; he then turned to stones. He was fortunate. One day he found an interesting stone in the river while he was bathing in a mountain resort near Tokyo. He sold it for five thousand yen, a sum which paid for his hotel and travelling expenses and encouraged him to pursue his lucrative hobby.

Collectors are pushing up the prices in their quest for rarity. Recently a greenish stone was quoted as being worth three million yen. You have to be a connoisseur to appreciate those curiously shaped and coloured boulders which are capable of fetching such high prices in this limited but interesting market; many Japanese believe that westerners are incapable of such sensitive appreciation.

Stone appreciation is a traditional art and as such the Japanese are attuned to it; their values are less sound where new and modern arts are concerned. This is true of all ancient civilizations whose culture seems to have completed a circle and come to a dead end without being capable of renewing itself.

Mass production has hastened the process and most of the potters who used to turn out individual pieces are now obliged to follow the modern trend and work quickly to fill the shelves of the department stores. There are exceptions, of course. One of them is

Sakujiro Kamiguchi, the 'mad potter' as he calls himself, who lives and works in the heart of Tokyo although he detests the city and all it stands for: modern acquisitiveness and the crushing of the Japanese artist's individuality. He belongs to the small band of artistic hermits who work in silence and solitude, pursuing their own inspiration outside fashionable trends.

When Kamiguchi was a young man he wanted to be a tailor, the best tailor in Japan. 'To do so,' he decided, 'I must learn with the best master, and who could be better than the Emperor's tailor?' So he became his apprentice until he was proficient enough to set up on his own.

He became successful, orders poured in, and he liked his work. But after some time he realized that even his most perfect creations were ephemeral and the most splendid costumes only last for a few years. He determined to devote his creative abilities to something of a more permanent nature and so he chose pottery. This may seem surprising to a westerner who thinks of pottery as something fragile, but in Japan pottery is more lasting than paintings on silk or wooden sculptures. Each piece is carefully looked after and kept between thick layers of material in a special brick safe called a *koura*.

It usually takes some time before Kamiguchi confides his ideas to foreigners. He often devises a kind of psychological test to find out whether or not they are 'genuine'. Even his Japanese patrons are subjected to this initiation ritual. Once he presented a bowl of tea to a V.I.P. on which the word 'idiot' was written. The V.I.P. took it and drank from it without a murmur. He had passed the test.

Kamiguchi's patrons do not buy from him, they merely look and admire, because, 'I never sell anything,' he says. 'I make pieces of pottery in the same way that others paint, sing or play the flute. If an artist sells his works, sooner or later he becomes the slave of his clients. I want to remain free and that is why, for two days in every week, I am a tailor. On the other days of the week, I am the mad potter Kamiguchi.'

Bending down to scoop up a handful of earth, the third element in the Shinto trinity, Kamiguchi launched a tirade against westerners who are responsible for the lowering of taste in Japan, the Japanese who stick to the past without trying to improve upon it, and potters who jealously guard the secrets of their art and the name of the locality from where they obtain their material.

Kamiguchi uses the soil from his Tokyo garden and he does not object if an occasional crushed pebble produces a bump or a hole in the finished product.

'Look at this bowl,' he says, handing you a piece which at first sight appears to be rather gross and rustic but which closer inspection reveals to be full of delicate shades. 'Turn it slowly,' he commands, 'and you will see here a mountain, there a cliff, and a valley; when you pour green tea into it, the bottom of the bowl becomes a mountain lake. I want people who look at and use my pieces of pottery to feel calm and rested. I create to bring consolation to the heart of man, like a bonze who meditates or reads a *sutra.*'

This is in the true spirit of the tea-ceremony and it is not surprising to discover that Kamiguchi has built his own tea-house. Like everything he does it is quite different from the classical, traditional form. Instead of the usual elegant, rather precious little building, refined and polished as a temple, Kamiguchi's tea-house resembles a peasant's hut. In its roughness and strength it has a close affinity with his pottery.

The tea-house and the tea-ceremony were elaborated in the sixteenth century, when the art of pottery was flourishing, by priests who wished to curb the violent passions of the aristocratic Samurai. While they were being forced to be calm and concentrate on the intricacies of the tea-ceremony, they had no time in which to cut off people's heads. The threshold of the tea-house was the only place where the proud Samurai condescended to leave their inseparable swords.

'Permanent contact with nature is at the basis of our art,' said Kamiguchi. This contact can at times provoke a salutary shock, the Zen 'moment of truth', by descending to the scatological. Kamiguchi has amused himself by producing potteries in the shape of excrement. 'Are they not natural?' he exclaimed. 'No school. No style. All my works are like that—natural, devoid of artificiality. A work of art should be born without any effort, without any preconceptions, naturally, without ceremony—then one feels relieved. Art is a necessary, sometimes an urgent function.' These products of his sense of humour are destined to illustrate his theories; he does not consider them to be works of art. But he wishes to stress that art began to be decadent from the moment that sanitary notions began to appear, creating a barrier between the clean and the dirty.

Kamiguchi's love of caricature is very 'Zen'. 'Look!' he said, pointing to a paunchy, slightly lop-sided *sake* jug. 'That one has drunk too much!' I picked up a tea bowl from a log of wood that lay like a sunken crocodile in the middle of a pond. 'Hold it firmly, like this,' said Kamiguchi. 'Clasp it with both hands. You are accustomed to western tea-cups with their silly little handles. A bowl is meant to be grasped, then you can feel its rotundity, its substance. Doesn't that convey something to you?' 'Yes,' I said 'I am holding the whole of Japan in the palm of my hand.' Kamiguchi shook his head. 'More than that. Far more. The earth, the womb of the earth, from which we are separated in this senseless sort of life,' and he waved his sturdy arms in the direction of the monotonous skyline of office buildings and of that crude, red, steel horror: Tokyo Tower.

Modern Kabuki

*T*his afternoon Mrs Matsuo took me to a modern Kabuki play at one of the many theatres lavishly decorated outside with artificial cherry blossom. I am surprised that the Japanese, who have organized what amounts to a cherry-blossom cult—singling out individual trees for special viewing, taking days off to picnic under them—should tolerate this rash of paper petals which are not even good imitations. Real cherry-blossom is a delicate pink, not this German measles tint. Mr Kamiguchi is right—the Japanese are losing the contact with nature which was one of their main qualities and the source of the best they have produced in art.

Mrs Matsuo fluttered round the ticket office trying to obtain an English programme of the performance—most theatres provide at least a summary of the plot in flowery English—but today there was none. So she went up to the manager, a jovial, bearded man with the relaxed attitude of show business people everywhere and asked him to give me a verbal summary of the play, which he did in quite understandable English.

The story is quite old but it has been modernized, cut by about half, and it is acted in a less stilted manner than the classical Kabuki. The plot as he relates it awakens no enthusiasm in me. The heroine is a woman who is in love with one of her husband's clerks. She asks him to lend her five hundred yen from the safe to send to her ailing mother, because her husband has refused to help, promising that she will return the money shortly. The faithful clerk hesitates—conflict between love and duty—because, as the manager put it, 'he loves her inside but does not show it', but he finally succumbs and takes the money from the safe. He is seen by a villainous colleague who blackmails him and his employer's wife. The ex-faithful clerk and the wife decide to elope. Nobody will take them in. Winter comes—they commit a double suicide, off-stage.

The foyer is about three-quarters full of well-groomed ladies, most of whom are wearing black and white kimonos; this colour combination is all the rage at the moment. Nobody smokes and there is a clean, fresh atmosphere which western theatres would do well to emulate. Perhaps this is impossible, because a good deal of it must be attributed to the cleanliness of the Japanese audience, These well-scrubbed people never smell. (They evidently expect *us* to, since one of my later hosts remarked to me one day, with obvious surprise, and in the injured tone of a person who has been wrongly informed, 'you don't smell anything special'.)

The curtain rises on the vast stage and I settle down, expecting to be bored. The first scene takes place in the husband's counting-house, in an old-fashioned and therefore tasteful Japanese décor, with the clerks sitting cross-legged on *tatami* mats in front of huge ledgers. They wear the long-haired hairstyles of olden times and flowing black costumes that stand out boldly against the light bamboo background. The faithful clerk is too old for his role, but he looks amiable and expressive.

Soon the boss's wife appears, trailing her kimono, in the S-shaped posture of Japanese dolls, with two long thin wisps of hair straggling over her face. No doubt this is intended to denote an agitated state of mind. She speaks in a high-pitched, weepy voice and looks very distraught. How can the clerk be in love with such an intolerable woman? She never leaves off complaining from the beginning to the end of the play. Nevertheless, she exercises a certain fascination, even over me and I watch her, entranced. She is quite unnatural, her poses are affected, yet she glides into them so uncannily, her gestures are so smooth, her hands so expressive that one gradually merges, half-unbelievingly, into the strange half-dream world of Kabuki.

There is a charming mime scene during which the clerk asks the wife whether she will elope with him and she nods her reply. Not a word is spoken—they are clasped in each other's arms in a highly stylized gesture from which lust is entirely absent. They finally disappear to commit suicide at the end of the 'flower path' which is a feature of all Japanese theatres.

Mrs Matsuo yawned. She is looking forward to the arrival of a colourful troup of Mexican dancers hired by Mr Matsuo, whom they are to meet tonight at the airport. Nobody here has ever seen any Mexican dancers and they hope for a big success. This is the sort of thing that the public wants.

Kabuki is rather *vieux jeu* and not many modern Japanese really enjoy it. Noh plays are even more esoteric and nobody can understand them except a few scholars. (A French artist has been so entranced by them that he is adapting the technique to modern stories.) You attend a Noh play with the text in your hand, like an opera fan, except that fewer people can read the score. Bunraku, the famous puppet plays of Osaka, are on the way out too—the Government is being asked to subsidize them and turn them into 'a national cultural property'. One of the Bunraku musicians has already achieved this distinction. I am beginning to think that it is not so comical after all to bestow this curious title upon living beings; it is even rather pathetic—they are the last representatives of artistic dynasties, rendered impotent and barren by the times in which they live. The nation is right to salute them respectfully before they pass to history. It is an original, Don Quixotish idea which nobody could have thought of but the Japanese.

Geisha party

This evening I was invited to a geisha party by two civil servants who wished to entertain me and a middle-aged journalist from New Zealand.

Male foreign guests are titillated by the very idea of a geisha party. What do they expect? Nothing happens; or is it the idea of what might or could happen, that makes them blush like school-boys at the mention of the word 'geisha'? There is more sex in a strip-tease show (*not* a Japanese one). The geishas are well-covered up and the carefully whitened nape of the neck, which is so alluring to the Japanese male, leaves a westerner stone cold.

I suppose that the charm of the geisha, for the foreigner, resides in the aura of mystery with which her profession is surrounded. The Japanese are so discreet about their own love affairs and goings-on in geisha houses that one is left guessing—and it is so delicious to guess! Since all element of mystery has been ruthlessly cut out of western novels and general treatment of sex, since all the fig-leaves have been removed, it is exciting to find that there is still one country in the world where women whose profession is to entertain men retain the appearance of demi-Goddesses, the demureness of virgins and the gorgeous apparel of a nation that revels in colour. The foreigner may be momentarily interested in the spectacle, but for him it always remains a spectacle; at a superficial level.

By this time I had seen a number of bourgeois wives, the kind of wives to whom my hosts were probably married, and it interested me to be able to set eyes on their rivals. Is this the right word? Perhaps not. There is no rivalry. The wife belongs to one world, the decorous formal world of the home and family to which the average Japanese male is deeply attached; the geisha belongs to the fantasy world to which the harassed business man can escape from his dull, money-making routine. The geisha world is a day-dream world which satisfies the innate Japanese need for visual beauty and reassurance. The reassurance comes from the traditional character of the geisha's accomplishments: they are essentially Japanese, with roots in a mythological past. At the very commencement of Japanese history, the goddesses danced before the Sun goddess: in the beginning was the dance, and the display was combined with an element of eroticism and buffoonery. Likewise the geishas, who glitter and sparkle like deities, perform complicated steps which only a connoisseur can appreciate and, when they are over, they sit with their patrons and play childish games to the accompaniment of much giggling and, sometimes, horseplay.

In this company the middle-aged Japanese male, usually so glum and rigid, relaxes and behaves like an adolescent. I have seldom seen him like this at home where, even with his wife, he feels he must assume the heavy role of father and tyrannical husband. An element of respect enters into his relations with his wife. To her he talks differently, his gestures are more studied; he is the master, and fifty per cent of all wives call him so, according to a recent magazine survey. With the geisha he uses free language, he lets himself go, he literally sits in his shirtsleeves and laughs.

The geisha knows how to entertain him *à la japonaise*, since this is her business and vocation; she is just as adolescent as her clients. First-class geishas are said to be clever; one of them is said to be interested in economics and she can talk intelligently with Cabinet Ministers, but such blue-stockings are an exception. Japanese males do not like clever women any more than the majority of their western counterparts do. They want to be amused, served, danced and sung to. Fundamentally insecure, suffering from a deep inferiority complex, the average male wants to feel like a powerful Samurai. None more accomplished than the geisha to provide him with the momentary fulfilment of this day-dream.

Patrons pay dearly for these privileges. Geishas are an expensive hobby, but this is part of the game. An element of prestige and vanity is involved. It is stylish to have a first-class geisha and although both clients and geishas are dwindling in numbers, there are still enough 'old style Japanese gentlemen' left to ensure their continuity for quite some time. And if the younger generation revert to type in their middle-age the system will probably continue for a long time. 'So long as kimonos are worn, the geishas will continue,' I hear it said, and there is probably a good deal of truth in this. The kimono is a necessary part of the décor, and three-quarters of the geishas' attraction is in the décor.

The geishas who served us this evening were truly charming. They twittered like birds, they seemed to be so happy to see us, they behaved as if they were enjoying themselves and the dancers among them were resplendent—the image of the expensive dolls one sees in glass cases in the shops which are so stubbornly given away to foreigners as parting gifts—even when the donors know that they are leaving by plane and liable to pay excess luggage.

I was enchanted, too, by the variety of types. How untrue to say, as so many unobservant westerners do, that 'the Japanese all look alike!' The dancers were heavily made up, but the others wore hardly any cosmetics at all and they had soft, clear complexions. It is equally untrue to say that the Japanese have yellow skins. Some of them have, but not all.

The geishas looked after me as attentively as if I had been a male guest. (I have been told that a number of them are Lesbians.) They passed favourable comments on my fair hair, tried to guess my age, a pastime which I discouraged amid much giggling, asked me questions about my life as a writer and pretended to be genuinely interested. I complimented them on their appearance, applauded their dancing and *samisen* playing, and felt quite sorry that I could not afford to take a geisha back home to keep as a pet and produce at cocktail parties for the entertainment of guests. My geisha peeled tangerines for me, poured out endless thimblefuls of *sake* and laughed like a schoolgirl.

The heaviest make-up cannot disguise the fact that the geishas are artless and unsophisticated. In public they are the most abstemious entertainers in the world. They do not smoke, they do not drink, they do not eat, they never wink or betray by a change in their expression that the gentleman at their side is pinching their thighs. They are as expressionless and circumspect as the famous Hakata dolls that hide lascivious male dolls beneath their kimono.

The two dancing geishas are sumptuously attired; they wear wigs over their sleek, modern hairstyle—few girls have long hair nowadays—into which are fastened flowers and glittering ornaments which fall like a tiny waterfall in a dark mountain glade over their tiny ears. They smile delicately, without showing their teeth. Their mouths are very small and their lips thin. Few Japanese have thick, voluptuous lips. Their slanting eyes make them look arch; but some are more slanting than others. Japanese eyes can be as bright as jet, almost unnaturally brilliant; their eyes are so narrow that there is hardly any room in them to express emotion; one has to look closely to detect any. Can they be tender? I have not seen any tender eyes yet but tenderness is not an emotion which the Japanese display in public.

The Japanese rarely touch one another—there is little skin-to-skin communication between them; in this they are as formal as the old time Chinese. The other day I saw the unusual sight of a young married couple (with two children) who had fallen asleep in a bus so that their heads were touching. This amused the other passengers but it embarrassed them even more. They were quite evidently *gênés* by this lack of modesty on the part of their countrymen.

The *sake* has been flowing in rapid thimblefuls, alternating with light Japanese beer. It has no effect upon me, but I have probably drunk less than the New Zealand journalist who is beginning to behave badly. His voice has become thick, he is leering at the geishas who look uncomfortable, and he is pouring lavish flattery upon our hosts, who look contemptuous. His face has gone very red and he suddenly looks elephantine and ridiculous sitting at the low table over the delicate pieces of china.

The Japanese get drunk too—very quickly and quite often—but they behave differently and the geishas know how to pack them off home without protest. In the case of a foreigner they are nonplussed, and we are getting fidgety. Four of us—the two civil servants, one of the geishas and myself—want to go to a night-club to dance.

How shall we get rid of this drunken bore? We make a move and proceed to the entrance, along the slippery polished floor, down the steep and narrow staircase (most Japanese staircases are like ladders) to the step, below which our shoes lie patiently waiting. A smiling little attendant, bent in two with politeness, fetches a long-handled shoehorn. Somebody has called a taxi for the journalist and we stay behind until he has been packed into it and sent back to his hotel. The geishas smile and wave and titter until he is out of sight then another taxi is hailed for us. One of the civil servants turns reproachfully to the middle-aged geisha who plays the *samisen* and keeps an eye on the girls: 'You must teach them how to deal with foreign drunks!' One of the bright-eyed dancing geishas sidles up and informs us 'An American came here the other night—he was so handsome. Wasn't he?' She turned to me and simpered, 'He is married. So—triangle trouble—not good, eh?' And she laughed mischievously behind her fan.

Of course 'triangle trouble' does not worry them at all. They live in a world apart and it is better fun being a geisha than a wife, until you grow old and then, who knows what may happen? You may be lucky, like the geisha of a high government official who has installed her in his home after his wife's death. She has been his geisha for over twenty years and she is not particularly beautiful, but she is charming, talented and a good listener. This geisha is visible only to intimate friends. Only one foreigner has seen her. He considered it a great honour and mark of friendship.

Many geishas and their patrons stay together for years, which seems to contradict the theory I put forward earlier—that the geisha represents an element of fantasy and romance. The middle-aged geisha looks very much like an ordinary wife to an outsider. An elderly Japanese with whom I discussed the point surprised me by his answer: 'The Japanese are sentimental—sentimental and conservative; they do not want to go through too frequent emotional pangs. The geisha–patron relationship is more complex than you think. Most patrons follow their geisha's artistic career, encourage her, applaud her at her first public performance—they give annual displays of their talents—share her triumphs and failures; she, on her part, is the confidant of his joys and sorrows so that the tie between them is very strong, just as strong, in an entirely different way, as the tie that links him to his wife through their home and children. The middle-aged geisha is still attractive, still the perfect hostess. Several of our ambassadors are married to ex-geishas. They make excellent ambassadors' wives.'

At the night-club we went to, the little geisha danced decorously with her patron and nobody else. She looked astonishingly young (she was only twenty) and innocent with her lack of make-up and her light kimono with a white background. The modern Japanese night-club hostesses, smoking ostentatiously, wriggling their low bottoms encased in tight-fitting western dresses in an attempt to be 'sexy', looked positively indecent by comparison. Some of these hostesses are on the payroll of big companies as 'part-time employees' to entertain foreign guests. They earn good money, sometimes more than executives, drive their own cars, live in their own flats. They look bold and uninhibited and one presumes that they are less selective in their choice of patrons than the traditional geisha.

One rarely sees wives at a night-club. It is not customary for Japanese husbands to take their wives with them anywhere—social life in Japan is a very one-sided affair—but, on the other hand, older generation wives are not attracted by night-club life. 'My wife has never set foot in one,' said the civil servant who did not have a geisha. 'She has seen them on television and decided she does not like them.'

The second civil servant, whose geisha had excused herself because she was booked for another party (they generally go to three parties in one night and sleep until noon), called one of the club hostesses to our table and fondled her affectionately. 'Our wives don't like going out,' he said emphatically. 'They prefer to stay at home. What they want,' he banged the table and looked to his colleague for confirmation, 'is security. Yes, that's it. Security. So long as they have a good home, food, a nice new kimono every once in a while—so long as they know the children are having a good education—that's what they want. In return they never bother us with unnecessary questions, do they?' His colleague nodded his assent. 'I often get home late—I have to in my job— but never does my wife ask me where I have been or with whom. Does yours?' His colleague shook his head. 'Of course they don't. They know perfectly well that we are faithful to them. I have never spent a night away from home in my life—except strictly on business.' 'Nor have I,' said his colleague, draining his glass of lemon squash.

The band struck up an old-fashioned waltz. 'Let's dance,' said the unaccompanied civil servant, springing to his feet. 'The waltz was the first ballroom dance I ever learned. My mother taught it to me . . . how it takes me back . . . she was so graceful' and he began to dance with a nostalgic smile. We danced until midnight, when night-clubs officially close, but if you really want to lead a life of sin, there are plenty of possibilities. The latest are the private call bars. Our hostess provided us with details. She was probably one of the 'introducers' to this new type of fun, which is intended for couples. The usual procedure is for the prospective customer to obtain the address from a bartender or a chief waiter in a cabaret who obligingly telephones a mysterious number and escorts the client in his own car to a modern apartment building.

The bartender takes the clients up to an apartment and pushes the door button. A peeping window is pulled aside, then the door quietly opens. Inside the couple find a luxurious apartment provided with a bar. A housemaid or a bartender waits on the customers and then discreetly disappears leaving them to enjoy what our hostess euphemistically called 'a pleasant home atmosphere'.

These '*koru* bars' (Japanese for 'call bars') are quite profitable. They are open from 10 p.m. to 5 a.m. and the owner of the apartment does not require to lay out any capital or pay for a licence. It costs about four thousand pounds key money to open a bar in downtown Tokyo in the Ginza area and two thousand in Shinjuku. But all the call bars charge customers Ginza prices.

Since it is illegal, a call bar is cautious in accepting customers, the majority of whom are movie stars, people in show business or wealthy playboys. As for the people who operate them, 'they can be divided into three types,' our hostess informed us with un-Japanese precision.

'One is the "Madam OB type" run by a former bar madam.' ('OB,' she explained, 'comes from "Old Boys", meaning a graduate of a college.') 'Then there is the "Future Madam" type run by a woman who plans to open a legal bar soon but has temporarily hired her apartment in order to raise the necessary funds. Here you will often find a bartender whom she has hired for her future legal bar. Thirdly, there is the "Amateur type". This is almost domestic —it is run by the wife of an employee or a financially incompetent husband who cannot support his family.'

'I don't see the point of such bars,' said one of the civil servants, echoing my own sentiments. 'What have they got that other places haven't got—except that you can go there at different hours?' 'That is an advantage, for some people,' replied our hostess, 'but I think the main attraction lies in the mystery that surrounds it—the atmosphere of secrecy. Most men love that.' She looked round and smiled invitingly. 'At any rate, that is what I have found. Most of us hostesses working at night-clubs run a bar in our own apartments. A little sideline, you know. It's quite simple. Mine is very cosy. Would you like to run over and have a look at it?'

*A luxury
modern block*

*T*oday I regretfully moved out of the Matsuo's house to go on to my next hostess, whom I shall call Mrs Yoshiko.

Mrs Yoshiko called for me in her car, which she drives herself. She needs it for business purposes, because she manages a Chinese restaurant where she took me for lunch. Her husband is in the lucrative import–export business and owns another and larger car. They have a daughter who is studying Spanish in the United States and wants to spend a year at Madrid University. What do I think about that? the mother asks me anxiously. What kind of a city is Madrid? Would it be safe to send her daughter there? I assure her that Madrid is one of the 'safest' cities in the world. Spain still has a strong family tradition and you find less violence and juvenile delinquency there than anywhere else. Besides, I have friends who would be delighted to entertain a Japanese girl. Mrs Yoshiko looks relieved and decides to discuss the proposition with her husband that evening.

The Chinese food in her restaurant is good, but the interior architecture is Japanese and depressing since one eats in solitude. Apart from the food, half the fun of going to a restaurant is to see people, what they wear, what they eat, how they eat, and occasionally eavesdrop on an interesting conversation. This feminine point of view does not correspond to a man's ideas and, until recently, only Japanese men went to restaurants. Now that women have become more emancipated they are venturing out too, but mostly in groups of their own kind—graduates celebrating a university success, elderly ladies eager for a change and *sake*. (They can drink a surprising amount of *sake*.)

A stag party was going on in the room next to ours. The loud singing and boisterous laughter ended in a slow, typically Japanese rendering of 'Auld Lang Syne', to which the Japanese have put their own words. This tune, being sentimentally lachrymose, is a great favourite in Japan.

None of these guests are visible, only their shoes, when one passes in front of the carefully concealed apartments between which jolly waitresses scamper to and fro in kimono, from which their white *tabi* heels peep like rabbits' tails.

After lunch I accompanied Mrs Yoshiko to her *kouta* lesson. *Kouta* are short Japanese songs, highly classical, monotonous to the non-initiated, and difficult to learn even for the Japanese, because the music is unscored. The patient pupil sits on her heels in front of the teacher and listens carefully while the latter intones something that sounds like plainsong chanted by an expiring monk. Mrs Yoshiko does not look like the sort of person who would be interested in *kouta*: she dresses in severe western style and one would imagine, to hear her discuss her business interests, that she had turned her back on old Japan. I am beginning to realize, however, that very few people ever turn their backs completely on old Japan. The younger generation may be different, but the in-betweens, the people whose life is astride the old régime and the new, tend to get more and more Japanese as they grow older. Some of them, like the writer Tanazaki, end their lives in a cloister-like retreat.

Mrs Yoshiko's singing teacher lives in a similar kind of cultural retreat but it is in the middle of Tokyo, a little room above a dingy café in a busy thoroughfare from where one hears the incessant din of traffic; not, one would have thought, a propitious place in which to cultivate the arts. And yet, after five minutes in the dim atmosphere, subjected to the Buddha-like calm of the slow-moving teacher, one falls into a state of semi-hypnosis through which the harsh notes of the archaic songs pierce the consciousness like an incantation.

When we slid the door open we found the teacher coiled like a serpent-goddess before a small, low table, bending over her book of songs. We bowed until our foreheads touched the *tatami*. Meekly, Mrs Yoshiko took up her position, looking more like the disciple of a priestess than the pupil of a singing teacher. 'We are going to sing a love song,' she explained. It sounded more like a funeral dirge to me, but I reminded myself that love in ancient Japan was nearly always crossed and deals, like medieval troubadour poems, with the themes of death and separation. Double love suicides are still fashionable among the very young. The Press reported at least a dozen while I was in Japan.

After the lesson, we drove to the Yoshiko's flat in a large apartment block facing Tokyo bay. At the moment, the bay is invisible. It is raining hard and a slate-grey mist droops forlornly over the jagged rooftops and the television aerials. Flat-topped modern buildings, uniform as barracks, surge between dark old houses with upturned roofs, survivals of the bombardments, remnants of the old Tokyo where people live behind barricades of shutters, high walls and carefully tailored trees. There are still whole streets of these houses, but they are slowly giving way before the resolute army of builders and labourers who advance day by day, probing into every corner of the ever-widening city, replacing the old by the uniform new. Drilling goes on day and night.

Occasionally one comes across an old house being repaired; it is a fascinating sight. The scaffolding is of the flimsiest nature, wooden poles tied together by old pieces of string and twine. Labourers crouch on the cross-beams, barefoot, pail or tool in hand. Sometimes they fall off their precarious perches or the scaffolding gives way, but not as often as one would expect.

Everything in Mrs Yoshiko's flat is western style: beds, bath and toilet. It is almost a novel sensation to sit on a toilet again—how quickly one loses everyday habits—and it feels lazy. I occupy the one guest room where I am able to hang up my clothes. It is not a large flat, the L-shaped living-room merges into the dining-room and the maid sits near us when her chores are over, poring over an exercise book. She is learning English, like her mistress.

Mrs Yoshiko's husband has got home before us. He is sitting in his slippers and kimono watching television. He speaks good English and we converse in between programmes.

After dinner, the telephone rings to announce that Mrs Yoshiko's father has unexpectedly arrived in Tokyo from Kyushu and will be with us in half an hour. 'But what will you do? I am occupying the only guest room!' I exclaim in alarm. Mrs Yoshiko smiles. 'That is quite all right—you do not need to worry on his behalf,' she says. 'My father cannot bear to sleep in a western bed so we keep a *futon* for him which will be laid out later on the *tatami*.'

The *tatami* is the one concession to Japanese customs that is preserved in modern blocks of apartments. Even here there is a step in the hall—a small one but a step nevertheless, before which one leaves one's shoes and puts on slippers.

It is said that the expectation of life in Japan is shorter than in the West but I am continually coming across very old and very energetic people of both sexes. According to the official statistics, Mr Morita, Mrs Yoshiko's father, should have died five years ago, but he is well over seventy and seems likely to live for another twenty years. His energy is boundless. He is a Councillor of Dazaifu, a little town near Fukuoka, famous for its Shinto shrine, and as far as I can make out, the unofficial P.R.O. attached to the shrine, a function for which, as an ex-newspaperman, he is well qualified. Thirty years ago he went on a voyage round the world and stayed in London for four days. While he was there he enrolled at the London School of Economics and attended one lecture; this convinced him that his knowledge of English was insufficient. He could not understand the lecturer and regretfully abandoned his project.

Father's presence in the house is not obtrusive yet it is felt. His tall, gaunt, commanding presence subtly changes the atmosphere. Mrs Yoshiko and her husband are politely deferential—the son-in-law warmer and more intimate than his wife. I tell Mr Morita that I shall be going to Kumamoto in Kyushu later; he kindly asks me, through his daughter, to stop at Fukuoka, where he will meet me and take me to Dazaifu which is only an hour away. I am invited to spend a night at this historic shrine. The head priest is young and progressive and he speaks good English for he has studied in the United States. Mr Morita is so insistent that I am convinced his invitation is no mere formality, but his son-in-law whispers in my ear: 'Send him a telegram a couple of days before you arrive, just in case he forgets. He has so many projects in hand. . . .' We make careful notes in our respective diaries and I promise to send a telegram, although I foresee that this could be a complicated operation. I have not yet set foot in a Japanese post-office—so far I have used the facilities of the large hotels.

I had a one hundred per cent western breakfast this morning. No seaweed. By 8 a.m. both men had gone to work. Mrs Yoshiko put on some classical western records after breakfast and we looked through a stack of photograph albums. Every self-respecting modern Japanese family has a large collection; I should think that every Japanese over the age of ten possesses a camera of some sort which he uses on every possible occasion. (According to the un-flagging statisticians, ten million Japanese own a camera.) There is a nation-wide passion for taking photographs and being photo-graphed in serried rows with a complete lack of any artistic sense. Composition is the last thing they bother about.

The sun came out after breakfast and Mrs Yoshiko asked me timidly if I should like to visit the famous Sengakuji shrine where the forty-seven *ronin* are buried. It lies practically at the foot of the block of flats, in one of the 'Japanese' corners of the city of which there are far too few.

I had heard the story of the forty-seven Samurai who avenged the murder of their lord but I had always believed that it belonged to the realm of mythology. Their graves convinced me that they had really existed. The forty-seven tombstones lie in a separate cemetery on a slope behind the shrine. Incense was burning before every one of them, and each one was decorated with a fresh sprig of the sacred *sakaki* tree which plays an important role in Shinto ceremonial. Several visitors were mooning about absorbing the atmosphere. The Japanese are very sensitive to atmosphere. They are far less interested than we are in historical facts and dates but they have recently adopted the American fad for measure-ments; every pagoda, every temple has been measured from top to bottom to cater for this particular aspect of American tourist gluttony.

*A modest
modern block*

The multiple storey building has caused a social revolution in Japan—it is a tangible sign of the post-war break-away from the traditional family pattern. Most of the apartments are occupied by couples with their children; there is no room in them for parents or in-laws, except on short visits.

There is still a lingering guilt complex in young people's minds about the abandonment of mother-in-law. I am often asked, rather anxiously, by young men and women: 'What do you think about newly-weds living with their in-laws? Do you believe it is a good thing?' It was not customary before the new Constitution to discuss private affairs and probe into the dark psychological motives that lie behind the behaviour of the various members of one's family. An Ivy Compton-Burnett was unthinkable. But all this has changed, and the awful extent of the mother-in-law problem frankly revealed by papers, magazines and Family Courts. The Japanese mother-in-law has been shown up and proved to be very much like mothers-in-law everywhere else. The Japanese have still not got over the shock of this revelation and of their own feelings on the subject. They still feel the weight of the taboo on a public exposure of family rifts.

This afternoon I was taken to the suburbs to visit one of the new, modest types of housing estates for the lower middle class income groups. My guide and interpreter was Miss Harada, the Secretary of the Federation of Housewives' Associations, one of the startling new pressure groups to have arisen since the end of the war, under the presidency of Mrs Obu, a woman member of the Diet and an indefatigable social worker.

I had already visited the headquarters of the Association in a modern building where a variety of activities take place, from the cooking of hamburgers to the performance of Shinto wedding ceremonies. The first is connected with the cookery school which teaches, like others of its kind in Japan, both foreign-style and Japanese cooking. The second activity is connected with the Association's drive to lower the high cost of weddings; a Shinto wedding can be held anywhere, from a department store to a well-known shrine (the latter carries a certain amount of snobbish prestige; the Meiji shrine in Tokyo has cashed in on this source of revenue since the end of the war to restore its depleted funds).

The Housewives' Association's badge is the large round wooden spatula with which rice is dished out from a bowl placed on the *tatami* at meal-times; this badge is wielded during processions when members, clad in the Japanese housewife's traditional white overall edged with a narrow flounce, walk through the streets of Tokyo in protest against the rising cost of living, the municipal authorities neglect to collect garbage and other vital everyday questions with which housewives are concerned. The Government takes notice of the Association's demands, and sends observers to their conferences.

It has always been usual for countrywomen to band together to get certain jobs done, and now that many of them have come to live in town they occasionally extend the system to the capital. The other day, for instance, I heard that the women of a certain Tokyo ward had got together to cut down the jungle-like growth of weeds in the plots near their homes in an effort to discourage sex crimes. (Forty-four were committed last summer in empty lots in the neighbourhood.) Even crimes are seasonal in Japan. It is said that there is an increase in sex crimes in the summer, while spring is the season for double suicides—either poison under the cherry-blossom or the more modern method of throwing oneself under a train.

Miss Harada was waiting for me outside a small suburban station with the resolute expression of a woman waiting for a banner to be placed in her hands. With her straight hair, square jaw and lack of make-up I likened her to a domestic Joan of Arc ardently cam-paigning for an improved standard of living and housewives' rights. Miss Harada sleeps on a sofa on the Association's premises, 'because of the shortage of accommodation'. She belongs to the dedicated without whom little progress would be made in a man's country like Japan where women, despite the assurances in the Constitution, are not men's equals or even their complements.

Miss Harada is a recent convert to Christianity. There are only half a million Christians in Japan, in spite of the strenuous efforts made by so many diverse missionaries over the centuries, a small number compared to the membership of some of the 'new' religions, e.g.

Reiyukai	3,465,668
Rissho Koseikai	1,349,905
The House of Growth	1,533,784
Perfect Liberty	701,550
Daijo	816,856

and a host of others. Even the new Sun Goddess sect has over a hundred thousand members.

The parents of some of the converts I have met complain that Christianity is 'a foreign religion'; when I remark that Buddhism is just as foreign since it originated in India, they look blank and it is obvious that the argument has made no impact. Maybe India is less 'foreign' than the West and anyway Buddhism has been Japanized over the centuries to the point that many people worship indiscriminately in Buddhist temples and Shinto shrines. On the other hand western missionaries were—still are—inclined to be aggressive, to boast of western superiority and alienate the people from their own culture. The Japanese are not really interested in dogma—they prefer a vague religious 'atmosphere' induced by natural surroundings and they have not been able to assimilate the Christian ambience conveyed by an ugly alien architecture that does not fit snugly into their landscape as shrines and temples do. Every mountain, every beauty spot in Japan has its god and its temple. There is no room left for church spires that pierce the skies so sharply, almost forcing the deity to come down from his heavenly abode; Japanese gods are invited more gently. They are very accessible and can be summoned in the same way that one calls a Continental waiter: by a clap of the hands.

I have met several Japanese Christians and I am trying to assess what they have in common. Perhaps it is rather futile, perhaps it is impossible, but it is an interesting pastime. Those I have come across so far can be divided into three classes: people who have been converted to Christianity because they are blind admirers of the West, particularly of the 'American conquerors', and they feel that to be one hundred per cent western, modern and 'accepted' you have got to be Christian. Their knowledge of the Bible is scanty but they contribute handsomely to charity bazaars and send their children to Christian schools. Then there are tender-hearted Japanese who find their own religions cold and are attracted by the element of compassion in Christianity; they shed tears over Bible stories and find it 'the most poetical book in the world'. Thirdly, there is a tight little core of genuine believers who try to put the principles of Christianity into practice in their daily lives. Miss Harada is obviously one of these.

There is a streak of Victorian prudery in the Japanese—particularly among young ladies—and I do not think that Christianity will do them any good. It all depends, of course, on the brand of Christianity they come into contact with; those which lay emphasis on Original Sin, guilt and hell are not going to help to make the Japanese more optimistic or relaxed. And they do need to relax. There is far too much solemnity in their faces, too much formality in their social relations, too much pessimism in their outlook.

Miss Harada has given me a magnificent pamphlet to look at, published by the Ministry of Housing; it is full of glossy pictures of new housing estates, but there are still not half enough blocks of flats for the increasing population; Tokyo is a giant octopus with tentacles spreading far out into the paddy-fields of the countryside, on the one hand, and almost into the sea, reclaiming land from the bay, on the other. I looked at the pamphlet dutifully but I was more interested in our fellow-passengers on the suburban train.

Most of them looked as though they belonged to the *churyu kaikyu* (middle class) or the *chukan-so*: middle social strata, an expression which most Japanese dislike, because it gives them the uncomfortable impression of 'being left in mid-air in society'. The *chukan-so* are the salaried people, the kind of people who live on housing estates like the Lark Hill apartments, where we are going, and earn approximately thirty-five pounds a month.

They are clean, neat and odourless and, after eyeing me with polite curiosity, most of them fell into a doze. I have never seen so many people asleep in trains or buses as in Japan. Is it because they work so hard, or because they wish to gather strength for their next job or because they become mentally exhausted quicker than people who use a Roman alphabet? I cannot help thinking that all those Japanese characters with their demon shapes must prey on people's minds. Japanese brains must be hopelessly encumbered.

This is apparent when they engage in a telephone conversation. The shortest message, which could be delivered in three or four short English sentences, is expanded by a Japanese to such extraordinary lengths that one begins to doubt whether he is referring to the subject in hand or whether for some mysterious reason he has launched forth into his autobiography. This is always happening to me, and since other foreigners tell me that it is always happening to them, we cannot all be mistaken. Ask a Japanese to ring up Mr X and cancel an appointment—he will be on the telephone for ten minutes, if you are fortunate. Ask him to ring up and fix an appointment and he will be away for twenty minutes. One must, I admit, make allowances for the lengthy directions without which one could never find a Japanese house. Another peculiarity of the Japanese is to ask questions about one's ancestors and lineage on what appears to us to be irrelevant occasions. If you ring up in answer to an advertisement to rent a house—to take one example—the owner will want to know what your father and grandfather did, which university you graduated from, where and when, and, of course, your age. It is only after you have been properly pigeon-holed that negotiations can begin. All this takes time.

We got out at a drab little station in a drab little suburb and crossed the lines to find a bus. (Bridges are built for more ornamental than practical purposes in Japan.) It had begun to rain; we joined a small, dejected-looking queue while passing traffic, bouncing up, down and round the numerous holes in the road, splashed large abstract mud patterns on our legs and coats. Eventually our single-decker arrived and a dapper little conductress in a green uniform with a small green cap stuck jauntily over one mischievous slanting eye welcomed us in with the air of proprietorship. As the door slammed, she murmured '*orrye, orrye, orrye*' which I mistook for a Japanese word until Miss Harada told me that it was a Japanese rendering of 'all right'. This hang-over from the American occupation is found all over Japan.

We bumped along narrow, muddy roads in a flat landscape for a quarter of an hour, and I began to commiserate with the wage-earners who have to spend so much time travelling to and fro to Tokyo every day from the housing estate. Our bus took us through the groups of blocks and left us near the shopping area. Small as it was there were two flower shops.

After consulting the coloured map of the estate at the crossroads we walked up to the central office, where the manager and a young woman assistant were waiting to welcome us. Several chubby children peered round the sliding door separating the office from a hall where a busy group of mothers was diligently sewing. Others were knitting or embroidering. They belonged to the 'Meeting of

Taste' circle which meets two or three times a week to cook, sew or arrange flowers; it is a good way of bringing together the young wives on the estate who might otherwise feel lonely.

Nine thousand people live on this estate. The flats are allocated on a lottery basis. There is no priority system for families with children. Rents, for a small two-roomed flat with dining-room and kitchen combined, toilet and tiny bathroom (Japanese style, of course) cost approximately six pounds a month.

After tea and sweet, sticky cakes filled with dark brown soya bean paste, which has no taste and adds pounds to one's weight, Miss Mori, the assistant, took us round the estate. She is a tall, slim efficient-looking person, dressed in western clothes (I saw very few kimonos on the estate) whose main job is to deal with 'human problems'. I would have liked her to give me some examples of actual cases, but nothing is more difficult than to extract concrete data from the Japanese. (When they do so, however, they are as meticulous as the Teutons.) Most complaints, I discovered after much prodding, concern noise made by neighbours' radios and television sets. There are no laws about this and Miss Mori was astonished to hear that we are not allowed to disturb our neighbours after 11 p.m. in England. Young couples complain about lack of space—they have less than their parents would because they insist on having western-style bedrooms. The advantage of a *futon* is that you can pack it away in the daytime and use the space for other purposes.

I asked to see one of the apartments—a contingency which had been foreseen, and the occupants forewarned. It was, said Miss Mori proudly, the best-kept apartment on the estate. I should like to have seen the worst, too, but I did not dare to ask.

There are no elevators in the blocks—only stone steps; each block is numbered in large black letters; there is plenty of space between them, with a well-kept lawn and room for children to play. The roads leading to each block are lined with shrubs.

A well-dressed young woman opened to us when Miss Mori knocked at her door on the second floor of block 93. We advanced in single file; it was a squeeze for the three of us to take off our shoes together in the miniature hall and shuffle into the slippers provided for us. The young woman's husband, an architect, was reading a technical magazine in the living-room. He works in Yokohama three days a week. The rest of the time he spends at home on various projects. The young woman showed me the bedroom in which there was only just enough room for a large double bed, a wardrobe, a dressing-table and a chair. 'It is much too small,' sighed her husband.

There was everything in the flat that a modern couple want, according to the requirements advertised on television and the galaxy of women's magazines: a television set, a washing-machine (they make them cheaper in Japan), gay plastics in the kitchen, stiff western-style furniture. An artistically arranged vase of flowers and a square wooden tub of a bath in the closet that served for a bathroom were the only 'Japanese' touches. It was a small flat to have a baby in, but there did not seem to be any for the moment. Population figures are fairly static now that the Japanese have been told all about birth control. They use the Ogino method, which has been discredited in some western countries, but it seems to work in Japan—that and, of course, abortion, which accounts for two million interrupted births a year. The operation is legal and costs approximately six shillings but many people believe that it should be more strictly controlled.

There is no provision in these flats for a Buddhist alcove or a Shinto god-shelf. Mrs Yoshiko has not got one either in her luxury flat. There does not appear to be any demand for them on the part of the modern generation.

Admittedly these young couples on the housing estates do not enjoy the same kind of life that we do—they cannot afford holidays (nobody in Japan ever seems to take a holiday except the very wealthy who go on world tours); members of the *chukan-so* can rarely afford a car, but they are not doing at all badly. Basically they are not very different from our own *chukan-so*; the gap between us is growing narrower. The young couple I had just seen are fairly typical and inclined to disappoint foreigners who prefer to regard the Japanese as exotic little creatures of purely ornamental value—when they are not wickedly spoiling our markets.

The husbands on the housing estates are not the sort who keep geishas. Miss Mori estimates that about half of them hand over their pay-packets to their wives. On the other hand, housework 'has no standard of economic evaluation' and the lack of it occasionally produces heated legal arguments.

A little while ago a forty-five-year-old housewife of Yokohama was knocked over and killed by a hit-and-run driver while she was on her way to the station with an umbrella to meet her husband, for it had begun to rain in the afternoon. The driver, who was drunk at the time of the accident, gave himself up the following day. His family offered two hundred pounds 'consolation money' plus the three hundred pounds legally fixed amount of insurance against loss which the family of a victim in a traffic accident is entitled to in Japan. But the lawyer acting on behalf of the widowed husband considered the offer too small and demanded consolation money of three thousand pounds plus another three thousand as 'compensation for damages'. The case was finally brought to the Yokohama District Court where it has attracted public attention, because the lawyer is trying to establish a precedent with his argument that 'a housewife enables her husband to earn income in peace by devoting herself to housework and child-care. Accordingly, half of her husband's income belongs to her.' So far it has been the rule that if a housewife is killed in an accident the family only receive consolation money; her housework does not count. If her husband is killed she gets both consolation money and compensation, depending on the estimated number of years the victim would have lived and the salary he was earning at the time of the accident. Nobody believes, however, that the Yokohama lawyer stands a chance with his revolutionary theory.

A Tokyo husband recently evaluated his thirty-eight-year-old wife's work at eighteen pounds a month. He worked it out this way: the forty-five-year-old merchant husband, with a monthly income of £150 took a mistress last year and kept her in an apartment. His wife came to hear of the relationship and begged her husband to break with his mistress. Her arguments being of no avail she began to neglect the housework to such an extent that her husband was forced to hire a housekeeper, whom he paid at the rate of eight shillings (plus meals) a day. Some months later the husband told his wife: 'We have merely lived under the same roof for the past half year. To manage the housework I have only had to hire a housekeeper. From now on you are only qualified as a housekeeper and I shall pay you eighteen pounds a month. So— please leave me alone!'

Miss Harada did not think that we had accomplished enough for one afternoon and she insisted that I should pay a visit to a doll-maker; it was still raining and it was late. 'But I told her that we would be coming,' said Miss Harada anxiously. 'Can't you ring her up and tell her that we have been delayed and cannot make it?' I asked her. 'But she has brought out all her dolls especially for us, we *must* go,' she insisted with surprising obstinacy. After fifteen minutes, when no bus had arrived I again began to protest. 'We will have to take a taxi,' said Miss Harada. She was evidently bent on my seeing the doll-maker and nothing I could do would deflect her.

After another twenty minutes, and a phone call from a box near the shopping centre, a large 80-yen taxi came prancing up with the windscreen wiper in rapid action like an agitated Japanese fan. 'The doll-maker's house is on the road back to town,' said Miss Harada apologetically as we scrambled in. But the taxi-driver was not sure of the way; he missed it several times and it was getting later and later. 'I can't stop—I have an appointment at Shibuya station,' I said. 'We must,' insisted Miss Harada, almost hysterically, 'let me phone and tell your friends that you will be late.' The taxi paused while she rushed off to a call-box by the side of the road. I resigned myself to a fifteen minutes' wait while she delivered the message. It took twenty.

It was almost dark by the time we reached Miss Y's house which was not easy to find for it lay buried like an ancient tomb behind a mass of dripping foliage and a tall, sulky gate at the end of a winding drive.

Miss Y opened the door and beamed at Miss Harada. They evidently knew each other well. We removed our wet shoes and Miss Y led us along a corridor and into a dark Japanese room where the dolls had been laid out upon shelves. It was cold but it was above all the atmosphere that made me shiver. The house seemed to be soaked in sad memories. Miss Y switched on an electric radiator, then her mother came in and bowed, till her wrinkled forehead touched the floor. She looked very old and very crushed, more like Miss Y's grandmother; she sat on her heels with her hands meekly folded on her lap while Miss Y made us tea and brought out more dolls. Miss Harada looked relaxed and pleased. I looked surreptitiously at my watch. I had been invited to the theatre and I did not wish to make my friends wait in the rain at Shibuya.

The dolls on the shelves were traditional style 'Girls' Festival' dolls, but those which Miss Y makes are quite different—they are modern, and impish like Japanese versions of Mabel Lucy Attwell's creations. They are made of painted pawlonia wood, and they have wide, plump faces with mock-innocent expressions. None of them are for sale. They have been exhibited at department stores and

they have won prizes. After ten minutes, a bowl of tea and two
sticky cakes (our hostesses had also bought a large cream and
strawberry cake for us) I made a determined move to go.

Miss Y, still beaming, led us to the door. Her soft-spoken
mother bowed and bowed. Out in the street I began to ask questions. 'Why doesn't Miss Y sell her dolls?' 'She does not make
them for money,' Miss Harada retorted sharply, as if I had made an
immoral suggestion. 'She works in an office all day. She is a clerk.
It is only in the evening that she can make her dolls.' 'But if she
sold them,' I suggested, 'she could make them all day. She would
probably like that better.' 'Perhaps.'

Little by little, the story came out. The Y's are very poor. They
lost everything in the war. The father was a Captain who died of
war wounds. They have only got their old house which is full of
scars and Miss Y works to keep the three of them: herself, her
mother and the house which means so much to them. She is
twenty-eight—quite old, by Japanese standards. 'A very respectable person,' said Miss Harada emphatically. They are good friends
and now I began to understand why Miss Harada was so anxious
for me to meet Miss Y. It was not every day that a foreigner called,
and a foreigner who was writing about Japan. Miss Y leads a hard
life and she needs encouragement. It would give her pleasure . . .
Miss Harada, as her devoted friend, had made up her mind that I
should call. It was for her that she had forsaken her bland, polite,
almost meek manner. Although the Japanese have few close
friends, they are devoted to the ones they have; I have known quite
poor people to undertake long train journeys, at great personal
sacrifice, to advise a friend upon a personal matter which a westerner would have been content to discuss by correspondence;
friends are much more demanding than in the West.

By a curious coincidence, the modern play I was taken to this
evening deals with emotional conflicts on a housing estate; the
block of apartments on the revolving stage looked just like Lark
Hill. The occupiers, however, were very dissimilar. I could not
imagine the set-faced ladies of the 'Meeting of Taste' behaving as
wantonly as their counterparts on the stage, who were constantly
inviting their neighbours in for a drink and a bit of love-making;
in the play a middle-aged doll-maker who lived on the ground
floor made mischief and tried to break up happy marriages; it
turned out that she was frigid and she ended by going stark raving

mad. The Japanese are inordinately fond of melodramatic endings.

Tomorrow I move to the suburbs—more specifically, to the residential suburb of Seijo, to stay with a lady whom I shall call Mrs Michiko. She is taking me in her car and I am terrified because she is a nervous little woman who drives in a series of fits and starts that correspond to her changing moods. Her car snorts and snaps like a wild animal under her trembling hands. So far, however, she has not had an accident. I hope that fate is not waiting until I am with her. It is quite a long drive to Seijo—about an hour, through the traffic of Tokyo.

In the suburbs:
bathing in public

April 8th   *A*ll is well, we arrived at Seijo safely after having infuriated numberless drivers on our way. Mrs Michiko's house is situated on the slope of a steep hill and it is not easy to drive down and round the narrow muddy lane that leads to it. We nearly bumped into a lorry and only just averted an accident. Mrs Michiko bowed apologetically and the lorry-driver bowed back. I cannot imagine an English lorry-driver behaving with so much restraint. Mrs Michiko apologizes to everybody. She is always saying '*Sumimasen*'—I am sorry—for reasons which are not at all clear. But this streak of apparent meekness cannot disguise Mrs Michiko's fundamental purposefulness. She knows what she wants and like so many Japanese, she is prepared to fight to achieve it. Her sixteen-year-old son is an aspiring violinist who is studying in the United States. Mrs Michiko is taking her car over to tour the States with her son next summer. In the meantime, she is negotiating to sell her present house in exchange for another. She expects to make a handsome profit out of the transaction. Japanese women have shrewd calculating little heads. I have observed that several members of the International Women's Association are either in partnership with their husbands or in business on their own account. One member, a charming young essayist who writes for women's magazines and looks so feminine in her flowery kimono, is the director of an oil firm; that is the side of her life which is publicized on her visiting-card—not her literary pursuits. Since the end of the war, women have begun to dabble in stocks and shares; they are called 'Investment Madams'.

For the time being, the Michikos live in a three-storeyed wooden house overlooking paddy-fields and a village; Mrs Michiko points out the primary school which is used for Baptist church services on Sundays. She tells me that she is a Christian and that her father, who has been a Buddhist for fifty years, has recently been converted too. Her mother prefers to stay as she is. She likes the Bible stories, says Mrs Michiko, and even goes so far as to believe that they may be true, but she is conservative and does not wish to break with her ancestral traditions.

My room, or what will be my room when we have finished dinner and my hosts decide that it is time the *futon* should be brought out of its hiding place, is on the third storey at the top of the usual highly polished steep staircase which I find so difficult to climb in the outsize slippers provided for me. There is a writing desk, a low table, a few flat cushions on the floor, a television set, and a very loud cuckoo clock on the wall which fills me with dismay for I am a pathologically light sleeper. I fear that I shall not be able to sleep, even with ear-plugs.

The plant on the writing-desk is intriguing. It is a pink azalea on which a branch of white azalea has been grafted. The experiment has succeeded although I am not sure that the result is aesthetically satisfying.

Mrs Michiko's parents come in and I am formally introduced to them. I try to bow as gracefully as possible. The father is a chiropractor, one of the first in Japan, a benevolent gentleman with large, capable hands. The mother is as brown as an autumn leaf, from her kimono to her sallow face. The elderly couple have just celebrated their Golden Wedding; after dinner I was shown the film of the celebrations, which traditionally include a ceremonial fan dance by the old pair who wear special masks for the occasion and advance slowly, extending their arms in a gesture which signifies the length of their happy life together. Later they are given brooms with which they sweep up imaginary leaves indicating that they are in the autumn of their lives. The dance took place in the garden, watched by the younger members of the family, and was followed by a banquet.

In addition to Mrs Michiko's parents, there is her young brother, who works with Mrs Michiko's husband at the Family Planning Association, her nephew, who is studying English at Tokyo University, and her fourteen-year-old daughter who promises to become a very good pianist. She is shy, like so many Japanese girls, giggles a lot and hides her face in her hands. I am getting used to this form of self-defence which can last from several hours to several days, according to the individual.

Dinner is brought up in stages from the floor below. There are so many dishes, bowls and plates of all colours, shapes and sizes that the table is too small to hold them all. Some will have to remain on the *tatami*. Wine is produced—Japanese white wine. It is such a long time since I was offered a drink that my eyes sparkle with the lust of a deprived alcoholic. Alas, it is served in a liqueur glass which is not refilled. Warm *sake* follows but it is obvious that my hosts are not partial to alcohol. One dish follows the other— each one as pretty as a picture. One of them contains only three small objects: one prawn, one tiny cockleshell and one lotus flower— a charming subject for a still life. It is surprising that the Japanese should not have painted *nature morte* inspired from their dinner-tables. There is scope in this idea for a western artist.

After dinner and the film show, I am taken down to the basement, which overlooks the lower portion of the garden, to meet a Japanese English teacher and her three pupils—shy, teenage boys who bend over their books in embarrassment when I speak to them very slowly in English. The teacher, whose first name is Edna, was educated in the United States and speaks such fluent English that at first I could not guess where she came from. When I asked her she replied with a wry smile, 'I'm supposed to be Japanese.' She is one of the 'in-betweens'. 'I married a Japanese in the States,' she told me, puffing at a cigarette and leaning against the piano, 'we both thought along the same lines then. But since we came back home, he's become all Japanesy—expects me to do the slave-girl stuff. That doesn't suit me at all—I've grown out of it for keeps—so now we go our separate ways.'

Edna is certainly not the slave-girl type. She looks *Bohème* in her jeans, with her hair falling to her shoulders, her cigarettes and her unconventional ideas. She likes western music, goes to all the concerts she can afford, and walks home in the dark when she has no money to pay the fare. She warmed up as she talked, and probably felt closer to me than to many of her own countrymen. I know of a similar unadjusted case in Tokyo—except that the woman in question is single. 'I felt like rebelling when I first got back from the States,' she told me, 'but I've got used to it now.' Maybe she had, superficially, but at a deeper level a sense of discontent remains and like Edna, she looks sad. The worst kind of incomprehension, the one that really wounds, is to find oneself a foreigner in one's own country, cast aside like a mongrel without a pedigree. And in Japan, of all countries, it is extremely important to have a pedigree.

When I climb upstairs again I find that the *futon* has been laid out in the middle of 'my' room and the table has been placed on one side. I should like to hang some clothes up but there is no cupboard or wardrobe, not even the traditional clothes-horse.

The old couple bid me good night. The father looks round before he leaves the room and gently walks up to the cuckoo clock which he stops and silences. I am grateful to him for his thoughtfulness which proves that Japanese men, when they want to, can be just as kind and attentive to details as their women.

April 9th   It is Sunday and I am expected to go to church with Mrs Michiko, her father and her young brother. In return, I ask her whether she would be kind enough to accompany me to the public baths in the afternoon. I have heard so much about them and wonder what they are actually like, and how they are run. My hostess is just as ignorant as myself. Japanese ladies of the upper middle-class never go to public-baths and Mrs Michiko is obviously embarrassed by my request. I am sorry to cause such a flutter but I am firm: I want to know. I do not realize that Mrs Michiko is very modest and the idea of appearing in the nude before other women does not appeal to her. She says she wants to go soon after opening-time, 'when the water is cleaner'; her maid tells us that the baths open at 3 p.m.

What a pathetic little affair it was, the church service in the village hall, conducted in fluent Japanese by an American Baptist minister with the aid of his wife, a ginger-haired lady in spectacles who played hymns on the piano! One of them was by Charles Wesley. My mind went back to the tumultuous, hysterical scenes which followed his brother's open-air sermons in eighteenth-century England. There has been nothing like that here. Only the new 'dancing' religions can work the Japanese up into anything approaching a frenzy.

The congregation was pitifully small; the Michikos and I accounted for over one half of it. Three students, one of them tubercular and still living in a sanatorium, and the Minister's secretary, were the only other members. They pored over their Japanese Bibles—twice the size of our English one—and looked terribly earnest. The Minister said a few words in English for my benefit. He told them about Adam and Eve. I prefer Japanese Creation stories myself, especially the one about the Sun Goddess hiding herself in a cave because her brother teased her, and how the other Gods lured her out—the world had become dark without her—by means of a lewd dance which made them all laugh.

After the service I spoke with the Minister. He is pessimistic and sees signs of a possible renewal of emperor-worship in Japan. There *is* an extreme Rightist element, it is true, but I doubt whether the majority of Japanese youth will ever take this step backward.

We drop father at home and go for a drive. Seijo is quite attractive. Many well-to-do Tokyoites have built houses here, some in Japanese style with upturned eaves and carefully clipped cypresses in the gardens, others in modern style with flat roofs and large windows. Small houses are being built too, and new schools—lots of new schools.

The shopping centre of Seijo is doing brisk business. Few shops close on Sundays. We lunch on beer and sandwiches in a snack-bar frequented by students. Some of them are immersed in books—examination time is drawing near.

After lunch we call on an old English lady, married to a Japanese, who has made her home in Seijo for nearly forty years. Her husband is a scholar; he also cultivates orchids. We find the old lady wandering about her garden; she smiles slowly when I am introduced and extends a limp hand in the way people do when they are not accustomed to western forms of salutation.

This lady is the opposite of Edna—she is a Japanized westerner, and I feel my way cautiously, not quite knowing how to treat her. From time to time during our conversation she reacts like 'one of us', laughs whole-heartedly at my interpretation of the Japanese scene and is in complete agreement with my way of looking at it. At other times she shakes her head, becomes expressionless and gives the impression that she has retreated to an inaccessible sphere. Her gestures are quiet and oriental, her manner of speech slow and unEnglish, her eyes reflect an introspective eastern calm, even her complexion is unEuropean. The metamorphosis is so unusual that I keep on asking myself: is she truly English or is she a Japanese acting a part in a play? The front door opened and her husband appeared for a moment in the doorway in his *yukata*, a tall, gaunt man with the detached expression of a thinker. He bowed slightly and closed the door. His wife explained that he had been ill and was not fit to talk to visitors. As if in answer to my thoughts, she added: 'He is very gentle. I have been very happy. He lets me do what I like.'

The public baths are situated in the most rustic part of Seijo, tucked away at the end of a path opposite a paddy-field. There is nothing to show the casual visitor that they are baths at all, not even the usual sign consisting of three wavy upright lines, signifying flames, above a curved horizontal line no doubt representing a cauldron. We arrive a few minutes after three and find a few bicycles propped against the outer wall. One or two stoutish women walk up the path with their babies on their backs, their little round faces peeping inquiringly over their mothers' shoulder. They blink slowly when they see me—they will blink even more when they see me sharing their bath.

It is obvious that Mrs Michiko is not quite sure how to proceed. She laughs a little nervously as we approach the entrance and confront the rosy-faced woman in a white cap who appears to be the custodian of our shoes. We leave these in one of the lockers provided for the purpose and enter through the left-hand door. The one on the right is reserved for men.

Beyond this door is an undressing-room, under the supervision of a manageress seated on a postilion-like box, to whom we pay our thirty yen (approximately 9d.) and with whom we leave our valuables: watch, rings, etc. A fluttering curtain separates this recess from the corresponding one on the men's side; when the breeze blows, I catch a fleeting vision of several men in various states of undress on the opposite side. Those I catch sight of are skinny; I observe with interest that they are devoid of hair on the chest.

Apart from this recess, the partition between us is solid and extends from the floor to the ceiling so that there is no danger of peeping Toms. The room is very light, there are large windows all round, over-looking a fenced-in garden. We lift a lacy willow basket from the pile on our left and begin to undress. We have each brought a plastic basin, a face-cloth, soap and towel. Japanese towels are small and narrow; they have nothing that resembles our voluminous bath towels.

In the centre of the room, a couple of mothers are unwrapping their plump babies in the raised compartments provided for the purpose; the babies gurgle happily. There is a placidity about most Japanese mothers that has a soothing effect upon their offspring; the constant devotion to which they are subjected no doubt gives them a sense of comfort and security. The real business of life does not start until they go to school; then and only then is the notion of discipline severely inculcated in them.

It is my first visit to a public bath and I feel slightly embarrassed. I feel almost too shy to look at my neighbours. I observe, however, that they take their little towels with them into the bathing-room next door, held in front of them like a fig-leaf. This intimate part of their anatomy is never revealed to anyone at any time—not even in a strip-tease show. I also observe that Mrs Michiko wears a different kind of underwear from the kind I had been shown in the department store. I caught a glimpse of a very long chemise in what looked like thick cotton, and—but it would be indelicate of me to add more.

We tripped across and pushed open the sliding-door to join the bathers. There were already about a dozen of them inside. Some were seated on tiny oblong wooden stools, vigorously scrubbing themselves and were in the process of pouring basins of water over their backs; this was obtained from one of several taps placed round the bathing-room opposite the large pool at the level of the tiled floor, in which one plunges after a preliminary soaping. I have never seen bathing water dirty even when, as was to happen later, I frequented crowded public baths in humbler areas, long after opening time. In private houses, being a guest, I was asked to use the bath before everybody else. (I was so careful to soap and rinse myself thoroughly beforehand that my bath water was crystal clear when I had finished soaking: so much so that sometimes my hosts would ask me next day: 'Did you really get into the bath?')

Those ladies who had completed the initial stages were soaking in the large rectangular pool, blue as the Mediterranean, thanks to the tiles at the bottom. The walls of the bathing-room were tiled and gleaming; so was the floor. It was much more pleasant than any of the private bathrooms I had used, and also much warmer.

None of the ladies had ever seen a westerner in the bath before, but they were too polite to stare overtly. Only a two-year-old baby boy opened his narrow eyes wide when I entered the pool and could not take them off me. Another woman was holding a two months-old baby wrapped in a cotton towel in her arms. His eyes were half-closed and he slopped on her shoulder like a drunk. Perhaps he was feeling the heat. I like a hot bath, but this one was very hot indeed. The Japanese are able to withstand extremes of heat and cold; they live in cold houses and bathe in boiling water. I am sure there must be a parallel extremism in their emotional make-up.

Everybody expected me to find the water hot. They know that foreigners have tender skins, and they kindly offered to open the cold water tap for my benefit. Since I was in a minority of one I could not bring myself to accept their thoughtful offer. I climbed in gingerly and lowered myself little by little but found it impossible to stay in longer than five minutes.

I was altogether in too much of a hurry. Everybody else took their time over the various operations that constitute the bathing ritual. They scrubbed and scrubbed as though they had not had a bath for months, whereas they all bathe if not every day at least three times a week. The difficulty of back-scrubbing is resolved by your neighbours, one of whom will always courteously perform this task for you with your own face-cloth. A very old lady had offered to do mine and I felt in duty bound to offer to wash hers. This she acknowledged with a broad smile and the scene was watched, obliquely, by everybody in the bathing-room. It is not every day that a westerner is seen rubbing a Japanese lady's back, and vice versa.

It struck me for the first time that our own bathing system at home (apart from showers) is dirty and unhygienic. Fancy soaking in dirty water with soap suds clinging to the sides of the bath—ugh! I was already beginning to feel less embarrassed since my fellow-bathers were so unselfconscious—that is all of them except poor Mrs Michiko who was crouching unhappily in a corner of the pool with her eyes modestly lowered—and it interested me to observe how different the average Japanese figure is from our own. Some Japanese women have full breasts and attractive bodies—as one can see from the colour slides sold in the basement of the big western-style hotels—but one does not see many of them at the public baths, certainly not in any of those I have frequented. Most Japanese nudes fall short of our ideal standards in several respects which can be summarized as follows: (1) Chests: too flat and low;

(2) waists: too straight; (3) legs: too short and often bandy. The national dress hides most of these defects and that is why a Japanese woman is at her best in kimono.

There is also something unusual about the nipple area which is often deep purple, almost black. Knees are often calloused as the result of sitting for prolonged periods on the *tatami*.

The old lady who had rubbed my back expressed surprise that I was not going to shave my face. Several ladies were already squatting in front of the mirror above the taps, shaving the dark down from their cheeks and upper lips. I told her that I did not think it was necessary in my case.

A young, perhaps sixteen-year-old girl was squatting in front of the mirror, pretending to comb her long hair and admiring her slender body. I noticed her as we came in. She had not stirred since. What an interesting group for a painter! What a pity one could not take photographs! Perhaps in the dressing-room next door, on the pretext of photographing the babe who was being slipped into a pink silk quilted bag, rather like the kind the Bretons used to carry their babies in. No—the supervisor would not allow it, but I could photograph the baby outside, if I wished. I liked the baby anyway and so he was carried out, still half-asleep, and held out by his mother—a rosy-cheeked young woman in the wide blue trousers and white overall of the typical lower-class Japanese housewife.

I glanced at myself in the mirror as we went out. I was as red as a lobster and fully deserved the old-time Chinese epithet of 'Red Barbarian'. Perhaps some of the bathers were now laughingly discussing me. Perhaps they were saying, as a country-woman said about me later in northern Japan: 'Do you know, she has fair hair *all over. . . .'*

Another
bourgeois home

April 10th   *T*oday I moved back to Tokyo, to the roomy house of a wealthy family situated in Shinjuku ward. It is on a hill with a clever garden enclosed by high trees which obliterate the view of factory chimneys and office rooftops. My hostess, Mrs Yoko, speaks little English, but she is counting on her twenty-seven-year-old son, who has studied Industrial Relations in the United States, to make up for her deficiencies. Her husband does not speak English either. He is a tall, broad man who is always presiding over committees; he owns a large printing-works and everything about him spells ease and affluence.

Mrs Yoko is a kindly, plump little woman who wears kimono but admires everything that is 'western style'. She is very anxious that I should be comfortable—over anxious, in fact. Strangely enough she knocks at the door before re-entering the sitting-room where I am engaged in conversation with her son. What can she think we are up to, after so short a time? It embarrasses us.

To my delight, I am offered a drink. This is the son's idea. I have two and begin to expand. Mrs Yoko sips her cocktail politely, and nods happily to hear us talking in English. She likes the sound of the language even though she cannot speak it, and it pleases her to hear her son expressing himself so fluently. Soon she brings out the inevitable photograph albums. I see countless pictures of weddings; fashionable girls attend the Shinto wedding ceremony in traditional kimono with a broad white headband over the various ornaments in their wig but they appear at the modern wedding reception afterwards in a flowing white western dress and veil. Then they leave for their honeymoon in a tight-fitting costume and helmet hat, looking like butterflies that have been shorn of their wings.

I am also shown pictures of Mrs Yoko's world tour with her husband, from the time of their departure (photograph of the aircraft, of the friends and relatives who came to see them off, etc.) until the time they came back (photograph of the aircraft, of the friends and relatives who came to welcome them, etc.). In between one saw familiar views of Washington, San Francisco, the Tower of London, the leaning tower of Pisa, St Marks and many cities in Germany.

Mrs Yoko's son is a serious young man who works long hours and does not seem to have much time for leisure. Like all self-respecting, well-to-do young Japanese, he plays golf. He tells me he has never set foot in a geisha-house but I am sure he would like to.

We sit down to a *recherché* western meal; some of the dishes have been prepared by Mrs Yoko's niece, a pleasant young girl who is studying domestic science. Mrs Yoko is already worrying about what I shall want for breakfast. I tell her that the meal she has given me should last for twenty-four hours.

The son is deferential towards his father. However modern he may be as far as education is concerned, I am sure that when the time comes for him to marry, he will accept his parents' choice for him as part of the inevitable Japanese pattern. In this class, the *nakodo* or go-between, is still important. The role may be played by a friend—perhaps by another member of the International Women's Association. One of them is an active matchmaker. The other day I overheard her trying to arrange a match for a friend's daughter; when we lunched at her house she introduced her secretary, informing me that she was very happily married and that she—the 'boss'—had found a husband for her. The girl smiled shyly and did not seem in the least put out that her husband should have been *found* for her by other people.

Whenever I express dissent from this way of doing things, my Japanese interlocutors point to the drawbacks of our western system: the frequent divorces, the instability of the home, the break-down of family life. (It is true that we have unofficial matchmakers ourselves, especially in the 'higher' classes.) On the other hand, as far as Japan is concerned, there are less opportunities for young people of good family to meet. Social life as we know it does not exist. There are no parties in people's homes to which friends of both sexes are invited. The sexes are still segregated to a large extent. Co-education has made a difference, it is true, and one hears of many romances in the upper forms that eventually lead to marriages but, until the general pattern of society changes, the *nakodo* will still be in business.

Slumming

*T*oday I went to see one of the darker corners of Tokyo, the slums by one of the stagnant canals which are due to be filled up; until that happens, people will continue to build shacks beside them out of old planks, empty petrol tins and pieces of corrugated iron and vegetate there free of taxes and rates.

None of my bourgeois Tokyo hostesses know where to find these dark corners and if they did they would not be able to introduce me to the occupiers for they live in different worlds. Not that my hostesses lack compassion, far from it—they raise funds for many charities; social welfare has fortunately become the fashion and much of it is still dependent on voluntary bodies, because the Government is not lavish in this field. But the slum dwellers in Tokyo, as elsewhere, close their drab doors to outsiders.

Luckily I have met somebody who can introduce me: Hideto Mori is an extrovert, an *original*, who writes about the classless peoples of Japan; labourers, dockyard workers, miners, outsiders. Hideto, now in his late twenties, is a grocer's son who graduated from Waseda University. He does not speak any English and so he brings a journalist friend along with him to interpret, often at inconvenient hours for his friend who, nevertheless, makes the effort. He has not been used to interpreting for such a long stretch at a time and after a couple of hours he buries his face in his hands and groans. When this happens Hideto laughs apologetically and offers him another beer.

I like Hideto. He is open and warm-hearted and I regret the language barrier between us more than with any other person I have met so far. His face is expressive, like all Japanese whose roots come from the people in the country and his eyes jump merrily in a head which is always seething with ideas and mad schemes. Lack of money prevents him from travelling outside Japan; like many other young Japanese he resents his country's geographical isolation from the rest of the world. The younger generation are eager to meet people of different nationalities and explore the world. 'I should like to go with you to the heart of Africa and study gorillas,' said Hideto inconsequently as we trudged down an uneven alley-way in the heart of Tokyo.

People eye us—especially me—with curiosity. It is all right here, Hideto explains; people are poor but not violent. There are other slum areas where it would be dangerous for me to go, especially at night. Violence is on the increase with more than a million and a half crimes a year for the country as a whole, but the trends do not appear to differ from those of other countries: juvenile delinquency is on the upgrade and the nature of crimes tends to become more 'sophisticated'.

Hideto bids us pause while he goes and asks the leader of the group of shacks whether we can go in. He knows them well, has written articles about them, endeavoured to get the authorities to do something about re-housing them—and it is obvious from the way they nod and smile when he approaches that they consider him as a friend. After a few whispered confidential words, Hideto turns and beckons and we join him at the entrance of the home-made dwellings.

I walk warily along the planks leading to what looks like a prehistoric lakeside dwelling. The shacks are built upon poles and some of them look perilously like sinking. The stench from the canal is suffocating.

Four families appear to be living here, in 'apartments' separated by thin wooden partitions. They built them overnight, to foil the authorities who had forbidden them to erect shacks in the area. Once the work was accomplished, however, they turned a blind eye and let them stay on.

Apart from the communal corridor running down the entire length of the long house, each apartment is private and built in the traditional Japanese way, with an inside step separating the *tatami* covered floors from a tiny hall. The cooking is done on individual stoves in the corridor. There is one tap, outside the long house, for everybody to share and a stone sink where the women do the laundry and washing up.

At the far end a ramshackle door opens on to the 'toilet' over the canal. The tiny individual rooms are dark, cluttered with boxes and tins. An old grandmother passes us, almost bent in two, carrying a small bundle of faggots. A middle-aged man and his wife peer out and bow. The men are casual labourers, when they can find work and the women work as chars. The children are apt to grow out of hand. They have built a playshack and call it 'the Apaches'. One of the older men shook his head and said he thought they were up to no good. Oh yes, they are supposed to go to school, but it is difficult to control them when their parents are away most of the time. 'And this isn't much of a place for them to come back to,' he added.

These people are poorly dressed, and their faces have the tight, inward expression of people who have suffered for a long time without hope, but they have not lost their dignity or their Japanese pride. They know how to bow gracefully, with no trace of servility, and when they smile, they become alive and friendly, momentarily

forgetting the trials of their existence. 'We want peace, and friendship with everybody,' said one of the older men, and his wife asked
us in to their warren of a home where she insisted on giving us tea
and a bowl of rice, with slimy species of seaweed rolled up in tight
balls which was new to me. It was the only article of food I ate in
Japan which ever made me feel like vomiting, but, in this instance,
it is possible that the slimy unctuousness of the seaweed reminded
me of the plant life growing along the banks of the canal and on
the posts of the house in which we were eating.

There is no false shame about these shack dwellers, and they are
still persons with a definite identity. They are affable, and at the
same time fundamentally tough. They have not given up, and just
as they struggled to build their miserable home overnight, so they
will go on struggling to try and improve their position. Like all
Japanese they are soft-spoken. One hears little of that constant
nagging, bickering and shouting that is always associated in
western minds with the 'lower classes'. I wished them good luck
and they thanked me for coming to see them and sent their warm
wishes to 'the workers of England'. Hideto lingered behind and
inquired after the member of one family who had died since his
last visit.

We took an electric train back to the main station. As it was still
early and Hideto's friend did not have to report at his foreign news
desk for another hour, we went into one of Tokyo's famous little
'story-tellers' ' theatres which carry on a centuries-old tradition in
the heart of the teeming modern city.

A short flagged path, a small stone lantern, and a gnarled tree—
the three 'musts' to any Japanese entrance, whether it leads to a
house, an inn or a traditional place of entertainment—only just
succeeded in warding off the modern shops that hemmed in the
tiny theatre off a busy main thoroughfare.

The theatre could not have held more than a hundred and fifty
people and it was so full that we had to stand at the back most of
the time. The audience ranged from students to workmen and
modest families complete with baby strapped on to mother's back;
one of them looked at me rather than at the stage and stretched out
tiny, inquisitive fingers with an amused expression—as if I were a
novel toy.

The stage—devoid of props—the walls, the seats, are all made of
a light, well polished wood. I am beginning to realize what a

friendly substance it is to live with. There is a warm, friendly atmosphere in this theatre in which the wood of the walls and stage participate as if they had been brought to life again. Maybe the wood comes from ancient trees near shrines where dances and Noh plays were staged and so the theatre is not a novelty for them.

Some people drop in for half an hour's entertainment, but many more come for the *pièce de resistance*, the storyteller, who is billed half-way through the performance, after the secondary items: singers and dancers and acts in which two or three people take part.

When the *rakugoka* advances in a black kimono, a ripple runs through the audience followed by a murmur of satisfaction. Their eyes are riveted on this man with the nearly bald head, broad, lined face and large, flexible hands who kneels in front of a low table in the centre of the stage and with only a fan as prop acts a dozen roles, mimes comedy, tragedy and satire: word-perfect, without a single falter, and a fine clear diction. I follow the pace although I cannot follow the words and am transported like the rest of the audience by the command of his gestures and inflections of his voice. From time to time, a sharp rap on the table with the closed fan indicates a change of character and of scene. A burst of applause greets him when he comes to the end of his act, bows, rises slowly and strides off the stage with a majestic air. Hideto tells me that this *rakugoka* is famous, and often appears on television. This medium finds room for people like him as well as for westerns; both are in demand. The *rakugoka* still holds his own; he is no vulgar market-place storyteller, repeating fables and myths to the unlettered, but a polished actor with a fund of witty modern stories which appeal to his literate audience.

A juvenile court

April 16th $\mathcal{O}$ his morning I assisted at the proceedings of one of the juvenile courts—Family Courts as they are called here, following the American pattern. Judge Morita was in charge, a kindly man in his early forties who has studied juvenile delinquency in other countries. His wife is a doctor. While we were talking his son, a high-school boy, telephoned to ask for more pocket-money and said he would be coming round to collect it. What would *he* do if he did not have a father to give him what he wants? The youths who slouch into the court-room to confront the judge and the probation officers are weak-willed fellows who took the easy way. . . .

I talked with Judge Morita before the proceedings opened in an office lined with maps showing the areas where delinquency is particularly bad. All the stations in Tokyo are surrounded by ominous black dots, as well as the Ginza shopping area where touts, pimps and prostitutes approach foreigners.

The gangster system thrives, and many hoodlums depend on children to do their dirty work. Recently a highly organized gang system was found in a high school in direct link with adult criminal groups. One of the probation officers shakes his head when I point out that we share the same kinds of problems. 'Ours have a peculiarly Japanese twist,' he says. 'Our gangsters use methods involving a strict code of behaviour which stresses duty, honour, loyalty among their members. In my opinion this is a form of feudalistic revival, just as the increase in crimes like extortion and blackmail among adults is part of an old feudalistic pattern. The younger generation responds to the discipline imposed by the gang leaders. It is a kind of discipline they do not find at home or at school where the traditional fount of authority has broken down in the name of democracy. Our youngsters need discipline, they want a firm lead. They also crave excitement—they find both these desires satisfied by working for adult gangsters.'

'There is a decline in the moral quality of the Japanese way of life as a whole,' added another probation officer. 'It affects even traditional pastimes. Take *karate*, for instance, a science which teaches how to deal lethal blows with the hand. (Aspirants practise on tiles, logs, etc.) This art, once widely practised in self-defence, is being misused. The *karate* clubs of our universities are coming into the news because of this. In a recent instance a *karate* student engaged in a brawl with two labourers in a bar and hit one of them. The man died thirty hours later with, according to a medical report, severed intestines. At schools, freshmen have been roughly handled for trifling reasons. Not long ago an American teacher at Rikkyo University was killed by a drunken student who had a smattering of *karate*.'

It was time to open the court, and we passed next door. I sat at a little table by the window with my interpreter. Three or four chairs had been placed in front of the judge's table. The judge was in everyday clothes and the proceedings were informal, more like a family council presided over by an impartial but well-meaning outsider.

The first boy came in with his father. He was a tall, flabby youngster in tight-fitting jeans and a hip-length sweater with a hairstyle current among the beatniks. He looked pale and anxious and he never once took his eyes off the judge. He had a weak face with a round chin and looked adenoidal. His father was a short, brown, tough little man with a slightly dazed countrified air who seemed incapable of handling his lanky town-bred son. His son had stolen a watch and other valuables from his colleagues in a factory where he had worked for a time; he was lazy and always being reprimanded for arriving late. There were four younger children in the family; the mother was out at work all day. The father was temporarily unemployed, but he had refunded the value of the stolen watch. It seemed that the boy quarrelled with his mother and was always asking for pocket-money. When his mother refused, he stole the watch. The only positive feature about him was that he had been a champion runner; the judge made as much of this as he could. He told the boy, gently but firmly, that life was like a race for which one must train and work and observe rules.

The boy's eyes reddened and he swallowed hard. The father sat with lowered eyes. The probation officer said that the factory manager had agreed to take the boy back provided he made an effort to work harder and be honest. The judge nodded, told the boy that in future he was not to leave home at night without his parents' permission and that he was to visit the probation officer regularly twice a month. He entreated him to work and not to quarrel with his parents whose life was already hard enough. The boy nodded vigorously and in a low voice promised to amend.

The second boy was sixteen and a *pachinko* parlour assistant. (This pin ball game, a post-war development, is the most popular form of gambling in Japan. It hypnotizes thousands of devotees in every city, like a drug.) The boy had donned his school jacket which may have been a significant gesture because while he was at school he lived at home in the country with his mother, who had pampered him. His aunt and elder brother accompanied him to the court, since the mother now works in a sanatorium, and lives too far away. The *pachinko* boy looked like a 'little boy lost', attracted by the big city, unstable, constantly moving from one job to another and stealing in between. When he was out of work he frequented cheap cafés where he often fell asleep. His aunt looked very respectable in her dark grey kimono and black lace three-quarter length jacket—too respectable to want to look after her wayward nephew. The elder brother, to whose care the judge confided the boy, was a jaunty, self-reliant fellow; he did not appear to have much time for the black sheep of the family.

The third boy was a nineteen-year-old *dafuya*. This is the name given to the youths who sell cinema and theatre tickets outside the doors when the house is said to be full. I have never quite understood how this system works, although it is widely practised in several western countries. The *dafuya* said he did not make any money out of his trade because he worked for an 'employer' who merely provided him with food and lodging in return for his work. He lived in a dormitory with other *dafuyas* and he had stolen in order to get some pocket money. He was alone in Tokyo. His father was dead, his mother lived in the country. His elder brother was a taxi-driver in Tokyo but he never saw him. It was not the first time that he had been in trouble—he had previously been sent to a training centre from which he had run away.

'What would *you* do with him?' asked the judge smilingly when the boy had been sent out and the judge and the probation officers held a consultation. The probation officer wanted to send him to another training school. Since I had been asked, I volunteered the opinion that he would probably run away again. Wasn't there some private family who would take the boy in and keep an eye on him? He looked desperately lonely, but the probation officer preferred to have him submitted once more to the discipline of an institution.

And so it went on, the long procession of youths, most of them weak-looking, gangly and faintly scruffy, some pale, some flushed, nearly all of them from homes in which the tight traditional pattern had broken down, boys without the character and stamina to work and fend for themselves.

Invisible men

April 18th *I* saw a fascinating programme on television the other night about the Ninjas, or invisible men, who used to be employed as spies by the feudal lords. Only a few men are keeping the old tradition alive, but I should not be surprised to hear that their services are in demand, since spies and assassins are not unknown in present-day Japan.

I suspect that Yuso, who introduced me to Mr Toshiro, faith-healer and Ninja instructor in his spare moments, is one of his disciples. It does not seem to be a lucrative profession, for the two-storey house in one of Tokyo's lesser-known suburbs where the master lives is quite humble.

Ninjutsu, explained Mr Toshiro, is a martial act perfected over the centuries. It originated in the twelfth century when small bands of defeated warriors took to the hills and began to live on their wits. As they lacked arms they had to make up for them by resorting to trickery, stratagem and unorthodox devices. The first thing they had to learn was to merge into the landscape like chameleons. Their 'uniform' was—is—dark blue and when they are 'on duty' they conceal their face in a hood. The Ninjas became so adept that their talents were recognized by the warlords and their services were highly paid for. From that time on they enveloped their profession with an aura of mystery, forming a tightly closed brotherhood. Anybody who revealed his true identity to an outsider was immediately murdered by a colleague.

For a long time the Japanese believed that the Ninjas were capable of almost superhuman feats. They were said to run at incredible speeds, to scale high walls at a leap, to make themselves invisible thanks to a magic powder. They appear in films about Samurai times with the aid of trick photography.

All this, said Mr Toshiro candidly, is absolute nonsense. The genuine Ninja is a highly trained man, an expert in Judo, Karate and Kendo (Japanese-style fencing) plus a few extra tricks handed down from generation to generation of Ninjas. 'We are taught the art of deception,' he said, 'and muscular control.'

Mr Toshiro took a grape and swallowed it but he continued talking in a perfectly normal voice. A few moments later he opened his mouth and revealed the grape. This was useful in the old days (one can conceive that it could still be handy in certain present-day circumstances) for hiding secret messages. I should have thought it would be difficult to get a message into a grape in the first place, but the Japanese are pastmasters at wrapping things up small. I do not think a westerner would ever be capable of such a feat.

A Ninja acquired the reputation of being able to make himself invisible by such simple devices as throwing powdered resin contained in an eggshell into his pursuer's eyes or jumping into the air and grabbing a beam in the ceiling by means of metal hooks bound to his wrists.

The Ninja carries ropes armed with hooks which can be used for a quick get-away over a wall or gate (when not in use they fold into a bamboo pole), spiked wrist-bands to ward off sword blows and deal pretty deadly ones and knives. . . . But even without weapons, thanks to his training in judo and *karate*, the Ninja is a formidable opponent.

The 'master' demonstrated some of his skills by grappling with his student and then climbing on to the roof by means of his grappling hook—loops tied in the rope were used as the rungs of a ladder. Such sprightliness he said was the result of years of training. He had started at the age of eleven.

Mr Toshiro has a small group of 'serious students'. I should have liked to know a little more about their background. Perhaps the police would have been interested too. A fully trained Ninja is not a person to be taken lightly. The 'master' was not only sprightly— he also looked very tough. And, surely, one doesn't learn all these tricks for fun! Would it not be a waste of considerable talent?

Gypsies

I am constantly coming across references to people with unusual interests and pursuits. The other day I read about a well-known

novelist and newly made doctor to whom the Department of
Sociology of Tokyo University has awarded a degree for his unique
study of Japanese gypsies. His name is Kan Misumi and he is the
only outsider to have studied the Sanka or Mountain People, as the
gypsies are called, and to have gained their confidence. Professor
Ishida, of the Cultural Anthropology department of Tokyo University, kindly arranged an appointment for me, and the Foreign
Office lent me an able member of their staff, Mr Koichi Tsutsumi,
to act as interpreter.

Kan Misumi is much more striking in appearance than any of
his gypsies. He is a tall, well-built man with long white hair and
well-defined features who looks extraordinarily like the French-
Canadian anthropologist and folklorist Dr Marius Barbeau. He
had never even heard of the Sanka when, in the nineteen twenties,
as a young reporter for the *Asahi Shimbun*, he covered the case of
an elusive burglar who had made headlines for three years by
victimizing the inhabitants of the northern outskirts of Tokyo.
One day he overheard an old police detective murmur, 'may be
that burglar is a Sanka'. 'Who are they?' he asked, but the detective
could give him no information except that they were nomads who
called themselves Sanka. Nobody else seemed to know anything
about them either. He asked his editor for permission to make a
special study of these people, but this was refused on the grounds
that it might involve him in danger. So, unknown to his editor, he
began to make investigations in his spare time. Summer after
summer, he would disappear into the mountain districts near
Tokyo until his face became familiar to the shy nomads and they
began to invite him into their tents.

Little by little, Mr Misumi found out that the Sanka were to be
found in other mountainous districts of Japan, in Kyushu and east
of Hiroshima. They earn their living by making baskets, brooms
and above all winnows, which farmers still use for separating the
rice chaff from the grains. They move rapidly, covering thirty or
forty miles in a day, following the course of river-beds, sleeping
in crude canvas open-ended tents, on thin straw mats.

The twentieth century is not kind to nomads and they are rapidly
disappearing or, more accurately, becoming assimilated. As with
our own western gypsies, the Second World War brought them
into contact with the 'civilized' world and lured them into munitions factories. Now many Sanka send their children to school and
some of them have even gone to universities. Their numbers have

decreased from about 160,000 in 1910, according to Mr Misumi, to 14,000 in 1949. There are probably less than ten thousand roaming about today in the traditional Sanka way.

The Sanka speak an archaic form of Japanese and they also have a curious written language in which no trace of Chinese appears. Physically they are a sturdy people with well-developed legs (unlike the Japanese) but otherwise there does not seem to be any marked racial difference between the two. They are robust, and their life span averages eighty years.

In feudal times, the Sanka were used in a similar capacity to the Ninjas—except that their natural faculties were relied upon rather than acquired ones. They were so fleet of foot that they were used as message bearers, and their excellent sight made them useful spies. But when the General Army staff of the Second World War tried to train them for commando operations in jungle warfare, they failed because the Sanka could not adapt themselves to discipline. Their life in the mountains is not exactly free, they have their own conventions, but it is certainly freer than in the army. Likewise the Sanka, forcibly employed in munitions factories, ran away and back to their mountains as soon as the war was over.

So long as farmers continue to use the *mi*, or winnow made out of willow branches, the Sanka will be able to make a living. They can make two or three winnows a day which they sell for five hundred yen (ten shillings) each. Their monthly income in the good season often amounts to thirty pounds, which is more than enough for their few needs. They have no housing problem, they live on their surroundings, eat river fish, fruit (they are mostly vegetarian and rarely eat any meat) and make their own *sake* which they call 'Monkey Brew'; Kan Misumi described this as 'a strong alcoholic beverage distilled from wild fruits'. They cure their injuries with dry viper skins and are skilled in herbal lore. Their money goes on tobacco and a few clothes, for they are becoming more sophisticated in the matter of dress.

Mr Misumi asked his male secretary to fetch some samples of *Sanka* clothes. He returned with a pair of navy blue pants, a blue and white striped jacket and a white sash. The leaders wear wider stripes to distinguish them from the rest. There are three types of leaders: the *kuzushi*, who is at the head of a given area, the *kuzuko*, who is in charge of one 'river-road' followed by a group and shuttlecocks between the tribes as a messenger, and the *mureko* or ordinary group leader who decides upon such things as the order of march, the times of departure from a given spot, etc. All disputes are settled by the *kuzushi*. The group leaders also act as priests. Their religion, said Misumi, 'is an ancient form of Shintoism. Ancestors are worshipped and a great feast is held in their honour every year. The dead used to be hanged from a tree but this custom has now disappeared.'

The women used to be bare to the waist like the Balinese but nowadays they wear a sleeveless vest on top of their draped sarong-like skirt. Married women wear large flat bamboo hairpins to distinguish them from the virgins.

Girls are married off at the first sign of menstruation, and the marriage is arranged by the group leader with a boy from another group. Her mother-in-law gives her a new red skirt for the wedding; the old one is ceremonially thrown into the river by the leader. The various groups meet in different localities every year for their festivals, the most important of all being the Autumn Festival which is celebrated by simple dances, accompanied by drums and bamboo flutes, songs, and 'Monkey Brew'. (The masks and clothes they wear on these occasions are stored for them during the rest of the year by sedentary villagers.)

The Sanka are a cheerful, hard-working people with a strong sense of duty; they lead a chaste life and allow divorce only in the case of impotence. Their women have occasionally attracted outsiders and two or three of them have married and joined the roving community.

The Sanka believe that they are the descendants of the true aborigines of Japan and in their own language their ancestors are called *kunitsukami*, native inhabitants, as distinct from the *amatsu-kami* or those who came from across the sea.

Like the rest of the Japanese, the Sanka are a clean people and they contrive to have hot baths even in the middle of their jungle habitat. For this they dig deep holes in the ground in which they light a fire under large flat stones gathered from the river bed. The bather sits on the stones while a helper pours water into the hole. The stones retain heat for quite a long while.

In the summer, they have cold baths; nowadays they line the holes with a plastic material. Of course when they are on the move along a river-course, they do not need to dig holes. Even in the heart of winter they have a hot bath at least once a week.

Much of their music has been tape-recorded by Kan Misumi. It is quite unlike Japanese music. The gay rhythm reminded me of

North African Berber music. The words of the songs are free and uninhibited. Here is one of them, as transcribed by Mr Misumi:

> Vast plains and mountains,
>   These are my country,
> I am happy wherever I go,
>   As my husband is always in my arms.
>
> We kiss and make love in the tent.
>   I am happy and never troubled,
> Like a worm inside the heart of a willow tree,
>   Free from the danger of wood-peckers.

The language was archaic. My interpreter could not understand it. Kan Misumi presented me with a Sanka-made bamboo cup and a couple of Sanka hairpins as a gift. Before we left, he showed us the sixty-three volumes of stories which he has published on these little-known people, and his large doctoral dissertation. Thanks to him, the Sanka will be perpetuated in literature and history. And thanks to the Sanka, Kan Misumi seems to have found a lucrative source of inspiration. Donning a lined silk jacket and a lavender satin kind of alb which gave him a priestly air, he told us that he was going to a party given by a famous sculptor—would we like to join him?—and away we sped in his chauffeur-driven car.

The inevitable
cherry-blossom

*O*n the letters written to me by my future hostesses before I left England, they had remarked that I would be in Japan in time for the cherry-viewing season. How lovely it would be to go for cherry-blossom picnics together!

Signs of the approaching festivities began to appear in the streets about the middle of March. I have already mentioned the irritating rash of bright pink artificial blossoms in front of theatres, but soon I began to see more and more of them every day, entwined round pylons and street lamps in various quarters of the city.

Real cherry-trees are on the decline because of city grime and the authorities' ruthlessness in cutting them down when they stand in the way of progress. Certain trees were protected by wealthy patrons who cherished them like geishas, for more or less the same reason: because they represent an ancient Japanese tradition linked with the arts. During the war the Kamikaze suicide pilots used the cherry-blossom motif as their official seal.

Famous cherry-trees are disappearing fast. In 1961, the famous Sakura No Sono tree in a park in Kyoto prefecture was 'forcefully requisitioned', according to one newspaper, 'to make room for the Meishin Super Highway'. Two other well-known trees, purchased by the business magnate Mr T. Takasaki had been 'drowned by the building of the Miboro dam in Gifu prefecture'. There are hardly any worthwhile cherry-trees left in Tokyo. (The best is said to be 'Baba-no-Sakura' in Korakuen gardens. It is a three-hundred-year-old, drooping variety.)

The *Japan Times* commented in an editorial upon the Brueghelesque scenes which are enacted during cherry-viewing time: 'When the cherry-blossom season comes, there are fights and other forms of rough behaviour all over the country.... Just recently, a man was dragged off a suburban train in Tokyo and given a drubbing by three men just because he had cautioned them about smoking in the train.... Another man, who removed a newspaper lying beside a man sleeping on the seat so that he could sit down, was hit by the second man and received serious injuries which required three months' medical treatment. No other passengers intervened....' It is well-known that cherry-blossom time is an excuse for excessive *sake* drinking. Perhaps, in olden days, the Japanese treated the festival as we did our May 1st celebrations, flowers being euphemistically used to cover up orgiastic celebrations in honour of the vital force that once more ran gaily through men's veins after the long cold winter.

In ancient Kyoto, capital of Japan for a thousand years, the geishas were preparing their *miyako-odori* or cherry-blossom dances; in the hope that these would be worth seeing I decided to leave the capital and travel south.

PART II

In

And Around

Kyoto

Asleep in a
Japanese home

Stream-lined journey

*M*y last hostess in Tokyo lived out of town and so, not wishing to oblige her to accompany me to the station, I spent the night in a hotel close to Tokyo tower. Service here was acknowledged to be slow and a warning notice propped up on the table in my room advised guests to 'Order tomorrow's breakfast tonight'. A girlish voice took my order and carefully repeated, like a diligent pupil: 'Tea—with milk—two rolls—butter—marmalade.' If you speak slowly you usually find the staff get your order correctly but if you speak too fast they become flustered. The Japanese panic very easily. The calm, impassive look on so many Japanese faces is deceptive.

I was a little flustered myself when morning came and I suddenly realized that I was going to travel alone for the first time. There would be no smiling Kazuko this time to deal with porters and train attendants; would I find the right platform? Would the porters pretend not to understand me?

I need not have worried. The central station *akabos*, or porters, recognizable in tight navy-blue breeches and red peak caps, are accustomed to dealing with foreigners and they know in advance that you are bound for the limited express Hakone when you turn up at the station shortly before 9 a.m.

My taxi driver kindly hailed an *akabo* for me and doffed his cap politely when I paid him, although there is no tipping in Japan. 'Kyoto,' I said to the *akabo*, as softly as I could to make up for my ignorance of the language. Foreigners sound so unbearably arrogant when they shout a key word to a native all unwrapped without any accompanying 'please' or 'will you' to tone down the imperative. 'Kyoto,' I said to the *akabo*; he nodded and replied tersely: 'Platform number fifteen,' with an American accent.

To reach platform fifteen we had to cross the station and wend our way through grim crowds of white-collar workers pouring out from suburban trains on their way to the *zaitbatsu* district—Marunouchi and its neighbours—the throbbing heart of Japanese big business. The office girls looked sullen, as though they were contemplating a strike to protest against all the tea they are asked to brew for visitors; their male colleagues brushed past them, solemn as owls, and at least ninety-nine per cent bespectacled. (When a Japanese friend had the effrontery to say to me: 'I don't understand how you can see, with your eyes so deeply set in your head', I retorted tartly: 'I see better than you; most of you have to wear glasses.')

Eight forty-five a.m. in Central station is not kimono-time, and the general scene is as drab and uninspiring as in any of our stations at home. There was a little more local colour on the platform, but not of the best kind. The magazines on the stalls, for instance, had covers which outmatch ours in vulgarity. Their contents, I have been told, would not pass our censor, mild though he seems to be these days. Japanese educationists and other people concerned with moral welfare complain from time to time about the porno-graphic contents of magazines so easily available to young people. The Japanese have always been interested in a clinical type of pornography, their literature is full of graphically illustrated 'pillow stories', but it has never been sold so openly and so cheaply; many good writers unashamedly earn a good living by turning out pornographic stories for these pulp magazines.

The air-conditioned limited express was poised lightly between the rails, cream, sleek and shiny and as aseptic as a hospital. White-uniformed attendants, grave as male nurses, dealt with the luggage and ushered me to an adjustable seat by the window. The wide corridor in the middle led to two types of toilets: a western-style toilet at one end of the coach, a Japanese-style one at the other. A red light visible from every seat in the coach warned us when they were 'engaged' to avoid unnecessary journeys. One felt as cosseted as in an aeroplane.

There were still a few minutes to spare before the express left so I got out and walked up the platform to look at people. Many

passengers were already queuing up methodically for the next
train, which would be slower, cheaper and altogether less grand
than the Hakone express. Passengers would be seated according to
their queue priority. They were waiting patiently, with neat little
parcels beside them wrapped in attractive-coloured *furoshikis*; a few
nasty plastic bags and baskets were also to be seen. An American
fellow-passenger exclaimed to her husband: 'Look dear, they have
ever so many more plastic bags than when we were last here. They
are getting more modern every day!'

Some of the queues were composed of lanky schoolboys and
girls in dark, military-looking uniforms. Everybody must have
heard by now that one of the latest fads in Japan is the 'educational
tour'. Every school in the country organizes a couple of these per
year, and since there are thousands of schools and hundreds of
thousands of school children, one cannot go anywhere without
running into them. Most of the tours travel in superb coaches, but
others take trains. So far, however, their parents do not seem to be
able to afford the more expensive limited-expresses and this is about
the only place where one is safe from the determined advances of
ruthless teenagers who wish to practise their English on you or hear
you speak this language which they are taught for five hours every
week (at high school) with little effect as far as conversational
English is concerned.

These shrewd young people are aware of the deficiencies in their
teachers and extremely anxious to make up for them at every
opportunity. I was constantly accosted by boys and girls whose
entrée en relations varied from: 'Herro, herro' (the Japanese, having
no 'l' in their language, cannot pronounce this letter) to a brazen:
'May I have free English conversation with you, please?' I was
glad to have the chance of speaking with these young people, but
when I began to ask them questions, they became shy and tongue-
tied. They could cope with concrete questions such as where do
you live? How many members are there in your family, and so on,
but as soon as I asked anything of an abstract nature, or their
opinion on any subject, they hesitated, blushed and shook their
heads. Young people are still not taught to think for themselves.
They were never asked or expected to give an opinion in the old
days when all adults from parents to teachers were a cross between
a god and the emperor, but I had expected the post-war generation,
brought up in a new atmosphere, under a new (American) system
of education, to be different.

In addition to the sombre queues of school children quietly waiting for their train (they are usually well-disciplined; I never saw any signs of anything like a rough-house—they wait for that until they are university students, when they break out in a big way, organize strikes, become affiliated to extremist political organizations and occasionally assassinate Prime Ministers), there were equally sombre queues of dapper little men lined up behind a leader bearing a large banner. This would probably be a group of business employees off on a spree; the banner served to rally them like the wings of an immense mother hen, so that they would not stray or be lost at the point of departure and later at their destination, which would no doubt be a famous and overcrowded beauty spot, shrine or temple.

I never saw any young women out together, but I saw plenty of middle-aged and elderly ones (members of rural Women's Clubs), tottering about on *getas* at an astonishingly rapid pace and occasionally curling up in a corner of a shrine to enjoy a smoke.

I have heard foreign visitors in Japan express the belief that half of Japan always seems to be on vacation while the other half holds its nose to the grindstone of school, office or factory, but in fact there is much more grind than vacation. As I have already mentioned, very few Japanese can afford to take an annual vacation. They have two weeks' holiday—on paper—but it never materializes. Most boys and girls stay at home for the greater part of their holidays. The people one sees out and about: children buying up souvenirs for their parents at home, old ladies smoking and occasionally drinking a little more *sake* than is good for them, drunken young men staggering through railway coaches patting ladies affectionately on the head, are all letting off pathetic little puffs of steam. They do not get much of a chance to in their everyday life. Everyday life in Japan is very humdrum indeed.

At the top of the platform, women sweepers armed with tiny shovels and long brooms were meticulously sweeping up dust and odd bits of litter. They were trim, neatly dressed in trousers that fitted them, unlike women train and platform sweepers at home who wear baggy trousers and look as unkempt as the survivors of a shipwreck.

A general consultation of watches indicated that the train was about to leave and I ran back to my coach. The Japanese, like the Spaniards, like seeing people off at stations and the more important you are, the larger the number of senders-off you may expect. A group of immaculately dressed men outside my coach formed a ring round a pompous, fat 'boss' man who was about to enter the train, and appeared to be engaged in an early morning Shinto exercise, bowing from the waist: down, still further down, now raising themselves slightly then, evidently afraid they had not stayed down long enough, bowing again two, three times, and, tentatively, up again, with a side glance at the depth of their companions' bows. There was no synchronization until the last moment, when they all dipped in unison. The 'boss' man bowed less deeply, indicating his superior rank; anyway his waistline was not so supple as that of his employees.

The express glided off on time in smooth Japanese style, seats were moved back, one or two old ladies bent down to remove their sandals and placed their *tabi*-encased feet upon the foot-rest, looking as if they had recently undergone a painful operation.

My neighbour had bought a string bag of tasteless Japanese tangerines which he proceeded to peel with grave deliberation. A female announcer chirruped to us in the lisping, affected style adopted by the department store staff; three or four scholarly Americans brought out their books.

In less than an hour we left the untidy sprawl of Tokyo with its garish billboards; patches of green became more and more frequent until they stretched, in neat, broad strips, to the foot of cone-shaped hills upon which pine trees clung tastefully as Japanese prints have led us to expect they should. One storeyed-houses clustered in deep valleys as thickly as fir cones, the cylindrical tiles on the roofs glistening after a spring shower.

The train sped impassively past the upturned eaves of a temple behind a wall of cypresses; a crimson *torii* marking the entrance to a shrine hidden upon some mountain peak; a glimpse of mossy steps flanked by a double row of stone lanterns leading up to a dark grove; a brash new hotel perched upon a cliff; factory chimneys; posters advertising Japanese beer spoiling a particularly lovely bit of countryside. . . .

Two girl attendants in brown linen dresses, white aprons and white caps passed down the corridor with a trolley of pretty, mysterious boxes and tiny pale grey china teapots which were eagerly bought by the old ladies. The deep lids were used as cups.

Presently a *maître d'hotel* in black suit and bow tie advanced with an unctuous smile, holding a menu from which we could select either a western or a Japanese-style luncheon, western-style meant steaks or hamburgers; these were the most expensive and cost from sixteen shillings to one pound.

The Japanese fish or rice lunches cost much less, a fried prawn and salad lunch, with roll and butter and coffee, only costing six shillings. Dessert—either cream caramel or ice-cream, was only served with the more expensive lunches and it was impossible to buy one *à la carte*. The Japanese do not eat dessert, only fruit, but it was never possible to get any on a train. When the time came for lunch—there were three services—the elfin girls in brown came to fetch us individually with an inviting smile and a gracious bow.

The first service was favoured by the Japanese passengers who usually eat earlier than we do: midday for lunch and five-thirty for supper, while the last lunch united all the westerners of whom there were plenty, Kyoto being the number one show-place on any tour of Japan.

Looking at them as they walked past on their way to the dining-car, I realized that my stay with Japanese families had conditioned me to Japanese physique; all these western people looked a trifle too big, their faces were too pink and their features too large. Those noses! I was surprised to read in the paper that a recent survey among the Japanese (surveys are very fashionable) had revealed that they are dissatisfied with *their* noses. Many people at home seem to think that all the Japanese have flat noses but this is not true at all; some do, and as a young Japanese told me 'when two people have flat noses it is much easier to kiss on the mouth—western noses are always in the way so you have to kiss sideways', but many others have delicious little noses.

The gentleman sitting in front of me at lunch was one of the solemn Japanese business types. He did not open his mouth until I broke the silence by asking him whether he could speak English. He immediately answered 'yes' and little by little I coaxed a little more information out of him. He was one of the men who had been surrounded by senders-off at Tokyo station, but by jovial not official senders-off. He told me that he worked for a big textile firm, that he had been transferred to Nagoya and that a band of ex-college friends had assembled the night before to celebrate his promotion and send him off the following day. Some of his friends had come from as far as the southern island of Kyushu; their host added that the dinner he had given them the night before had cost him over eighty pounds.

Once their college days are over, the Japanese seldom make new friends. Perhaps they are distrustful; competition is keen; or perhaps they do not want to reveal their character to a man who has not followed them step by step through life; whatever the reason, they have few close friends. Those they have are made in the carefree days of their adolescence. When they meet, they know that they can relax and behave like the adolescents they once were—nobody will reproach them or hold it against them, they are as united as a secret society.   Their wives, too, have an ex-college friend or two and perhaps, in memory of old times, they attend flower-arrangement classes together or *haiku* societies; the Japanese are always learning something or the other.

The clouds rolled themselves up and left the hills just before we reached Mount Fuji so that I had the unexpected treat of seeing the snow-capped sacred mountain silhouetted against a bright blue sky; the loveliest views are to be seen from the lakes at the foot, with choppy blue-green waves and a red *torii* in the foreground, but Fuji is always breathtaking—from a distance. The road to the summit is disfigured by litter—no place could look less sacred or be treated with less respect. At the moment the summit is being disputed by two Shinto shrines. My travelling companions had seen Fuji so often that they did not even look up and went on reading their papers. I felt like shouting: 'You *must* sit up and look! It is not often Mount Fuji reveals itself so clearly. This is your Parnassus. . . .' Parnassus on a Japanese scale, small, perfectly proportioned and feminine. Other sacred mountains of the world: Olympus, Meru, are rugged, inaccessible, masculine. Fuji is easily climbed and the Japanese have therefore been led to believe that heaven is close to the everyday world.

As we approached Kyoto, the delicate embroidery of the shrubs and trees became more intricate; the gods who fashioned Japanese landscapes were fond of variety and refused to make leaves too similar in colour. Our northern landscapes are too uniformly green, they do not blend with the same subtlety as Japanese foliage which even in spring retains some of the rich tints of autumn, the crimson of young maple trees forming a striking contrast with the feathery lightness of golden bamboos, while an occasional cluster of melancholy pine, graceful larch, long-leaved Japanese oak, prevent the colour scheme from becoming too riotous.

At all seasons of the year shrubs produce flowers in endless profusion. In winter, the sense of intimacy, of communion with

nature, is not dispelled by the snow and ice; the landscape is like
an ageing beauty who still preserves much of her youthful charm
thanks to a faultless bone structure; the shapes of the sleeping volcanoes are firm and compact, in harmony with the exquisite houses at their feet, the tilted roofs, the stepping-stones
in the gardens, each one placed with the cunning of a chess-
player, the stone lanterns and the tunnels of *torii* leading to the
shrines.

The hills finally melted into a vast plain where buildings rose
and fell according to their age: the smallest and oldest being the
wooden temples and shrines beside the railway line, the tallest were
the new multiple-storey buildings which are changing the face of
Japan's first capital. 'This is the heart of Japan,' one is told, but my
first impression, a few weeks before, had been one of acute disappointment. I had gradually discovered, however, that although
old Kyoto *is* disappearing, *is* being obliterated by garish shops,
traffic, popular coffee bars, new-look hotels, a great deal of it still
remains—where the hills hold countless shrines and temples to
their bosom, old palaces and model gardens recall the splendours
of ancient courts and learned scholars, dainty inns cluster beside
mountain streams in a tasteful blend of old and modern Japanese
style.

Old Kyoto, Japanese-print Kyoto, lingers even in the middle of
the hurrying city, in narrow alley-ways aflame with globular scarlet
lanterns and gaudy neon signs, in the geisha district of Pontocho
beside the River Kamo, in the *yukas*—temporary wooden verandas
along the riverside where people sup in summertime to escape the
heat of the town—in the hundreds of shrines—over fifteen hundred
of them—in scores of odd corners which would take one weeks to
ferret out. The people and pace of Kyoto are slower, more conservative than those of Tokyo and no modern Japanese looks
pleased when you tell him you prefer Kyoto to the capital. He
admits, rather grudgingly, that Kyoto is more beautiful, more
historical, and that it appeals to the tourist, but as a rule he is
secretly rather tired of temples and shrines, and impatient with the
many 'old-style Japanese' who obstinately follow the old ways and
traditions in the ancient city.

A male announcer apologized in Japanese and English because
we were three minutes late. The Japanese National Railways pride
themselves on keeping to an exact schedule and they do not like
their trains to lose face.

We surged out of the light, modern station to join the taxi queues—separate ones for the 70- and 80-yen taxis. There is nothing much to say about Kyoto station except that, in common with other large Japanese stations, it is thoughtfully provided with an entire floor of shops where one can buy anything from souvenirs to bread and groceries—very convenient for all kinds of traveller-shoppers, from those who have time to kill before their train to those who have had no time to provide for meals at home after a journey.

I noticed a group of American tourists standing open-mouthed before they climbed into their coaches. They were contemplating the extraordinary spectacle of several bus-loads of *sumo* wrestlers alighting and making their way to the station. A couple of *sumo* wrestlers is already an arresting sight, but to see scores of these giants in kimono, *geta* and their piled-up hair style running among their tiny, frail-looking countrymen, is like a scene from an eastern *Gulliver's Travels*.

I have often wondered how this race is produced, and whether *sumo* wrestlers, who, strangely enough, attract the fair sex, perpetuate the species or not. The quantities of food they consume cannot explain their immense height and girth although it may account for the pounds of fat and gristle in which they are encased —but they must have been born extra large. If all the Japanese were as big as this there would not be enough room for them, so it is just as well they have been made small, in keeping with the proportions of their landscapes.

Living in a barber's shop

*O*n Tokyo I had stayed with well-to-do bourgeois families living in semi-western style, but I was anxious to know how the humbler and more traditional Japanese lived if they would accept me into their homes.

In Kyoto, I was fortunate to meet Shizue, an orphan who lived with her aunt and cousin in a barber's shop in one of the most populous quarters of the town; her interest in English was such that she asked me to stay in spite of certain domestic deficiencies.

These were carefully explained to me from the outset. 'To begin with, our house is very dirty,' Shizue told me, 'because my aunt is a semi-invalid and cannot do much housework; I go to the office every day and get home late, and my cousin is busy all day in the barber's shop. So,' she repeated earnestly, stressing every word, 'our house is very dirty indeed.' This was difficult to believe. I had never yet seen a dirty Japanese interior, not even in the slums of Tokyo.

'Secondly,' pursued Shizue determinedly, 'the only free room we have is over the shop and overlooks the main street where the trams run. It is therefore very noisy. And thirdly, what will you do about meals? My aunt is too busy—she has to cook for my cousin, the apprentice who works in the shop, and my cousin's two little boys. Besides, we are very poor.'

This was just the sort of family I wanted to stay with. Shizue's sincerity was pleasing. I liked her from the moment I set eyes on her. She was tall for a Japanese, slim as they nearly always are, rapid—almost nervous—in her gestures. I guessed she must be in her mid-twenties. Her wavy black hair fell to her shoulders, framing an extremely mobile face and kind eyes, wide for a Japanese. I was not surprised when she told me that she would have liked to become an actress; she was sensitive, intelligent, and eager.

The taxi drew up in front of the barber's shop where three customers were being dealt with by Shizue's business-like cousin and her two helpers. I thought it would be better to take my luggage through the door in the side-street, as soon as passing traffic allowed, for there was no pavement. The side door led to a gentleman's toilet on the immediate left with no prudish attempt at concealment. I became quite used, eventually, to the sight of urinating clients from the shop on my way in or out of the house. The 'ladies' was provided with a door but the hole was not provided with a wooden cover and the stench, especially on rainy days, was penetrating.

The rest of the room could be described as a storehouse cum scullery; it had a stone floor, a sink below which goldfish were swimming merrily in a large tin basin; baskets, bowls, utensils of every description were piled up in various corners, and firewood beside the large stone oven in a corner. A thin wooden partition separated it from the living-room where Shizue's elderly aunt lived and slept upon a raised platform beside the *kotatsu*, the Japanese-style fire, now often electrified, placed in a square opening in the floor, under a table covered by a thick quilt which can be pulled over the knees of the people sitting round. This is a superior version of the old Spanish *camilla* which is still found in parts of Galicia.

Opposite the *tatami*-covered platform a cupboard extended across the length of the room, filled with crockery, books, and papers. A sink and a small electric stove by the door permitted the aunt to cook and wash-up without having to move far. Beyond this room a small passage, containing a telephone upon a shelf and a couple of bicycles, led to the barber's shop, which was light, clean and modern, well provided with hot water and driers. It was here that we came to wash at night, when the shutters had been drawn and the last client had left—well after 10 p.m. We never went to bed before midnight.

A flight of narrow wooden stairs at the far end of the scullery led to the bedrooms on the first floor. Shoes had first to be removed and placed precariously upon a shelf under the stairs before the ascent; this was easy to do when one was on the way up, but to collect one's shoes on the way down one needed a flexible Japanese figure to bend, twist, collect and place them on the stone floor—being careful not to let them fall into a puddle (the floor was uneven and nearly always wet) and bend to slide one's feet into them, again being careful not to push them into another puddle beyond one's reach.

At the top of the stairs, a narrow corridor, sharp with splinters that played havoc with one's stockings, led to two *tatami*-covered rooms, separated by a sliding door; the barber's apprentice slept in the first, nearest the corridor; I slept in the next, overlooking the street. I never saw the bedrooms off the corridor where Shizue, her cousin and the little boys slept.

In my room I found a brass bedstead covered by a sheet, a blanket and a heavy Japanese quilt, a writing-table near the window, a folding table against the wall, a chair, and, surprisingly, a few coat-hangers suspended from a shelf.

One important item was missing, however: curtains, and the lights from the street and sparks from passing trams were dazzling; Shizue eventually found a counterpane that almost fitted the

window once we had used up a box of safety-pins in lieu of rings
and hammered a few nails into the wall.

There was no bath in the house; the family went to the public
baths across the road three times a week; they were not embarrassed like my Tokyo hostesses; it had never occurred to them that
we do not have the same kind of baths in England. I really was in a
genuine Japanese atmosphere. No chi-chi here, no self-conscious
striving after a 'western-style' way of life.

I had promised to give Shizue English conversation lessons in
exchange for my accommodation. Seeing how poor they were I
offered to pay for my room, but they would not hear of such a
thing, they had too much Japanese pride—and generosity.

There was a super-market across the road where I could buy
milk, butter and rolls for breakfast. And there were plenty of
Japanese restaurants in the neighbourhood, although I never had
occasion to frequent them, as I was nearly always invited out in the
evening and was too far away in the middle of the day.

Seated on the *tatami* before the low table in my room, I proceeded to give Shizue her first English conversation lesson. She
sat in front of me, her long, shapely fingers grasping a fat notebook,
her face raised expectantly, her eyes glowing with pleasure. She
obviously loved being taught.

Shizue already knew a good deal of English. She had wanted to
study the subject at the university but her aunt had not been able
to afford such an advanced education, so Shizue had had to take a
secretarial job in an architect's office and learn English at evening
classes in her spare time. She had heard of me through her English
teacher.

I asked her to tell me about herself and little by little, with much
prompting and prodding, pieced together the few strands of her
uneventful life. Her father, an army captain, had been sent to
Manchuria, and he took his family with him; her mother died of
tuberculosis, her father was killed in the war. Her aunt had been
a second mother to her. She did not mind being an orphan, she
said, but she did regret her lack of a university education and long
office hours that prevented her from joining a dramatic society.
She loves the stage—her face lit up when she spoke about it—but
'now it is a forbidden word'.

'One doesn't have to work such long hours in all offices,' I said.
'Why don't you find another job?' Shizue looked at me in

amazement. 'But I have been with my present firm for seven years,' she replied. 'Surely that is a very good reason to change,' I retorted, in my ignorance of Japanese ways.

Shizue explained patiently that it is 'not done' to change one's job. It would not be considered a responsible thing to do. If she were to apply to another firm, they would think she had done something wrong, or that she was a flighty person. This system is prevalent all over Japan and is only beginning to be altered in some of the more progressive industrial concerns.

It makes for immobility, lack of initiative and enterprise in the young, and a general lack of efficiency, since many older employees are kept on only because of the system; they cannot be sacked and they will not leave. Once the initial step has been taken, and an employee taken on the pay-roll after many inquiries—his commencing salary fixed according to the college he has attended—he remains in the same company for life.

Although Article 4 of the Labour Law requires that 'the employer should not treat a woman employee differently from a man employee in terms of wages, solely on the ground that the said employee is a woman', sex discrimination exists and it increases with time.

In Tokyo the average starting wage for high school graduates is twelve pounds for girls and thirteen pounds for boys. The gap is bigger among college graduates. The starting salary offered by a securities company is seventeen pounds for girls and twenty pounds for boys. A department store worker gets about five shillings less than a man to begin with, say at the age of twenty-two, and the gap will have widened to nearly six pounds by the time she is thirty-five. There is also discrimination in the nature of the work, girl clerical workers being made to do the 'dirty work', act as messengers, make tea, and so on. In small enterprises girls may have to report half an hour earlier than their male colleagues in the morning to clean the office. But working for a big company does not always mean higher pay for girl employees. One big shipping company pays only seventeen pounds a month to a telephone operator who has been in the company for seventeen years.

In Tokyo, girls in the clerical class tend to change their jobs after a few years and employers encourage it because they can always find younger girls who can be recruited at a lower salary. Two insurance companies even ask girl employees to sign a contract promising to resign when they reach the age of twenty-five.

Another insurance company encourages early marriage, with the understanding that the girls will resign as a result, by paying a marriage allowance to those who marry less than ten years after they start work, but not to those who marry later! The object is to keep down the average age of girl workers.

One progressive department store—Takashimaya—offers the same chance of promotion to both men and women workers—they are all required to pass the same examinations. A thirty-seven-year-old woman, who recently passed the fifth class examination, now holds the post of section chief of the home appliances section. But her case is an exception. And in Kyoto, such chances are even more rare.

'Have you got a boy-friend?' I asked Shizue, wondering where and when she could find one in such a tightly closed society. She blushed like a schoolgirl and put her hand in front of her face. Like many other young Japanese of both sexes, she was not quite sure what 'boy-friend' means. How is it different from an ordinary friend? (The younger generation of Kyoto appears to be more innocent than that of Tokyo. A twenty-four-year-old male student approached his English teacher one day and blurted out in spontaneous self-confession: 'Mr X, do you know something? I am no longer a virgin!' The teacher, after eyeing him for a moment in astonishment, replied: 'Congratulations!')

Shizue has one friend of the opposite sex with whom she occasionally goes to the pictures or an art exhibition; they share the same tastes and hold the same opinions. Is there a possibility of their getting married? Shizue did not think so. He is two years younger than her, she said with a gesture of finality. This would not make any difference in the West, I told her. 'It is better for the man to be older,' she assured me with a wise little nod.

Shizue is a Christian. Seven years ago, when she was ill at home, she came across a Bible which somebody had left with a friend. She began to read it out of curiosity and ended by weeping over the stories in the New Testament. It had opened up a new world for her—a world of tenderness and compassion. She had never heard of anybody as admirable as Jesus Christ. He felt nearer to her than the Buddha. The rest of her family continue to be tepid Buddhists. Her efforts at converting them have failed, but they do not mind what she does.

After our English lesson, we decided to go to the public baths. The usual preparations were made; soap, face-cloths, towels and basins collected and wrapped in a *furoshiki*. Shizue's cousin accompanied us, her hair in rollers. It was dark in the side-street but I could distinguish a number of other women carrying mysterious bundles bound for the same destination.

The public baths at Seijo had been rather splendid, and very new. These were small and much more modest, but they were clean. There was quite a crush. Once again I found myself a bit of an oddity but my fellow-bathers displayed the same friendly curiosity towards me as all the other women I had met. Shizue informed them proudly that I was staying at her house and they uttered loud exclamations of pleased surprise.

Refreshed after the bath, I suggested a visit to a coffee bar. At the 'Venice' we drank a glass of milk and ate sponge cakes to the accompaniment of classical (western) records. At one point Shizue tossed her head back and gave a deep sigh of contentment. She looked very young and very happy. So little ever happens in the average Japanese office girl's life! I was quite an event.

Back in my new home, I undressed in the dark—or comparative dark, for the street lights pierced the makeshift curtain. Next door, the silhouette of the barber's apprentice unfolding his *futon* and preparing for the night danced, larger than life, upon the paper screen. He had been watching television in the shop; he rarely went out. He ate, lived and slept on the premises.

When I awoke the next morning I found a slip of paper pushed under the screen. It was a note from Shizue, hastily written before she left for work, a little before 8 a.m. In it she expressed the hope that I had slept well in spite of the noise of the tram-cars, which she feared must have inconvenienced me. Did I want an egg for breakfast? If I did, I was to ask her aunt. A couple of sentences followed in romanized Japanese, which she assured me her aunt would understand if I spoke slowly. She thanked me warmly for the English lesson and was looking forward to the next one, that evening, 'if I liked'.

An ex-Zen
Buddhist
monk

While earnest Christian missionaries endeavour to convert the Japanese, foreigners are converted to Zen; Zen is big business in Kyoto where there are several study centres as well as a famous temple modernized by Mrs Ruth Sasaki, an American who married a Japanese scholar.

One of the correspondents who had written to me in reply to my letter in the *Asahi Evening News* introduced himself as an ex-Zen Buddhist monk who was 'bumming around looking for the Truth'. The American influence upon his vocabulary was the result of his sojourn with an American beatnik poet and his wife, who were interested in Zen but currently in India, searching for another kind of truth.

I was more interested in an ex-Zen monk than in a practising one, of whom there are so many, and so I anticipated Noboru's visit with interest. He came to see me one evening after his 'degrading work', as he called it: selling souvenirs, mostly lacquer work, in a shop, which enables him to earn a modest living of twenty pounds a month.

Noboru is a very small Japanese with a square face, large shock of hair, small features and smiling eyes; he is soft-spoken, like so many of his countrymen, and his manners are gentle. He is afraid to hurt people's feelings, but he is outspoken and sincere.

We walked through the gardens of the old Imperial Palace and sat on a bench in the setting sun until the evening chill drove us into town and a 'filthy Chinese restaurant' as Noboru described it, frequented by students, where we ate a good dinner by an open window (to escape the smell of frying) for about four shillings per head.

Noboru was born in the countryside, about four hours by train from Kyoto. His father is a Zen priest who brought up his family with great severity, almost cruelty. The only college to which he could afford to send Noboru, because it was cheap, was a Buddhist theological college in Kyoto. After graduating from this college, Noboru was more or less obliged to go on to a monastery. He did not have a religious vocation, however, and, moreover, he often felt the pangs of hunger. There were nights, he confessed, when he jumped over the monastery walls and slipped into the adjoining village to buy a bowl of noodles. Poor Noboru looked as if he had never eaten enough. First, the strict food rationing after the war, when he was a child—then the poor fare at college, followed by long fasts at the monastery, and now ... a dietitian would surely have advised him to eat more protein, in which the ordinary Japanese fare is deficient. 'I sometimes go on a spree,' he said, laughing, 'last night I cooked a splendid meal with the artist who lives below me: Liver and onions. It was excellent, but we drank too much *sake* afterwards and that rather spoiled the effect.'

It is not easy for Noboru to find congenial work; his qualifications are not of a practical nature and whenever he presents his diploma to a prospective employer, the reaction inevitably is: 'Why aren't you in a monastery?' A friend had offered him the salesman's job but Noboru is the first to admit that he is quite devoid of business sense. 'When a client comes in, asks me the price of an object and then exclaims: "But how expensive!" I nearly always agree with him. I have to, to be honest, because most of the objects *are* terribly expensive. I know the cost price, so....' 'So you had better find yourself another job,' I said. I seemed to be advising most young people I met to change their jobs ... but Noboru, unlike Shizue, had no compunction about the desirability of making a change. 'But *what* kind of a job?' 'We'll think about it,' I said. 'Let's meditate,' said Noboru, who is still permeated by his Zen background.

In the meantime, Noboru appointed himself my guide in Kyoto, in his spare time. That night, he suggested, we might go cherry-blossom viewing by moonlight at the Yasako shrine. It sounded an enchanting idea. It was also an idea that we shared with thousands of other Kyotoites. ...

Laughing and talking softly, the kimono-clad figures glided in the evening breeze up the street past the Gion geisha quarters to the gentle slopes of the Higashiyama hills and the great red *torii* beyond which stretch Maruyama park and a score of pavilions built at different levels, some hidden behind trees, some boldly thrust forward on a gravel path, others dim and inaccessible on a bluff, all part of the complex ninth-century shrine from which the gay Gion festival floats leave every July 17th for their annual procession through the town.

Up a small flight of steps, through the *torii* and into a land of enchantment where everything, even the gaudy souvenir booths, had been touched by the magic of a night illuminated by hundreds of stone lanterns from which candles, incense and resin sent up tongues of multi-coloured flames surrounded by haloes of sparks.

The large opal moon suspended above Maruyama park was the presiding goddess of the wide avenues of cherry trees in full, sub-dued pink blossom, shaded in silvery-grey. There was a happy sense of communion with nature, with the people round us, with the mysterious *kami* summoned from their sanctuaries by devotees pulling on white tasselled ropes in front of the pavilions; the sound of laughter mingled with the tinkle of coins thrown into grilled money-boxes, and the rhythmic double-clapping of pious hands. The gods felt very near.

A sturdy young Shinto priest saw us looking at the blossoms, and stopped to admire my fair hair with unpriestly pæans of praise. 'I look after the business-men's shrine, come and see it,' he said, and we followed him up a narrow path, round a corner edged with shrubs, to a diminutive shrine like a Swiss chalet filled with symbolic bric-à-brac—there is no other word for it—for none of the objects had any aesthetic value.

A couple of stone guardian dogs bared their fangs at the entrance to the pavilion; in the centre of the altar a round mirror, the Shinto symbol which symbolizes the stainless mind of the *kami*, shone like a Host; the priest pointed out the *gohei* consisting of a wand with strips of white paper folded zigzag fashion 'indicating the presence of the *kami* in the inner chamber', and small dried branches of the sacred *sakaki* tree. The usual thick straw rope hung with strips of white paper cut into four zigzags was stretched between the pillars at the entrance of the shrine. It has no religious significance, I was told; no doubt the meaning must have been forgotten, but nobody attaches much importance to these things; they are ornamental and traditional and that is enough.

The priest pointed with a satisfied smile to the rows of *sake* barrels stacked before the altar-offerings to the gods by the business men of Kyoto; the barrels are empty, the priests have drunk the *sake*. The Japanese may not be religious, but many traders are still superstitious, and the shrines depend on their support.

A Japanese may be a first-class modern technician and still believe in ancient lore. Only recently, one of Noboru's friends, an electronics engineer, had given up his beautiful country home because a fortune-teller had told him that it was built in an inauspicious direction. This old Chinese-inspired belief in 'directional powers' is still very strong in Japan.

Fortune-tellers do good business. They appear like moths in the evenings, sit on the pavement before tiny tables lit by candles that cast moving shadows on their faces, and form cabbalistic patterns with short sticks. Perhaps people are less susceptible to their appeal in the daytime; they wait until the light has gone, the world appears less secure and the mind—the restless, hybrid Japanese mind—feels the need of assurance, of a message from the world of supernatural forces.

Noboru, of course, did not feel such a need; he was above such childishness—his long Zen training had taught him to aspire to higher things—but he knew all the lore that has now been converted into playthings sold at the booths on the way to shrines. He explained what lay behind the little wooden models of a badger beside a cauldron displayed on the stalls beneath the cherry-trees: the legend of the devil who transformed himself into a badger and teased householders until one day someone caught him and tossed him into a cauldron hanging over the fire; and he explained the origin of the wooden Darouma toy—the pear-shaped object with the comical face of a whiskered old man with bushy brows which rocks from side to side but never falls over.

Darouma is the irreverent descendant of a venerable Hindu patriarch: Bodhidharama, the first representative of Zen in China, who is said to have introduced Zen to Japan in the sixth century. He was supposed to have spent nine years in meditation in northern China, where the cold forced him to wrap up from head to foot. Few Japanese remember his origin, but the Darouma toy is found all over Japan and represents stability, endurance and perseverance. Truth under the guise of buffoonery would no doubt not have displeased the old patriarch and advocate of Zen.

Noboru took me further up the slope to look at a famous cherry-tree, standing on a mound at a cross-roads in the park, protected by an iron railing. Its wide branches were heavily laden with double blossom, but the tree was so old, its trunk so gnarled and twisted, that it seemed almost indecent for it to be so overdressed in youthful blossom. The branches had had to be propped up by

poles and it stood there like an obstinate old actress determined to
go on with the show until she dropped.

Miyako-odori: the geisha spring dance

⊘here are three geisha quarters in Kyoto, and each one has its
special flavour: Gion has the best theatre and gives the most
polished cherry-blossom dances; it is the wealthiest and the most
publicized; Shimabara is the most mysterious; few outsiders can
penetrate the fastnesses of the old seventeenth-century houses
where the *Tayus*, old-style geishas, live in a traditional way, wear
gorgeous costumes and individual hair-styles; Pontocho, on the
banks of the Kamo, is the most picturesque, the most closely knit,
but equally impenetrable, unless one has the right kind of introduction.

None of the young Japanese I knew could introduce me into this
district; even Hideto Kato, the able young sociologist who has
written about the folk arts of Japan, had never set foot inside a
geisha house, but he was very willing to accompany me as an
interpreter. At last, I heard about a man who could, if he wanted
to, allow me to see a little more than the banal, expensive geisha
party available to any foreigner willing to pay the price. (The
official tariff at Gion is eleven pounds for a party with two Maiko
and one Geisha, eighteen pounds for three Maiko and two Geisha,
plus charges for drinks, room, tax, etc.)

Mr Perkins is an American who fell in love with Japan before the
war, and with a geisha from Pontocho whom he married; he plays
the *samisen*, speaks Japanese fluently and has become transformed,
like the English lady I had met at Seijo; a mental and physical
osmosis had taken place. I did not know whether I was speaking
to a westerner or an oriental when I sat in front of Mr Perkins's desk
in his Japanese house on a dripping wet afternoon with a pearl-
grey mist entwined between the branches like a giant spider's web.

Mr Perkins lives on the green edge of the city where old-style

houses have brooded in meditation for centuries, hiding exquisite
gardens and precious tea-houses behind walls as thick and forbidding as ramparts. On the other side of the wall one is absorbed
by the patrician atmosphere of an old Kyoto palace. Mr Perkins's
house once belonged to an aristocratic family and through the
broad central strip of the windows—half-glass, half rice-paper, one
looks out upon trees with graduated branches trimmed like clouds,
and a gourd-shaped pond, in and out of which frogs plop as merrily
as in the pictures by Sengai and squat upon stepping-stones in the
zazen posture which prompted the great Zen master to exclaim:
'I may sit in meditation for hours, just like a frog—but this will not
remove me from my mediocrity!'

Mr Perkins sat between piles of oriental books which he exports
to all corners of the world, dressed in a brown kimono, his once-
western face now the colour of old ivory remoulded by Japanese
thought and contemplation into an impassive mask from time to
time broken by a thoughtful smile. In the background, three
Japanese typists clicked away, two of them rapidly upon western
typewriters, one of them more slowly on an immense Japanese
typewriter manoeuvred with one hand, boxes of additional
characters on her right. One of the typists pushed her chair back
and a clink of cups announced that she was preparing the inevitable
pot of visitors' tasteless Japanese tea.

An hour later, I slipped away with an introduction in my handbag to Mrs Takae, an ex-geisha who owns a bar in Pontocho, and
whose daughter is a promising *samisen* player. The bar is not open
to foreigners; 'there would be no point in it,' Mr Perkins explained,
'because they could not join in the conversation which is usually
of a high standard. Mrs Takae's bar is a meeting-place for patrons
and well-known clients, connoisseurs of Japanese dancing and
music. A foreigner would be quite out of place and, besides, Mrs
Takae speaks no English. Take an interpreter with you and present
this card. She may let you see a cherry-blossom dance rehearsal.
The Pontocho performances take place later than the Gion dances.
They will be very busy and foreigners are not usually allowed
inside the theatre at rehearsal-time, but you can always try.'

Two days later, with the help of Mr Kato, I located the little bar
in the narrow street of Pontocho that runs parallel to the River
Kamo, near the playground where the geisha leave their children
when they are at their lessons—which never cease—or at the
theatre.

Every house in this street is a geisha house, with the names of famous geishas marked on the doors. They are so tightly shuttered that a stranger would think the district had been completely abandoned; but if he pauses long enough, he will see a door open ever so slightly and hesitatingly, to let out a bent old crone in a white overall with a shopping basket over her arm; if he is fortunate, he may catch sight of a gorgeous creature in brilliant kimono and shiny geisha wig clip-clopping up the street on her way home from a rehearsal at the theatre; he will look at her in raptures but she will not raise her eyes to his, nor will she smile as she passes by. Her world is not yours and she is not anxious for the two to meet. Her thoughts are far away, on some intricate step of a difficult dance, on her performance, on those of her rivals. . . . You realize with a pang of disappointment when she has gone that she was not so beautiful after all; her kimono, her hair-do, her glittering ornaments created the illusion of beauty; stripped of its wings, the butterfly is a very ordinary creature. But she is probably very talented and in great demand.

Mrs Takae is not beautiful either; in fact, she is extremely plain, with a thin face, protruding teeth and eyes that glitter with commercial sharpness behind her glasses. She did not seem pleased to see a foreigner but, for the sake of 'Perkins-*san*', who is one of 'them', she agreed to escort me and Mr Kato to the Kaburenjo theatre where the girls were rehearsing. Donning an aubergine-coloured kimono, she tottered up the street between us, slightly bent over her stiff brocade *obi* in the time-honoured Japanese style of walking, a cigarette between her teeth in more modern style. She was greeted right and left as we progressed; everybody knows Mrs Takae in the community of Pontocho where the geishas are born, brought up and die in what amounts to a matriarchal society.

Everything here is in the hands of women; the older and wealthier among them rule the *nyokoba* or business office that also runs the geisha school, the medical office and the practice rooms where music and dancing are taught; they select the dance programmes, the judges from Tokyo invited to comment on the annual performances, the musicians invited to compose the special music to accompany them; older geishas run the geisha houses, bars and tea-rooms; young ones flutter and learn, love and are disillusioned, bear children to their patrons and bring them up in Pontocho's ways—for they know no other, and there is no other. Nowadays, it is true, a few desert and dishonour the profession by becoming dance hostesses at night-clubs; that is hardly an improvement on the geisha way of life, with its long arduous training and striving for perfection in its arts.

You feel the matriarchal sense of community as soon as you enter the Kaburenjo—even outside, where groups of laughing young *maiko* approached from all directions, afraid of being late, while others who had finished their turn were coming out, chatting gaily among themselves; they all bowed to Mrs Takae and looked at us wonderingly.

The large hall inside was full of geishas and *maiko*, some sitting on long sofas eating a bowl of noodles, others dandling babies, while a stream of performers ran in and out of the adjoining theatre. A poster on one of the walls displayed the photograph of the liberal candidate for the forthcoming elections with the caption 'Pontocho recommends Mr X'—no doubt he is one of their patrons.

The theatre was filled with professionals: geishas come to watch their friends perform, severe-looking elderly ladies who obviously belonged to the geisha associations or were owners of tea-houses, and gentleman patrons. An old gentleman in a black kimono was pointed out to me as a distinguished composer from Tokyo; the choreographer, a younger man, was standing in a little box to the right, his eyes glued to the stage, on either side of which were two long undivided boxes holding thirteen musicians in each, the *samisen* players on the right, the drum and percussion players on the left. Mrs Takae sat between us at the back of the theatre, and pushed a programme into my hand to enable me to follow the dances as the tale unfolded. Every year, a different theme is chosen from classical literature or ancient history. This year the Pontocho association had chosen the *Tale of Ise*, which the programme related as follows:

The *Tale of Ise* is one of our classical works ranking with the *Tale of Genki*. The Prince Narihira, our Don Juan of the ninth century, is 56 years old and yet his amorousness is not wasted away. He is arranging the love poems in reply by many a lady with whom he had made a love's pledge from the day he had the rite to mark his attainment of manhood. Just then a playful spring breeze sweeps away the papers of the poems which float down on his garden. As he is to pick them up, he is suddenly attacked by a dizziness and falls down on the ground. All the blackness comes over him.

He was at the age of 25 when he was at last promoted to the Junior Grade of the 5th Rank. He had been carrying on a love affair with the

Lady Takai-ko, the daughter of an influential courtier, who was betrothed to the heir apparent of the Emperor. When the rumour reached
her family, a cordon of the guards round her mansion was intensified.
Her elder brother felt compassion for Narihira and allowed to meet her
just one night. Narihira madly in love betraying him stole into her
chamber and ran away with her. While the elopers were taking a shelter
in an old storehouse, her second elder brother wearing a demon's mask
on and his men pursued them there to take back his errant sister home.
Before leaving he cut Narihira's hair close as the chastisement.

As Narihira did not want to be a laughing stock in the capital because
of his round head, he taking with him his faithful retainer left for a
roving journey in the Eastern part of Japan. Coming to the village of
Yatsu-bashi, he met Miyoshino, the daughter of the provincial governor,
whose serene beauty reminded him of his wife, Itsuzu. Being lured by
her semblance in look, he spent the night with her.

Narihira having the pardon was back to the capital. It was one summer
night. When he was watching a group of maids catching fireflies on dry
river bed of the Kamo river, a flower of forget-me-not was held out to
him from the inside of a lady carriage. The presentor was a high court
lady, his former lover. They were again having a sweet love's rendezvous
in the carriage. His rival in love saw this and was furious with him. He
designed to have his wife, Itsuzu, in revenge who had been left alone in
the province of Yamato.

Narihira came to inspect the rice harvesting in his manor. The maids
working in the paddy-field were excited at their lord's visit and clamoured
for his handwritten poems. The quick-witted retainer of his made them
draw lots, saying that the winner only gets the one. Among the con-
testants was a grey-haired old maid. Knowing that he could rake out a
dying fire of love, Narihira contrived to make her the winner.

Narihira after over three years' absence came back to his wife. He
found out she had been misconducting herself with his rival. She asked
for his pardon as their marriage was the fruit of their long acquaintance
since their childhood. On the contrary her affair with the man was forced
on her. He turned a deaf ear to her implore. Itsuzu wrote a sad farewell
poem and threw herself into a well. Narihira now regretted and looking
into the well cried hard. The body accused him grudgingly. To the
self-reproaching man, the figures of the women with whom he had had
the affair appear on the surface of the well water one after another.

Narihira restoring his senses finds himself laying on the bed attended
by his wife. He now comes to know all is void and all is over. When he
expresses it in poem, the brush is dropped from his hand—and dies.

In between these distressing scenes, Mrs Takae gave me pieces
of factual information about present-day geisha life. Everything

costs so much more. Impossible to buy a really good *obi* under a hundred pounds—they are almost as expensive as a kimono. These can cost up to one hundred and fifty pounds or more—as much as a western model gown—and every geisha is expected to buy at least one new kimono a month. This is part of her stock-in-trade and the kimonos of Kyoto are famous. Thanks to the geishas, the artists and craftsmen continue to produce masterpieces. Without the geisha trade, there would be an inevitable decline. Few society ladies can afford to buy such gorgeous kimonos. (They might consider them too actressy for the kind of lives they lead.)

The geisha earns from fifty to a hundred pounds a month net, after deduction has been made for taxes and dues paid to the geisha association. She continues to take dancing and singing lessons, even when she is a fully-fledged geisha, at least six days a month at average cost of two pounds per lesson. The best masters are an expensive. There are a number of male teachers. Few of the women teachers have been geishas themselves. Their star pupils are allowed to take their names. Marriage? Mrs Takae smiled. 'Sometimes they get married, but generally speaking a geisha does not want to get married. She is wedded to her art, to the freedom of her life.' Inconsequentially she pointed to the row of *samisen* players and pointed out her daughter. 'She will be very good one day,' she said proudly. Then, seeing one of her elderly cronies in front beckoning to her, she suddenly got up, bowed stiffly and left us.

The Gion theatre is larger, more impressive and the dancing altogether of a higher order than at Pontocho. The entrance to the theatre is at the end of a wide street decorated with arches hung with gaily swinging rows of red and white globe lanterns. Even here, a few yards from Yasaka, artificial cherry-blossom had been archly drawn over street lamps and through the lanterns that decorated every house along the street leading to the theatre, but it was used with more discretion than in Tokyo.

The programme of the spring-dance performance was magnificent, full of colour pictures and photographs of the performers. Even the advertisements were attractive, since the most colourful geishas had posed for most of them. The choreography, by a lady member of the Japan Academy of Arts, was based on one of the stories of Oishi Yoshio, the leader of the revolt of the forty-seven *ronin* who avenged the murder of their feudal lord Asano and whose tombs I had seen in Tokyo. Oishi was not only a Samurai but a calligrapher, painter and composer of songs still sung in the geisha quarters of Gion. The origin of the annual cherry-blossom dance, however, does not go back so far. It was inaugurated in 1872, the programme informed me, 'under Government auspices as a means to restore high spirits to Kyoto on the occasion of the great exhibition held after the city had lost her status of the capital of Japan to Tokyo'.

I went to an afternoon performance and was surprised to find a mostly male audience. Some of the most eager patrons, I observed, had brought binoculars with them.

The curtains went up on the side boxes, revealing the row of *samisen* players in dark grey kimonos on the right, and the drum and percussion ladies on the left dressed in black and silver. The overture and song, 'Shall we dance the cherry-blossom dance', was sung and danced against an elegant silver-coloured paper screen with red-tasselled door fittings, supposed to represent the main hall of a tea-house; the next two scenes took place in the spring— one showed a bridge over the River Kamo and an old water-mill seen through willows, a delicate study in mustard-yellow and grey with a few touches of green for the willow branches and dark brown for the trunks; the other, in pale green, white and mauve, showed a combination of irises, snowdrops and wisteria under a pine tree with a waterfall indicated by six grey lines, beside two rocks; summer was represented by a mountain pass in deep blue and pale madder and by a love-scene enacted in the Gion quarters with an August moon reflected in a blue pond between the pavilions of a tea-house; the autumn scene was filled with maple leaves in the forest and winter, the most delicate season of all, showed Yamashina in the snow, a range of white hills against a blue-green sky, one naked tree on the right, on which a long-beaked bird sat watching two of its fellows in flight, and two snow-covered hayricks of the small, neat Japanese variety to the right; an evergreen pine tree on the left, and a few blades of rust-coloured grass, half enveloped in snow, completed the scene. The finale was a little overdone; it took the form of a group dance under masses of cherry-blossom, right, left and centre, with a sepia-coloured Mount Fuji in the centre, streaked with white forked lines on the summit like an advertisement for a caramel pudding.

The kimonos were radiant, extravagant, fabulous—indescrib-able in the variety of their patterns except for a Japanese fashion-writer. Impossible to remember the details of more than a few: a brilliant turquoise creation embroidered with pink and white peonies; a paler blue kimono with a design of three ranges of mountains in tones of russet and lime green separated by a white mist through which a plum tree emerged in full blossom; a graduated white and mauve satin kimono with a pattern of large brown and soft green leaves, lined in green and red: astonishing contrasts suddenly subdued by the appearance of a plain brown kimono worn with a blue under-collar, edged in beige.

Had the movements of the dances been rapid as in western ballet or music-hall the sight of so many vivid colours would have been unbearable, but the fastidious grace of Japanese dance-movements, the smooth, slow gestures, toned them down. The foreigners in the audience appeared to be stimulated by the colours and chilled by the dances. It took me a long time to appreciate them, but after I had attended several dancing-classes, I began to be interested and ended by being captivated. They are essentially tea-house dances of a past age, when women in order to be feminine imitated the curves of willow-branches; the body is seldom straight—the legs are always bent at the knees, the heels thrust upwards and exposed to indicate violence or temper; fans are turned in, out, round, opened, shut with a firm muscular control of dainty hands—dainty firmness is characteristic of much Japanese art.

The head and neck movements seem coy to a westerner who does not want women to look like spoiled children but one gets used to this convention and to the stylized charm with which the dancers use their kimono sleeves to express various emotions. I presume it is because modern girls can no longer hide a blush in a kimono sleeve that they put their hands before their faces instead, in a last concession to the old tradition whereby they were supposed to hide their feelings. Dainty, delectable, subtle—these are the adjectives conjured up by Japanese dancing; inseparable from the geisha who is its most able exponent.

I never saw the geishas of Shimabara, but I did walk through the narrow streets of this secretive district to visit the large, sombre seventeenth-century geisha house which is open to the public. It would make an admirable setting for a Samurai film. The ground floor is occupied by the descendants of the original owners, and most of it seems to consist of one big kitchen. Beyond it is a court-yard in which two stout trees have pushed their trunks up through the structure; the doors are painted with a cabbalistic motif like the seal of a Shinto shrine; somewhere a tap drips into a stone basin; lichens creep up the damp walls and the smell of decay reminds one of medieval churches where corpses lie beneath the crypt. It could be that buried corpses of murdered Samurai lie underneath the flagstones. Upstairs in the guest-rooms where the ceilings have been blackened by the smoke of thousands of candles burned at all-night parties, a wizened guide gleefully points out the marks of sword-thrusts on the walls—traces of long-forgotten fights and feuds after too much *sake* drinking.

The lattice-work in the windows and sliding doors is modernistic in its sobriety. I lean out of one window and see two cherry-trees in the minute courtyard below, forming a canopy over a dead tree-trunk preserved under a corrugated roof. This veteran is thought to be inhabited by a spirit; that is why he is being protected. I am sure that the house is haunted.

Rocks for export.
Soka Gakkai

The foreign relations department of the Municipal Offices to whom I had an introduction from the Foreign Office in Tokyo, have presented me with a gorgeous brochure illustrating Kyoto old and new. The thick cover is a reproduction of a painting from one of the sliding-doors in the old Imperial Palace, and represents the twisted branch of a lichen-covered Japanese pine, upon which an eagle is perched in regal meditation, against a dull gold background. It is a superb production; the text is in English and French, the illustrations begin with a bird's-eye view of the city, which enables one to see how it still follows the eighth-century Chinese plan—little rectangles cut across by long, straight streets—adopted by the Emperor Kammu (that is one reason why one can find one's way about in Kyoto, unlike Tokyo) and end in a prosaic modern note with photographs of the Central Telephone office, the gas storage tank, and the incinerator plant.

An introduction from the Foreign Office works like a talisman. All doors are opened to me. I talk to the courteous Public Relations

officer, who speaks English fluently; I am introduced to the deputy
Mayor, an ex-journalist who speaks French and lends me a car to go
and visit the Assembly Hall, completed in 1960, one of the architectural highlights of new-style Kyoto. The directors have published their own colourful brochure about this hall, with a reproduction on the cover of the impressionistic mosaic mural in the
main entrance. It is a striking building in glass and concrete with a
hint of traditional architecture in the upward tilt of the angles. It
contains two concert halls and a conference room. All visiting
artists and symphonies perform here and the schedule is full. Big
newspapers like the *Mainichi* and the *Asahi Shimbun* regularly
patronize artists and invite them to Japan. These papers also award
annual literary and scientific prizes.

After a tour of inspection we queued up for a cup of tea in the
glass-fronted self-service café on the ground floor where a group
of students were sitting over a rice curry, price approximately one
and six. The café overlooks a wide terrace and the splendid natural
backdrop of hills. This part of Kyoto, the rim of the city at the foot
of wooded hills, is incomparable. What a pity that the modern
centre should be so barren! The Kyotoites should do what the
Chinese have done in Peking: plant millions of trees.

It is easy to make a garden in Kyoto. The raw materials are just
a few hours' climb away in the hills where you can find all you need
from interesting stones to wonderful flowers and shrubs. So far as
I know there are no laws to prevent you from uprooting any of
them. There is no need because people are not interested in plant-
collecting—except the specialists. Japan is a land of specialists in
contrast to England, the land of amateurs.

Specialist gardeners, the famous landscape gardeners of Kyoto,
live along the green edge of the city where one can see their collections on display, ready for export, without even the protection of a
fence or barbed wire. People must be very honest or very dis-
interested not to want to filch them. Here you can see clusters of
stone lanterns of all sizes, trees twisted into irregular shapes either
naturally or artificially (Japanese trees, even in their natural state,
are more perverse than ours; they *like* to be complicated), mounds
of stones of all colours and forms, heaps of sand, rows of azaleas in
brilliant kimono shades.

Many theories have been put forward to explain the 'secret' of
the Ryoanji garden's magic. I have always thought that it was the
inspiration of a Zen priest who had either seen or heard about

deserts, in China. There are no deserts in Japan, no wide spaces like
the steppes, to satisfy the contemplative's desire for emptiness; a
desert had to be created artificially, re-invented by and for a
Japanese mind with the addition of boulders to represent mountains and thereby enable the imagination to grasp the universal
scale of the symbolic Ryoanji. The rocks are an important feature,
but the desert concept is the basic attraction and *raison d'être* of
Ryoanji, the only place outside Africa which, by an effort of con-
centration, produces in me the same sensations as the Sahara.

The Director of the Brooklyn Botanic Garden, believing that the
'tranquil mood of the Ryoanji would be good for busy New
Yorkers who need more chance for quiet and reflection', has asked
Touemon Sano, a famous Kyoto gardener, to find fifteen similar
rocks for shipment to New York, where he intends to build a
modified replica of the Ryoanji. Sano had recently spent two
months searching the mountains and rivers of Kyushu, Shikoku
and central Japan before he found rocks 'that he felt could match
the feeling of those in Ryoanji'. It looks as though the next export
of Japanese culture to America from Kyoto after Zen is to be
'rocks'.

It is not the first time that rocks have been exported from Japan.
A few years ago, Mr Yamaoka, who owed his fortune to the
inspiration of Dr Diesel, had fifty-six rocks assembled from all over
Japan and shipped to Augsbourg as a memorial. (The Germans
had not thought of putting one up themselves.) One of the rocks,
weighing over twenty tons, was inscribed with the words: 'Dr
Diesel, you are still alive all over Japan.' Mr Yamaoka had composed the phrase thinking of all the diesel engines in use in the
paddies, factories and lakes of Japan.

There are several Professors of landscape gardening at the
University. I was introduced to one the other day, a little bald man
with beady eyes, an expert on the history of Japanese gardens. He
graciously lent me one of his students to explain some of Kyoto's
best-known gardens to me. The student, however, was disappointing. He just would not or could not *explain*. We walked for miles,
rode endlessly in trams and buses to reach a particular garden but
once we got there he had nothing to say beyond what I read in a
guide-book: 'The garden (of the Daisen-in temple) designated as a
Special Scenic Beauty, is one of the representative Karesansui (dry
garden) laid out in the Muromachi period. It consists of rocks in
various shapes and sizes which represent mountains, a waterfall

and a stream, all in a small space' or, at the Tenryo-ji temple, 'The garden designed by Abbot Muso-Kokushi, retains its original beauty with its pond, white sand and rocks. There you will find a blend of the tradition that had come down from the Heian period and the new tastes which were being introduced by Zen Buddhism'.

At the Tofuku-ji temple, which contains a celebrated Zen toilet—the only toilet in Japan which has been elevated to the status of a national treasure—the student turned the tables on me and asked me what I thought of the garden. I expressed the opinion that the trees grew too far forward and destroyed the original balance; the student looked up and nodded. 'It is a good point,' he said, but he still refused to make any personal comments on any of the gardens.

Is this fear of expressing an opinion due to the old dread of 'losing face' or to the fact that young people are being indoctrinated rather than stimulated and encouraged to think for themselves? The official result of tests made in October 1961 at the behest of the Ministry of Education on second and third year junior high school pupils throughout the country confirmed what I found during my conversations at all levels. The children 'answered the simple memory questions with ease, but when they were called upon to exercise their powers of reason, to think for themselves, they floundered'.

When people do not think for themselves, there is a danger that somebody with a little more energy, ambition and a streak of fanaticism may think for them and appeal to their easily kindled emotions. This is probably the explanation of the spectacular achievements of the Soka Gakkai sect, a religious group which emerged from the July 1962 elections as the third voice in Japan's House of Councillors. Soka Gakkai is the only one of the many so-called 'new religions' in Japan to have grown into a major political force thanks to the energetic young men at the head of it who advocate conversion by force (*shabubuku*), promise their followers the world, and organize them from the bottom up with special emphasis on the young.

The smallest Soka Gakkai unit is the *kumi* or team composed of ten households. Five to ten *kumi* make a *han*, or squad. Five to ten *han* form a *chiku* area, and five to ten *chiku* form a *shibu* or chapter. Several chapters are organized into a general chapter. Policy decisions are transmitted from the general headquarters in Tokyo to the district departments. This sect, which founds its beliefs on the doctrinaire tenets of the thirteenth-century dissident Buddhist monk (saint to some) Nichiren, has a vague political programme. The leaders talk loosely about carrying out reforms 'in accordance with the change of the times by awakening the people to life through religion and using the good points of socialism or dialectical materialism. This is neo-socialism.'

It is anybody's guess whether it will eventually turn to Fascism or Communism, but the alarming fact is that Soka Gakkai is gaining adherents at the rate of 400,000 new families a year. (Every individual convert undertakes to bring his or her entire family into the fold.) The figures are eloquent: 1953 membership amounted to 200,000 individuals; by 1959 it had risen to a total of four millions!

It looks very much as though Soka Gakkai provides for the youth of the nineteen sixties, the only outlet (there is no army, nor any definite national ideology) for the firm discipline, military unquestioning obedience and shock tactics which appeal to the unthinking Japanese masses. Their activities disturb many Japanese. 'They should be watched!' they exclaim. But who is to do the watching? Youth is easily swayed and the emotional Japanese wants to be swayed by an ideological current which he believes is uniquely *Japanese*.

A new kind of love

*O*n Kyoto students jostle one another on the crowded pavements of Kawaramachi, meet their girl-friends in dimly lit coffee bars to the accompaniment of classical western music, or hot jazz. In one café girl-students work as waitresses and students of both sexes walk on to the little stage to sing and gesticulate in front of a microphone in the best television style. There is also community singing in which the youthful audience join in the choruses. Printed pamphlets are handed round; some of the songs are hill-billies, and the text is in English as well as Japanese. The atmosphere is gay but extremely proper. Many girls sit together at the tables and giggling seems to be the only way they know to attract boys' attention. In spite of co-education the average Japanese boy and girl are fairly naïve and bashful, especially in old-world Kyoto.

Round the corner, Mrs Tanaka runs a municipal youth club for young working people. She is young, alert, and her warm brown eyes sparkle with a sense of humour. She lets the club run itself. The boys and girls go to her when they want advice. A few boys stroll in while we sit talking in the first-floor lounge amply provided with leather-covered chairs, small varnished tables, a magazine rack, a record-player and a stack of records. A young couple are sitting at the soft drink bar in a corner of the lounge. A few boys and girls are playing ping-pong downstairs and the gymnasium is occupied by lads who still have some surplus energy after a long day behind a counter. Most of them work for local tradesmen. At week-ends they go hiking. 'It gives the boys self-confidence,' says Mrs Tanaka, 'and helps to override their innate shyness of girls; when you come to a steep bit on a hill and have to hold a girl's hand, for instance'—she laughed gaily. 'Many a boy has come to me and asked me how he should approach a girl whom he wants to get to know better. One of my boys is so shy that he wants to follow the old-style method and rely on his parents' choice of a girl. But his parents are more modern than he is. When he asked them to look for a bride for him they turned round and said, "why don't you look for one yourself?" '

The most up-to-date method of choosing a partner, one that is free of charge, worry and responsibility, and is respectably sponsored by the Municipal authorities, is the Municipal Marriage Bureau, a daring innovation which competes with the old-fashioned but not yet extinct *nakodo*. 'The truth is,' said marriage counsellor Mrs Okada, 'that people, even the "best people", are getting tired of *nakodos*.'

'The trouble with *nakodos* is that one is usually saddled with them for life. They assume obligations but they also meddle in family affairs; some *nakodos* expect to be rewarded and they can be a millstone round a family's neck. That is why we are getting applications now from better-class people who wish to be free of such associations.'

The Marriage Bureau was established ten years ago but it cannot be said that people are flocking to it. The idea is still too novel and perhaps it has not been publicized in the right way. Mrs Okada is the first to admit that people believe it is intended mainly for those who have remained on the shelf, the elderly and unattractive.

The Bureau receives just under one thousand applications a year, with forty per cent more girls than boys on the lists. As with marriage bureaux in other countries, young applicants in their early twenties are few; they begin to get worried when they reach the age of twenty-five, rising to the psychological peak of thirty years, with almost equal figures for men and women. Thereafter there is a steady decline tailing off at the age of fifty when only a very few women—four or five—dare to apply to the Bureau. As far as educational background is concerned, the bulk of the applicants are of senior high school standard, a number never went farther than junior high school, and there are relatively few college or university graduates—about one hundred young men and fifty girls per year.

Mrs Okada showed me the application cards which are sent to possible partners before a meeting is arranged in her office and in her presence, with the parents' prior permission. When they have been introduced she leaves the prospective couple to talk together alone. Later, if they are agreeable, they meet again outside; the young man may take the girl to an espresso bar or to the pictures. The parents know about it, of course, and the girl must be back home early. No evening meetings are allowed. The young people are advised not to make any decisions in a hurry and it is usual for them to meet for several months and only decide to get married after a year.

'Of course nobody would have come to a Marriage Bureau in the old days,' said Mrs Okada, 'Marriages *had* to be effected through a *nakodo* but now that the element of personal choice has entered into human relationships, everything is different. On the other hand, it is not always easy for young people to meet many members of the opposite sex. Our Bureau offers them a wider choice, in a perfectly respectable way.'

I asked her what qualities are sought for most in future husbands and wives. 'The men stress appearance first and then obedience; the young women stress financial security first and then they demand a virile character.' More young men are asking for educated girls.

The Marriage Bureau also provides a hall for wedding ceremonies at a reasonable rate, a miniature 'Palace of Weddings' with the difference that a Shinto priest can officiate if the parties wish him to.

Although many more young people are marrying 'for love', the western idea of romance having been introduced through films,

television, and magazines and coupled with the new popular concept of democracy, there are many families in which the old system
prevails in the case of the eldest son who has the important duty of
carrying on the family name and business, and of helping his
parents financially. It is they who choose a suitable bride for him.
They will probably allow the other sons to make their own choice.
During my conversations with young people in Tokyo and in the
provinces, I was surprised to find how many of them admitted that
although they would like to marry for love they would probably
follow their parents' advice.

Chastity is a 'must' in middle-class society and certainly nobody
could doubt that all those demure-looking little girls in the helmet
hats of the twenties whom one sees pouring into the offices every
day could be anything but virgins. Nevertheless, there are exceptions; there is a leaven of emancipated young women and of good-
timers, who do not object to meeting their boy-friends at the
'hotels for couples' that delicately advertise their amenities in
gracious Japanese characters by the euphemism: 'Here you may
rest for a few hours.'

These hotels are *not* brothels and the best of them are run with
characteristic Japanese delicacy. Prices vary from the humble but
clean hotels where a room may be hired for as little as six shillings
for two hours without a private bathroom—only a communal
wash-basin in the corridor—to thirty shillings a night for a private
suite with twin *futons* placed side by side in a bedroom, provided
with a *tokonoma*, fastidiously arranged vase of flowers and a television set, a small dining-room where Japanese meals are served, a
Japanese bath and a toilet. The daintily dressed maids look as
innocent as nuns and serve customers with cheerful attentiveness;
they are discreet and never make an appearance until they are
summoned by telephone.

The less refined types of 'hotel for couples' to which taxi-drivers
lead foreigners and less delicate customers, are run on more
obviously commercial lines. The manageress is much in evidence
and she generally looks tough; although she wears a handsome
kimono there is nothing of the Japanese butterfly about her and she
is as ruthless as any western 'Madame'. This is Japan without the
blossom. If 'Madame' sees a foreigner, she will propose a 'western-
style' room at thirty shillings for two hours without a bathroom.
For twenty shillings you may have a very small room with a
suspicious opaque glass ceiling which may not be so opaque on

the other side . . . and the telephone will ring ten minutes before time is up to warn you to get ready or—pay another twenty shillings.

April 20th   This evening I took Shizue with me to a large shrine in our district where an appointment had been arranged for me with the head priest. It was raining hard so we took a taxi. The taxi-driver went round in circles trying to locate the priest's house, which is just outside the wall on the eastern side of the shrine.

The head priest is a strongly built man with a commanding presence who must look impressive in ceremonial robes. He receives us in kimono and slippers and smokes contentedly while his son, a law graduate, interprets. His young wife leaves us to look after the baby, which is a pity because she speaks English better than her husband. She reappears only to bring us green tea and sticky cakes. She looks very bright and modern and does not wear kimono.

We begin the difficult conversation. The son refers even the simplest questions to his father. This is etiquette, but it soon becomes obvious that he knows nothing about Shinto; he ends by admitting so, adding that he has 'only studied international law'. The sons and daughters of priests, in shrines or temples, are often very ignorant on the subject of their father's religion. No attempt is made to indoctrinate the children, who are often quite indifferent. They seem to consider that their father's function is 'just another job', not a calling.

The conversation was frustrating. We were at cross-purposes, as the following example will show:

> Me: Do you believe in heaven and hell?
> Priest: It is not important.
> Me: But do you believe in them?
> Priest: We believe in immortality.
> Me: Do you engage in social work with the help of your devotees?
> Priest: The Japanese people are too proud to receive money, but the Koreans do.
> Me: Have you a moral code?
> Priest: There are no dogmas, but we have some old books about the creation of the world and things like that.

The trouble with me, as Shizue hinted delicately when we left and I tottered out exhausted into the inky-black street, was that my questions were too western, too direct, too analytical.

It had stopped raining, so we walked home, past the rows of weavers' homes from where the faint shuttling of looms pierced the stillness of the night, and discussed our different approach to religious questions. 'I do not think the Japanese mean the same by religion as you do,' ventured Shizue, picking her way carefully between the puddles. 'I am sure they don't,' I replied.

'You attach importance to dogma; one must believe this, one must believe that,' Shizue pursued, with puckered brow. 'To the Japanese that is not so important. The Shinto priests perform ceremonies—those are important.' 'But nobody can explain what the ceremonies *mean*,' I argued. 'Few people even understand the old language of the rites—what good can they do?' 'Good?' repeated Shizue reflectively, 'Good? I don't think they are intended to do good. They convey a feeling, a mood—I do not think that good and evil come into it at all.' 'Well, it hasn't satisfied you, has it?' I asked her. Shizue smiled and shook her head. 'No. I think Jesus is a lovely person. There is tenderness in Christianity. There is none of that in our religions—it does not seem to be Japanese. But we are learning.'

We had an English lesson before we went to bed. The next day was Sunday and Shizue was going to Osaka to give a lesson in book-keeping to three of her friends. 'You don't mind giving me an English lesson on a Sunday?' she inquired anxiously as she put her books away. 'Not at all,' I replied. She smiled happily.

Passing by . . .

I like to stroll near water and a grassy verge where one may sit and daydream and watch life passing by; there is always the chance that it will attract other specimens, like a water-hole in the jungle, and so provide a good observation post.

Here in the middle of the city is a willow-tree bending to reflect itself in a narrow stream at the end of an alley-way, but nobody sits on the bank. Everybody is far too busy. Motor-scooters bounce over the little humped bridge and into a main street where a raw-fish vendor has got off his bicycle to spread slivers of his pink and silver wares on a tray to attract housewives. They must be expecting him, for they come buzzing round him almost at once, shuffling along in *geta*, clad in white high-necked overalls, their hair screwed into tight little buns at the nape of their neck. When I raise my camera to take a picture they immediately put their hands before their faces and scatter with high-pitched mewing sounds like a band of frightened seagulls. I feel like apologizing to the raw-fish man, but he laughs and poses while I take a picture of him by way of compensation. I hope his clients will come back. In the mean-time, I move off so as not to spoil his business.

On the wide banks of the River Kamo, a row of plump, rosy-cheeked women in white caps and overalls are busily engaged in cutting the grass under the supervision of a bandy-legged foreman. They must be employed by the municipality. They work together like the Tiller girls dance, in a rhythmic row, all crouching at the same instant to cut a few blades of grass with a pair of scissors. I take a picture, the foreman bows, the women look up and utter little squeals of delight when they see my fair hair. During the tea-break they rush up to stroke it, surround me and touch my hair. I am mobbed and feel like a cinema star. The foreman walks up, ready to reproach his workers, but as he sees me smiling he turns back.

The Silver Pavilion was never covered with silver as was origi-nally intended; it is plain brown and cannot compete with the ethereal lightness of the Golden Pavilion, which has been covered with gold foil and is one of the loveliest sights of Kyoto, but the gardens on the slope of a hill are very beautiful, and so is the approach up a narrow path at the end of an avenue of cherry-blossom trees. The Pavilion was built as a villa for one of the fifteenth-century Shoguns and converted into a temple after his death but it still looks and feels like a princely summer residence. The garden contains a Japanese mystery: a white sand pile and a white mound of sand. Some say that they symbolize, respectively, a silver pavilion and Lake Seiko in China. Noboru stares at the piles, which to me look like left-overs from an unfinished building site, but they seem to afford him some inner Zen form of satisfaction. He smiles but will not divulge his thoughts.

On the way up we passed a melancholy-looking young man standing in the middle of the path, brandishing a banner. From time to time he stopped brandishing the banner and waved an arm instead, pointing with a long finger in the direction of a noodle restaurant. He was tall, long-haired and too intellectual-looking to be a sandwich-man. Perhaps he was a student. . . . I wanted to take a picture of him but he hid his face with his banner and turned round. 'Ask him why he doesn't want me to take a picture,' I told Noboru.

Noboru approached the tall young man, bowed and blushed slightly as he put my question to him. The sad young man answered him softly, with downcast eyes. 'He says he is an artist,' Noboru reported, 'and that he has to do this degrading work for a living. That is why he does not want his picture taken.' I bowed and tried to look sympathetic. The sad young man bowed back, and continued to point sorrowfully to the noodle restaurant.

Underneath the cherry-blossom trees that line the canal, a bearded old man in a black kimono and wide-brimmed grey felt hat advanced slowly upon a staff, book in hand. When he reached the mound of pink and green rocks that decorate one side of the bridge over the canal, he paused admiringly, took out a newspaper from the folds of his kimono, spread it carefully on a ledge, and sat down to read his book in the rocky landscape.

The grassy bank looked more inviting to the rag-and-bone man who pulled up his little cart by a tree and sat down to watch the blossom reflected in the placid water.

Rag-picking is quite a lucrative trade in Japan, although one would not think so to look at the rag-pickers. I had seen many of them, here and in Tokyo, some of them women, pushing and pulling heavily laden carts, often followed by two or three children. Two young sociologists in Tokyo, man and wife, had recently opened a nursery-school to look after rag-pickers' children while their parents were on their rounds.

The rag-picker on the banks of the canal seemed to be in no hurry to resume his work. 'Perhaps he will take the afternoon off,' said Noboru. 'Those people are inclined to be lazy. They lead a free life. Free and filthy. Most of them live in slums. You see,' he explained, 'it's quite an organization. Most paper manufacturers and canning industries make use of waste paper or scrap-iron gathered by rag-pickers. When they need material they get it through a network under the control of a boss who is in charge of a *shikiriba*, or rag centre. The slums are the places which feed the *shikiribas*.'

'Why don't the authorities clear them up?' 'It's being done in the big cities, but it's not all that simple,' said Noboru. 'The slum bosses are dead against it. I tell you, it's a peculiar set-up, feudalism persists, in a low-grade sort of way, even among the rag-pickers. The rag-pickers who live in the slums are not anxious to improve their conditions; they make a living, and they are all good friends together in their slums. They are not very intelligent people and they are easily controlled by the bosses. Anyway they usually pick up so much waste material that it is not practicable to carry it to any other place than their boss's centre. The boss usually keeps his "clients" rent-free in a tenement house or shack. In return the pickers agree to sell him the waste materials cheap. It's a vicious circle: the pickers are assured of a minimum wage but they have to obey the boss. They don't like outsiders prying into their affairs. They refuse to let welfare officers into the slums. They often protect criminals there. The rag-pickers live in a closed world of their own. Some religious groups have begun to take an interest in them. There's a place called the "Town of Ants", I forget where, occupied entirely by rag-pickers. . . .'

This afternoon I went to see an old people's club in a Buddhist temple. It is run by a jovial Buddhist priest and his wife who have put aside two unused rooms in their temple for the use of old men and women who live in poor, cramped surroundings and have nobody to talk to during the day.

The temple rooms are flanked by a veranda overlooking a small garden which, with the aid of a very little imagination, can be transformed into a magnificent panorama of lake, waterfalls, wooden slopes and mountains.

The old people squatting inside the rooms look very old, very brown, and very contented. They look up, smile, and bow when I walk in with the Buddhist priest, but two old gentlemen on the veranda are too engrossed with their game of Japanese chess, played with small pieces of square wood, to take any interest in a visitor. An old couple sit opposite each other, chatting, the man smoking, the woman brewing a kettle of tea on a small stove. A group of old ladies are playing cards. Before I left, the priest invited me to green tea and sticky cakes in his room and asked me to sign the visitor's book while he took a picture.

I walked into a very small branch post-office to buy some stamps. There were three bird-cages inside, with a different coloured bird in each; they were engaged in a singing competition and I could hardly make myself heard.

Out in the street householders and shopkeepers were throwing buckets of water to settle the dust of the day. This is another reason why it is difficult to keep western shoes immaculate in Japan. One of the householders was rearranging the flowers beside a roadside shrine. There must be hundreds of these religious dolls' houses on legs, filled with stone gods; Jizo, the children's god, is always among them, adorned with a bib of bright-coloured cotton.

Apart from song-birds, which are very popular, people keep haughty little white spitz dogs as pets (I rarely see any other breed), and short-tailed cats to keep down the mice in the wooden dwellings. For a long time I believed that Japanese cats must be related to Manx cats and I went round telling people how curious it was that this should be so, but that we had often thought the Isle of Man had had some affiliations with the Far East. Everybody listened politely but made no comment. Now Noboru has told me the truth. Japanese cats are born with long tails but as these are considered to be unlucky they are cut off.[1] Short-tailed Japanese cats have no connexion with their fellows on the Isle of Man. (According to the *Encyclopædia Britannica* 'the tailless or Manx cats, in which the tail may be represented merely by a tuft of hair without any bone, is common in the Far East. In the Malay regions and Philippines normal long-tailed cats are rarely seen, and kink-tailed or short-tailed cats predominate. Whether the tailless cat reached the Isle of Man from elsewhere or whether it developed there as a sudden independent mutation is not known.')

Today my lunch only cost me a shilling. I was hungry when I came out of Nijo castle, tired of looking at painted screens and sliding-doors, depressed by wax effigies of feudal lords and ladies and glad to plunge into a popular restaurant full of real people. The seating accommodation: long wooden tables and high-backed

---

[1] This must come from the old belief, once also current in Europe, that cats had a tendency to turn into demons. Their bewitching power was said to be centred on their tails and it was to check this that they were cut off as early as possible.

benches—reminded me of an English pub. I ordered *tempura* (fried fish) and a bowl of noodles and finished up with a bottle of iced coffee.

The atmosphere was friendly and I was welcomed with bows and smiles from the ladies present. We were a mixed company: lean students in thick spectacles, a couple of workmen, a dapper little man in a black suit who appeared to be a regular from some nearby office, three middle-aged ladies in kimono who sat in a row and chirruped like song-birds, a woman teacher in skirt and sweater accompanied by two chubby schoolgirls, and myself. A tea-kettle, from which customers were expected to refill their little bowls of tea whenever they wanted, whispered to itself on a gas-ring in the middle of a table.

There were days, however, when, after a surfeit of Japanese meals, I had a sudden urge to sink my teeth into a steak. A well-filled plate of meat and vegetables looks coarse after the one mouthful per dish of most Japanese meals, but still. . . .

On these barbaric occasions I lunch at the Miyako hotel on the slopes of the Higashiyama hills, with a superb view over Kyoto's temples and multiple-storey buildings. I had stayed at the Miyako on my official tour with Kazuko and had retained a sentimental attachment for its many amenities. On rainy days, when the damp heightened the smells in Shizue's house, I got into the habit of taking refuge—and meals—at the Miyako where, seated in a comfortable armchair in one of the many verandas, lounges or terraces, I could write letters, read, buy gifts in the arcade and indulge in an alcoholic drink.

The Miyako is more than an hotel, it is a show-place and as such guests are occasionally surprised to see hordes of Japanese families pouring down the carpeted corridors on the upper storeys; they have been visiting the Japanese gardens and tea-houses on the hill slopes at the back of the hotel.

The Japanese-style annexe, built by Togo Murano, is in the traditional *sukiya*-style architecture and after having seen it I cannot imagine how any visitor would want to stay in the western-style suites when, by choosing the annexe, they can genuinely feel they are in Japan, 'with western comforts and foam rubber mattresses' as the brochure tells them. The architecture which at first sight appears to be so simple, is full of Japanese subtlety. The roof, or series of roofs that cover the building, is made of copper sheet; a number of gables were made to curve downwards at the tips and these portions had to be reinforced with steel bands. To prevent them from standing out, Murano had them painted the colour of the surrounding wood—a solution which shocks the theorists but gives pleasing results.

The suites in the annexe are built entirely of wood, but the foundation is of reinforced concrete; this was made necessary by the slope of the site. The proportions are carefully calculated although it will not strike the casual observer, for instance, that the projection of the posts from the surface of the walls in the Japanese-style suites is no more than one and a half centimetres; the architect explained to a visiting critic: 'if the length of this projection is any greater than that, it seems to me that the building loses its elegance, and if *sukiya*-style architecture is not elegant, it is not *sukiya*-style architecture.'

The inner garden of the annexe, inspired by the Daigo-ji temple, consists of a flat area of white sand in which there are two beds of moss, one resembles a gourd and the other a *sake* cup. The garden is bordered by a rock-filled ditch which serves as a drain. The north side of the garden is bounded by a rocky slope dotted with pine trees, where a waterfall and a stream empty into a small pond. This water, which seems to flow so naturally, is pumped back up the hill to a point above the waterfall.

There is so much wood in Japanese hotels that it is not surprising to read notices in your room like one I had seen in Hakone: 'Please do not keep inflammables, explosives or other similar kind of articles in your room.' In Hakone, where families bring their spoilt children, another notice, addressed 'To Our Honourable Guests', expresses the hope that 'you will not disturb your neigh-bouring guests with your children's screaming or crying'. When I was there, an American boy was doing just this in the room next to mine. I then realized that the notice, written in English, is intended for *American*, not Japanese children.

The Miyako has evening entertainments of a refined nature, but it does not go in for anything as ostentatious as the Pool-side Bar in the Kowaki-en's night salon at Hakone, which the management advertise so enthusiastically: 'Alcohol is not the only one intoxicant here; rhythmic music, silhouettes of mermaids and mermen at the window pane! This is the only one human aquarium bar in Japan. You cannot say you have visited Kowaki-en unless you see this night-salon. Please come down after your dinner and enjoy the resort-evening.' We were there at the wrong time of the year; no mermaids were swimming in the aquarium in the early spring.

'Be Japanese at the Miyako,' suggests the prospectus, but I thought they were overdoing it a little the other day when I walked up the drive to spend yet another rainy day in its western rooms. The entire building was decorated with red flags. Maybe they were celebrating a festival? There are so many festivals in Kyoto that, as an English resident observed, 'you could retire here and spend your time going to a different festival every day'.

'What pretty flags!' I remarked to a managerial-looking man standing by the revolving door. He gave me a sour smile. I walked inside. The atmosphere was hushed. No bustle of grooms, no simpering elevator girls . . . what could have happened? The Japanese are so artistic and decorative it had not occurred to me that they extend their gifts to: strikes. The charming decoration of red flags of which I was to see so many all through the spring, all over Japan, was merely an indication that the employees were demanding higher wages. In the hall an apologetic notice signed by the Manager informed us, 'Dear Guests, We have been negotiating our staff union for past several weeks as to increase of their wages. Since we try every effort for new agreement in the meantime, please forgive for inefficiency of service. We appreciate for your co-operation.'

Another family

April 22nd   *T*onight is my last night at Shizue's. Tomorrow I move to a house in north Kyoto. I shall be sorry to leave the barber's shop in spite of all the drawbacks. Shizue and I have grown quite fond of each other in this short time. The old aunt is friendly too. She calls out to me to go and sit with her round the *kotatsu*, brews me endless bowls of tea, sends the little boys out for cakes and ice-creams.

Shizue's cousin came home at ten o'clock from a hairdressers' conference and insisted upon setting my hair when she saw me washing it in the shop. She must have been tired but she did not show it. Shizue looked on and helped, passing the rollers when required. The apprentice sat behind us on one of the swivel chairs used for customers, watching television.

I insist upon giving Shizue a last English lesson, promising that I will correct her letters when she writes to me at my home address later on. We talk until after midnight.

April 23rd   Shizue opened the sliding-door at 7.30 this morning to bid me a tearful good-bye and offer me a present: an exquisite scent flask and filler for my handbag, which must have cost her much more than she could afford. We embraced in unJapanese fashion. How affectionate she is, and how generous! I like the Japanese more and more. . . .

When I was ready and packed and had taken my suitcases down to the shop I was informed in sign language that there was a taxi strike on until mid-day; fortunately there were a few private taxis about and the whole neighbourhood was mobilized to find me one. Shopkeepers from both sides of the street sent messenger boys scurrying in all directions and one eventually returned with a 70-yen taxi. I wave to the smiling people assembled in front of their shops: the plump girl from the supermarket who has sold me so many cakes for the little boys and so many bottles of milk for my breakfast, the scholarly-looking man from the stationers' from whom I bought long, narrow Japanese envelopes, the pseudo-Beatnik types from the Venice café, the stolid matron from the public baths, and aunt, leaning on a stick in front of the barber's shop, smiling politely, but a little puzzled, as if my visit had not seemed quite real.

Yoshiko's house is in a quiet little street in a residential area. What a change from the dust and noise at Shizue's! I shall not hear the clanging of the tramcars here, nor the noodle-man's little bell as he goes on his nocturnal rounds. I shall not get to know the neighbours; I shall certainly not be able to walk into an espresso bar with my hair in rollers. There are no espresso bars here anyway. All the houses in the road are bourgeois and respectable, hidden behind high wooden gates at the side of which the owner's name and telephone number are inscribed upon metal plaques. Yoshiko's father has worked in the same bank all his life, in the traditional Japanese way. Yoshiko is about to study English and American literature at Doshisha University. She has written a thesis on Herman Melville (a great favourite with Japanese students) which she wishes me to read. There is a brother and a sister, of whom I shall see little, for they are very shy and do not speak English.

The family had a preview of me the other evening; the meeting took place in a tiny drawing-room furnished in western style where the members of the family were introduced one by one. Yoshiko speaks English slowly but quite well. I never cease to marvel at the way so many Japanese have mastered our difficult language. She is twenty-one and a staunch member of the 'life is earnest' category of Japanese student. She has a prim way of tilting her head to one side and smiling reflectively as she makes solemn pronouncements. I am a novelty, here as everywhere—the first foreigner to have crossed the threshold and be accepted as a guest. Yoshiko and her bright little mother ask me a thousand questions. They do not know how to behave or what to do; I entreat them to let me live as they do, for that is what I have come to Japan for, not to live the way I do at home. Yoshiko nods gravely and ends by saying, 'it is a good thing to be able to leap into other people's worlds.'

The new element, for me, in this family, is the grandmother, an active, lean old lady who evidently plays an important role in the household. Father, in brown kimono, was the last to be introduced for he, too, is shy. He is a mild, self-effacing man who spends long hours playing Japanese chess with a cousin from Tokyo who is spending a few days here with his daughter.

This is a matriarchal household, dominated by three women: Yoshiko, still young enough to be respectful but old enough tact-fully to assert herself, the acknowledged and admired intellectual member of the family, who hopes to be a teacher in a girls' high school. Tomorrow there will be a graduation ceremony, the President of the University will make a moralistic speech which Yoshiko will repeat to me almost word for word. . . . There is a Victorian streak in the Japanese who respond readily to exhorta-tions. I am surprised that no political leader has taken advantage of this—at least, not so far.

Yoshiko shows me my room on the first floor, with a veranda overlooking a small garden and, in the distance, an outline of hills and the upward curve of a temple roof. Yoshiko points to it and tells me that her ancestors are buried round the temple. I presume she means their ashes and I am rash enough to let myself in for another frustrating dialogue on the subject of religion. Yoshiko informs me that not only ashes but a few bones are buried under the gravestones. 'Which bones?' I want to know. 'The neckbone,' she says. 'Why?' Yoshiko tilts her head. 'I do not know. Let us ask my grandmother,' she suggests. Whenever I ask any question that impinges upon religion and traditions, Yoshiko is at a loss and appeals to the superior knowledge of her grandmother, the family repository of ancient lore.

We find grandmother mixing stomach powder in a bowl. It is a herbal concoction; being interested in folk medicine, I should like to know what it is, but nobody can tell me and the dictionary fails us; its compilers were evidently not interested in botany. Even grandmother does not know why a neckbone should be saved from the funeral pyre. This custom is not observed in other Buddhist countries.

An invisible bird is uttering in the garden; one cannot call a sound like the snapping of castanets 'singing'. Few Japanese birds are melodious; they often have a more striking plumage than our birds but their voice is inferior. Another bird of the same species snaps its reply to the first. 'What is that bird?' I ask, and again I draw a blank. The Japanese are only interested in nature in a general sort of way; they use it as a medium for introspection: all the talk, poetry and ceremony attached to cherry-blossom, chrysanthemums, and moon viewing, all the pictures of birds, mountains, clouds, proceed from detached, vague sentiments completely unconnected with the essence of the object. Few people, with the exception of the Emperor and a few specialists, are interested in bird and plant life. I never came across a naturalists' club or a bird-watching society, and this is one of the richest countries in the world into which nature has poured her bounties with reckless generosity!

Yoshiko listened to my impassioned speech with interest. 'I never knew,' she said when I had finished, 'that the English people could be so gentle about birds. It is interesting. You have taught me something new.'

*A prosperous
new religion:
Tenrikyo*

April 25th   Today Noboru accompanied me to the city of Tenri, south of Nara, once a farming village of less than thirty houses, now the centre of one of the most prosperous of Japan's 'new religions': Tenrikyo, founded in 1838 by Mrs Miki Nakayama. This religion, with its stress on divine healing, preceded Christian Science by a few years.

The post-war period in Japan, with its aftermath of depression and disillusion, was propitious for the resurgence of sects which had hitherto developed sporadically in the shade of official Shinto. Now they are booming. An important factor of their popularity is that they promise their followers a fair share of happiness in this world—not the next—if they purify themselves according to their various doctrines. This is sound Japanese psychology: religious leaders are fully aware that what people want is prosperity *now*. Christianity is much too evasive on this issue and is doomed to failure. Heaven is a long way off. So is hell, and these black-and-white distinctions are very unJapanese anyway.

Tenrikyo is particularly interesting because of its insistence upon education and the thorough training it gives to missionaries. Its university enjoys great prestige and has attracted professors from abroad. The foreign language courses are said to be first rate and the library of 700,000 volumes is the richest in Japan in the field of sociology and comparative religion. There are said to be over three million members of this religion and thousands of pilgrims visit the headquarters every year in specially chartered trains. Opponents speak darkly of 'forced donations' wrested out of devotees for the common fund, some go as far as to say that neophytes are made to give up all their material possessions when they join Tenrikyo. The least bitter comment I heard was that Tenrikyo is organized as efficiently as Moral Rearmament. Its doctrines? 'A volume has been published on the subject,' Mr Perkins told me, 'and they will be pleased to present you with a copy at head-quarters. They are very keen on propaganda.'

Noboru had never been to the centre and he was anxious to see the books on Buddhism in the library, so he took a day off from his 'degrading work' in the souvenir shop to guide me.

There are no streamlined diesel locomotives on the branch lines to Tenri, via Nara, only easy-going little trains full of informal people in everyday clothes. Passengers on the limited expresses give the impression of being dressed in their Sunday best; they are nearly all middle-aged and inclined to be stiff and formal whereas the cheaper secondary lines cater for a more youthful and unin-hibited set of passengers who sprawl, put their feet up on the seats, unbutton their shirts and lean out of windows.

Noboru had acquired a map. Whatever one's destination may be, a map is always available at the railway or bus station. The Japanese like to know exactly where they are going and they have a passion for maps which corresponds to the post-war boom—a fashionable word in Japan—in excursions. Never have people travelled or hiked so much.

On the train I was assailed by a bunch of schoolgirls who looked about ten or twelve years old but were in fact fourteen and fifteen. They wanted to know whether I was married to Noboru (they can never assess a foreigner's age; we have the same difficulty with them). Noboru blushed and put his hand over his face when the girls wanted to know how old I was. Noboru gave them a long lecture on western etiquette to which they listened attentively. Noboru is well versed on the subject; he surprised me, when I first met him, by his untypical courtesy—for a Japanese male—in such things as helping me on and off tramcars and walking on the outside of the pavement. When I remarked upon this, he smiled happily and explained that he had bought a book on western etiquette prior to my arrival. He had learned its lessons well. He had tried them out on Japanese girls before I came, but they had been unresponsive; they are so unused to polite treatment that it embarrassed them. They blushed, stammered, held back and made Noboru feel so awkward that he gave up the attempt to be gallant in the western manner in so far as his countrywomen are concerned.

From Tenri station a long arcade of shops led up to the extensive grounds occupied by the sanctuary and University of Tenrikyo. The street was full of girl and boy students wearing the dark blue *happi* coat of Tenrikyo inscribed with white characters. I scrutinized them closely to see whether or not they looked fanatical, but there was nothing to distinguish them from any other students and they looked gay, as befits people who are striving towards *Yokigurashi*, or 'the Joyous Life' enjoined by their Foundress.

On the way we passed a house decorated with black and white banners and long, cylindrical white lanterns. The front door was open and at the entrance a man in a black kimono sat at a little table with a pen and notebook. There had been a death in the house and it is customary for neighbours to make offerings towards the funeral expenses. One of them sits in the house receiving the money and carefully inscribing the names of the donors on a list which will later be made public.

At the end of the street a wide avenue leads to the main sanctuary of Tenrikyo, a magnificent building in a setting of low wooded hills. The grounds are well laid out, with spacious avenues separating the dormitories for visiting pilgrims, the missionary school and museum, the library, and the sports grounds. Tenrikyo is the brightest pilgrim centre I have ever seen. There are no mournful processions here, no sad chanting of sinners, lugubrious grottoes or dim cathedrals. All is gay, luminous, and modern.

We had arrived on a day when the Patriarch, the present head of Tenri and descendant of the Foundress (these new religions are nearly all founded on a hereditary basis) was engaged in a ceremony called *sazuke*, during which the gift of divine healing is imparted to 'sincere followers'. He was too busy to see us, which I regretted, because he sounds an interesting person. Apart from his important religious functions, the Patriarch is a judo expert, a member of the Olympic Games committee, and of Rotary International; he has travelled extensively, and brought back all manner of art objects and art facts for Tenri museum, which houses one of the best collections of Chinese art in Japan.

A Tenri priest in black and silver with a Samurai type of headgear directed us to the main office, from where an elegant, English-speaking Public Relations officer, Miss Tanaka, showed us round.

This modern, obviously well-educated young woman explained to us in front of the main sanctuary, that the 'interior is now made of wood but when the dew of heaven descends upon the whole of humanity, it will be rebuilt in marble'.

Inside the sanctuary, several people were consulting the priests kneeling upon the *tatami* and whispering urgently. At the far end, the apartments reserved for the Foundress are kept as if she were stil' alive. Meals are taken to her three times a day. . . .

This main sanctuary, called the *Jiba*, is believed to be the spot where man was first created. So said the Foundress in the holy book known as the *Ofudesaki*. These sayings are supposed to have been uttered by 'God the Parent' through the medium of the Foundress.

Many of the exterior trappings of Shinto are visible in the sanctuary: the sacred *sakaki* trees, the zigzag strips of white paper suspended on a cord, the architecture of the sanctuary. Sacred dancing plays an important role, and is performed once a month by specially chosen devotees. It is written that 'when this dance, *tsutome*, is performed in joyous harmony and with sincerity, God the Parent promises to grant all kinds of protection with his marvellous power. During the performance, ten dancers wearing masks move in unison to the music of nine instruments accompanying the sacred songs, each person re-enacting with gestures each of God's functions of creating human beings.

'Through this performance sincere people receive the gift of *kanro* or heavenly dew. When they receive this they will be allowed not only to complete the term of life of one hundred and fifteen years but also to extend it indefinitely if they so wish.'

The Tenri story of the Creation, as told by the Foundress, is quite literally—a fishy one:

Originally this world was an immense expanse of muddy waters, Tsuki-hi God the Parent found this chaotic condition unbearably tasteless, and thought of creating human beings so that He might share their joy by seeing their *yokigurashi*.

Therefore one day He searched through the muddy waters to see what materials He could find for the Creation. He found there a lot of loaches, and among them a merman and a white snake which promised to be fine materials for the creation of the first human couple. He called a sea-tiger from the north-west and a tortoise from the south-east, and when they came, He took them up with their consent, ate them to test their mental flavour and, discerning their respective qualities, decided to make use of the former as the 'first organ' of the sterner sex and also as the skeleton to support the body, the latter as the 'first organ' of the gentler sex and also as the skin to cover muscles and bones so as to keep them coherent. He put these materials respectively into the bodies of the merman and the white snake, which He had determined as the prototypes of man and woman.

More fish were used and finally the first offspring emerged, half an inch tall. They grew taller, half an inch at a time, and reached a height of three inches in ninety-nine years. Then they passed away. Human beings were reborn eight thousand and eight times before attaining human form, passing beforehand through all stages of existence, worms, birds and beasts. When they were born five feet high, the universe was completed. . . .

'What about donations?' I asked bluntly, 'People have told me. . . .' Miss Tanaka shook her head, anticipating the rest of my query. 'It is not true. There is a great deal of misunderstanding,' she said. 'What we do donate is voluntary labour. This is called *hinokishin*. Everybody has to do this. The Patriarch did it and his son does it regularly. We have all helped to build this sanctuary. Children do it—every summer since 1954 over one hundred thousand of our followers' children come here from all over Japan; they study the outline of Tenrikyo and enjoy the swimming-pool. *Hinokishin* for sweeping Nara park is performed twice a year, in May and November. . . .'

Great stress is laid on the indoctrination of children; followers send their offspring to Tenrikyo to be educated from kindergarten upwards. Visitors, according to Tenrikyo literature, 'get the strong impression that the infants are amicable and self-possessed children modified by freshness. The features of children who sing loudly the sacred music and dance, together give a beautiful and pleasant impression harmonized with innocence and piety; merry rhythms flow quietly and embrace the school building, the sentiments of children are automatically cultivated, and thus their bright characters formed.'

Tenrikyo followers are great believers in healthy bodies and sport is encouraged. Students compete in athletics, swimming contests, rugby, baseball. There is a university orchestra, a dramatic society and the extensive library where we saw the first Bibles to be printed in Japanese and early accounts of Japan by Spanish missionaries. In the modern section I noticed a first edition of *David Copperfield* as it appeared in *Every Saturday* and a letter by Charles Dickens.

Noboru began to ask sharp questions. Had not the doctrine been changed since its foundation—after all, the Foundress was an illiterate peasant woman—the so-called Holy Books were being rewritten by scholars . . .' Not rewritten,' Miss Tanaka corrected him severely, 'they were always there, inspired by God the Parent. But before the war we could not publish them for fear of being misunderstood. It was not easy when Shinto was the State religion.

Now it is different and we are going to have them published in a modern version. They are being edited.'

The missionary school is a large concrete building which turns out graduates versed in Tenri doctrine, sports and foreign languages. A mission was sent to London at the beginning of the twentieth century but it met with no success. It was reported at the time that 'the English are too conservative'. On the other hand, the Tenri missionaries weren't so tough in those days and they insisted on having special food sent to them from Japan; funds did not permit of such extravagance and they were eventually recalled.

At first, in the difficult economic conditions of the Tokugawa period the majority of Tenrikyo followers belonged to agricultural communities. Mr Kyoito, a young anthropologist from Kyoto University, knows a farmer who was born into a Tenrikyo family but gave it up in later life to found a community of his own; not a new religion—a co-operative farm; he has promised to take me there tomorrow.

Co-operative
farm experiment

𝒪𝑀r Kyoitu is a pleasant young man with a rather nervous manner; every now and then he brushes a rebellious tuft of hair off his broad forehead. He has a square face and I am not surprised to learn that his people are country folk; many country-born Japanese have square faces. This private bit of anthropological discovery on my part is probably very unscientific but it works. Mr Kyoitu is in his late twenties, married, with one child. He lives in a small flat in Kyoto, is keen on his work and full of fascinating stories. After two changes, we alight at a country station, eat a bowl of noodles in a modest restaurant and telephone Shinkyo, the co-operative settlement, to announce our visit. We take a taxi to Shinkyo; on the way Mr Kyoitu tells me about a village of horse-breeders in the south where houses have been built to accommodate both the owners and their horses. Since horses are no longer in demand the villagers are being trained in agriculture. They have had to sell their horses and they wept bitterly when they did so. Obligingly, Mr Kyoitu draws a plan of the house–stable on the back of an envelope, marking the rooms A, B and C with the precision of an architect.

The road is no more than a track, fit for jeeps; our taxi bounces up and down and the driver groans. Women in blue cotton trousers, their heads wrapped in a white cap like a Dutch bonnet, stand and stare at us. In the vegetable gardens, rows of infant cucumbers are carefully protected from the frost under plastic pokes; each poke is opened a very little every day when the sun comes out. The hay-ricks are small and slender, with overlapping conical covers; they stand in twos or threes, one always a little shorter than the others, like *kokeshi* dolls.

A long, low wooden building comes to sight round a bend. 'There is the rice straw mat factory,' says Mr Kyoitu. To the right, on a slope, a drive leads to a modern two-storeyed building with large windows. 'The Shinkyo centre,' says Mr Kyoitu. Between these two buildings, seventy people live and work, pooling their earnings. Beyond them, a straggly village of dark brown wooden houses edges off into the misty landscape.

There was nobody in sight at the centre but after Mr Kyoitu had called out two or three times, a robust little woman in navy blue trousers and a white overall appeared to inquire what we wanted.

We followed the little woman along the polished floor to the visitor's room upstairs, furnished with comfortable armchairs, a table, a case full of books ranging from detective stories to Dostoevsky; there was a splendid view from three large windows over the wide valley and hills. It was too cold to remove my coat but the little lady stirred the tiny pieces of charcoal in the centre of the round china *hibachi* with a toy poker about the same size as a chop-stick. A few minutes later, a plump girl brought a fresh supply of charcoal, four small pieces which she cajoled into place with attractive gestures, but they did not generate much heat.

The robust little lady who was manning the office that day (everybody takes turns at the various jobs to be done at the centre) went off to fetch Mr Osaki from the factory. Tea was served in the meantime with red bean jam cakes wrapped in paper and placed on bamboo plates in a delicate open lacework pattern.

Mr Osaki walked in with his sleeves rolled up and a half-smile on his face which broadened when he found out who we were and why we had come. He is a simple, unpretentious little man, every inch a rugged farmer, with muscular arms and hands, a heavy-jawed, earnest face and shrewd, sparkling eyes. He answered my questions readily, speaking in a slightly gruff voice compared to the soft tones of the townsmen, with unfanatical conviction, and accompanying his words with wide gestures as most country folk do in Japan.

He smiled broadly when he was told I had just visited Tenrikyo headquarters. 'My family belonged to that sect,' he said, 'they gave a lot of money to those people. You say it is different nowadays? I don't know I'm sure but they must have collected a packet to be able to build such an impressive centre. It's getting more and more like the Vatican every day!'

'I gave up Tenri when I was twenty but I admit I made use of them; it was the only way I could get an education. My parents were poor and couldn't afford to send me to a decent school. The Tenri people wanted to make a teacher out of me. I agreed—and left home for Osaka. But I didn't like their ideas at all. *My* idea was and is to raise the status of Japanese farmers. I'm a down-to-earth man and I believe that this can be achieved through sound economics and a spirit of co-operation. Not through religion or ideology. I have no time for that sort of thing. I believe in co-operation, hard work, equality. Outsiders often refer to me as the leader of Shinkyo. That's not true. There are no leaders here. We take it in turns to see that jobs get done. One month we may serve as treasurer, the next one as supervisor of the factory and so on. We have an executive committee, elected by the community, whose members are changed every so often. . . .'

I asked him how it all started. 'It's quite a story.' Mr Osaki screwed up his eyes and laughed. 'I was a bit of a fighter in my youth. I tried to convert the whole village—this village next door, where I was born—to my ideas. I told them to burn their Tenri portable shrines. I pulled down the village shrine myself with the help of a few young men who believed like me that we should start from scratch and work together to build a better community. We were banished from the village so we had to live outside like lepers. That wasn't much fun, so we decided to go to Manchuria and try out a community system there. Well, you know what happened. The Japanese were thrown out. We had to come home. A few more people joined us. Then the Second World War came. I was against it and was imprisoned for my views. I would have been shot if the war had lasted much longer.'

'When I came home again at the end of the war, the situation was pretty bad. We were growing plenty of rice but we didn't have any fish to eat—we couldn't afford it. One day I went to Osaka and got in touch with some fishermen. They said they were desperately short of rice-straw rope. This gave me an idea. We had plenty of rice straw on the farms in the village so I suggested we barter rope for fish. They agreed and that is how it all began. We got quite good at making rope and I thought we might try our hand at something else—why not *tatami* mats, for instance? There is always a demand for them. We started in a small way, then we built a factory in 1947. That was burned down so we built another one. We found an agent in Osaka to sell our mats for us. Little by little we brought in machinery. I daresay that if we were fully mechanized we could make even more mats than we do. But we earn enough to make a living.'

'How does co-operation work from the financial point of view?' I asked Mr Osaki.

'Very well,' he replied. 'I should like to see the system extended. Nobody earns any individual wages. All the money we make goes into a pool. We saved enough from 1947 until three years ago to build our centre. Last year we added an annexe.'

'What about the women? Don't they ever want to go on shopping sprees?'

'Of course they do. It is only human. From time to time we all go for excursions. We have three trucks and three motor-scooters. We stay overnight at an inn, go bathing' (Mr Osaki turned to the little lady at his side and asked her to bring out some photographs to show me how the workers enjoyed their leisure). 'And when we go for an excursion everyone wants to buy souvenirs. Sometimes a member of the community goes up to the treasurer and tells him he wants a camera or one of the women wants some new clothes. We find the money. Our people are reasonable. Whenever there are disagreements the question is thrashed out and a majority vote taken. One or two people have left the community—those who could not adapt themselves to our way of life. Others have come in from outside. Our people are very happy. When we come back from a trip to the outside world they always say: "It's good to get back home!" '

After visiting the centre I began to understand why they felt this way about their communal home. Granted you have no special yearning for privacy, which peasants rarely have, the centre is vastly superior to the average Japanese farmhouse or even town house. The spotless large kitchen (designed by the women) is much better equipped than the cramped little closet of the average lower-income group workers; the bathroom, obviously inspired by a visit to a hot springs resort and designed by the community, is superb—a vast tiled room with a semi-elliptical sunken pool, below a wide window from which bathers can contemplate a vast panorama of hills and sky.

There is a playroom for the children (who attend the village schools, the high school students go to Osaka) which the average Japanese house has no room for, a sewing-room, where two old ladies were kneeling on small cushions in front of the window mending clothes, several sitting-rooms, a large hall with ping-pong tables, and upstairs a long recreation room provided with a TV set and stage upon which stood a gilded screen. A red carpet ran down the centre of the room. This is where the members of the community hold performances of dancing and folk-singing, tea-ceremony and flower-arrangement, and even weddings . . . partners being sought for outside by *nakodos*, for the choice in the village is limited.

The bedrooms are identically empty but they command different views; to avoid jealousy a rotation system has been devised, each family occupying one bedroom for a month at a time before moving on to another. Clothes are kept in tall chests of drawers in a room put aside for this purpose. The tidiness is almost alarming.

But the special objects of Mr Osaki's pride are the two dining-rooms. His pet idea was to have two of them because, 'It is important for workers to have a sense of human dignity; this is very difficult for the ordinary run of farmers who work and live in mud or—as in our case—rice straw dust! I believe that there should be a marked contrast between their day life and their evening life. At midday our people come in from the factory in their working clothes and as they have to go back again in the afternoon their dining-room is plain, with large tables at which several people can sit. This saves time for those who are serving as waiters or wait-resses. . . . But in the evening, when our work is over we become human beings. We take a bath, we change into clean clothes, we sit down for supper at leisure and we want more aesthetic sur-roundings.'

Members do not sit on *tatami* for their Japanese meals. The 'evening dining-room' is quite elegant with its polished tables, covered with plastic, and green and red chairs. The flush, tiled toilets are another improvement over the average Japanese farm-house.

Women work in the factory on the lighter jobs. Mr Osaki is very anxious to raise the status of women who, he said, have been subjected to too hard a life for far too long.

When we returned to the visitors' room, a delicious lunch was served which would have done credit to a first-rate Japanese restaurant in town; soup, an array of vegetable dishes, fried prawns on skewers, and *tsukushi* or horsetail—a weed I spend so much time, always unsuccessfully, in eradicating from my garden and which is quite tender when cooked. It is eaten early in the year 'as a sign of spring'. The robust little lady poured us *sake*, and peeled apples and oranges for us—perhaps not with the polished grace of a geisha, but with maternal gusto. Photographs were brought out from a large box and we were shown jolly snapshots of the Shinkyo members at work and at play . . . rows of them in striped *yukatas* outside a seaside inn, stout women members in tight bathing costumes paddling in the sea, just like our matrons back home.

All these excursions, and visits to Japanese inns where guests are served with so much delicacy, have helped to rub off the labourers' rough edges. 'Bettering ourselves,' Mr Osaki said, 'does not only mean acquiring more objects, but learning how to use them gracefully. That is why the ancient arts of tea-ceremony, *ikebana* and dancing are not neglected here—they help to give our people poise.'

*Flashback: the
'water-drawing'
Ceremony*

On the way back to Kyoto we changed at Nara. I should have liked to stop and revisit this wonderful city, where the oldest wooden buildings in the world are to be found. It is a miracle that so many of them should have been spared the ravages of fire, earthquake and typhoon. Unfortunately the typhoons have changed course in the last few years and they now pass over Nara

Darby and Joan at the Noh theatre
Doll vendor outside a shrine in Kyoto

Trees in winter—one of my Tokyo homes
The Enoshima shrine near Tokyo

Baby and mother outside public baths near Tokyo
Slums by canal in Tokyo

Japanese gypsies bathing
Pontocho geisha

Raw-fish vendor, Kyoto
Goblin mountain temple, Kyoto

Members of the co-op farm on an excursion in hotel *yukata*
The annual moon ceremony, Kurama

Shinto priests, Nara
Hiroshima—ruin on right and peace monument left

'English conversation please!'
Miyajima—the torii

Miyajima—part of the shrine
Picnic under cherry blossom, Miyajima

The author writing her diary in the temple, under the Nichiren scroll
Mr Arito playing cymbals

In the temple garden. The priest's wife, Noriko, Yukiko, and Al
Al, Noriko and the author at a *sushi* bar

Tramcar driver's house, Kumamoto
Invitation to tea ceremony, Kumamoto

Sado island
Farmers' wives near Niigata

Peasant woman and baby, northern Japan
Working in the paddy fields

A Japanese wedding, Kumamoto
My hosts in Kahoku

Mr Hagashi dancing the Dragon dance in his Shinto shrine
The kindergarten reception

in the autumn. Last year they caused great damage and some of the buildings had to be repaired.

I had visited Nara in March with Kazuko, during my official tour. It had been arranged that we should spend the day of March 17th there, but the night before I heard from Francis King, the distinguished novelist and Director of the British Council at Kyoto, that *the* night of nights to visit Nara is the 16th, when the annual 'Water-Drawing' and 'Big Torches' ceremony is held in the great temple of Todaiji, the culmination of a complex of ceremonies begun in February, that originated in the eighth century and is said to have taken place without a break since the year 754.

Quickly changing plans, Kazuko and I rose from our beds at a Japanese inn in Kyoto after a short after-dinner rest and drove to Nara, arriving there a little after midnight. We left our luggage at the Nara hotel. It is refreshing to find that there are still old-fashioned hotels in Japan; Nara, as befits an impressive old city, has the most impressive old-fashioned western-style hotel I have ever seen. (I sincerely hope that it will not be demolished in favour of a less distinctive modern building.) The only accommodation available was a suite, an enfilade of large rooms with high ceilings and elaborately carved furniture that might have come out of the Castle of Otranto. What are guests expected to do with so many chairs, armchairs and sofas? Perhaps in the old Madame Butterfly days rich and mysterious foreigners up to no good held wild champagne and *sake* parties here followed by orgies on all those sofas. . . .

Downstairs in the hall, a hopeful attendant lit up the usual collections of colour slides on sale in all western-style hotels: brilliant sets of Japanese foods, Japanese weddings, geisha girls, nudes in colour, and the beautiful Mount Fuji photographed between cherry-blossom branches, maple trees, clouds at the edge of heavenly blue lakes. . . . To obtain such remarkable pictures in all seasons some able volunteer must have been posted to the sacred mountain by the Fuji colour company for at least a couple of years. This martyr for the cause of beauty—and commerce—must have lived in a hermit's hut or cave and taken little sleep so as to be at the ready whenever a particularly elusive view of the mountain was revealed to him. There must be quite a story behind that assignment, some typically Japanese story of devotion and sacrifice in the name of duty.

An American couple sat on one of the sofas in the hall (they even had one there) waiting, as we were, for a taxi to take them to Todaiji. They were pale and puffed with sleep but determined. They were too tired to talk either to us or to one another so the four of us sat grim, silent and semi-conscious hoping that the spectacle would be worth all the trouble and the lack of sleep.

At last our taxi crunched up the gravel drive and we went off into the night along an avenue of giant trees, up and round a hill which grew steeper and steeper, till we swerved round and into a clearing where scores of cars were lined up and hundreds of people were wending their way towards the temple pavilions. I doubted whether we would ever see anything but we pushed our way through the crowd to the foot of the long flight of stone steps flanked by stone lanterns and tablets inscribed with the names of pious donors.

At the top of the steps, to the left, the great wooden Nigatudo hall of the temple, the scene of the night's main activity, was ablaze with light. Great tangerine-shaped black and white lanterns suspended beneath the eaves swung lightly in the night breeze, the smell and smoke of incense filled the air, and suddenly the dense black crowd gathered round the entrance burst into the brilliant colours of festive kimonos as a lighted firebrand was rushed out of the hall crackling and sparking with diabolical life, borne by a ghostly figure in white running like a lunatic escaped from an asylum. Before he could do any harm, he was surrounded by a group of priestly figures bearing long torches who dipped the end into the heart of flame and sparks until they too were set alight; then, slowly turning and facing the palatial sweep of steps, they proceeded to descend with the slow, accomplished gestures of Kabuki actors. The light from their torches was so brilliant that it rendered them faceless like spirits bearing the-devil-knows-what magic from some hell or heaven unknown to our mythology, remote from the descriptions in our sacred books, strangely terrifying, alien and unreal.

'They are on their way to draw water from the sacred well,' somebody cried. 'Nobody is allowed to see that part of the ceremony,' said another. 'Soon the fire dance will begin in the Nigatudo hall,' whispered an old man, 'that is where you should go, if women are permitted.'

It took us nearly half an hour to reach the temple at the top and wriggle a passage through the crowd to the office where a priestly attendant and his wife were receiving V.I.P. guests and allowing

the ladies among them to peep behind the curtains at the holy of
holies inside, where the fire-dancers could be seen. Kazuko, armed
with the talismanic credentials of the Foreign Office, pushed forward with assurance, and we finally stumbled into the little room,
holding our shoes, for we were treading on *tatami*, sliding the door
behind us. Nobody complained as we trod on their toes; they
expect to be pushed about on the night of the Omizutori.

The porter-priest, a stout man with a broad, sallow face and bald
head, was unconcernedly brewing tea in the centre of the room
with the help of his wife. He nodded and smiled when Kazuko
explained who we were and parted the curtains so that I could get
a view of the temple interior where the congregation of male
devotees was seated. 'What is it all about? What is happening?' I
asked. Kazuko, who had never seen the ceremony before, had not
got the faintest idea; the priest said that it was extremely complicated but he thought he could find somebody who could explain
it to me, in English. A Miss Shimada. He would send for her.
'How can anyone find anybody in tonight's crowds?' I wondered.
'She will come,' said Kazuko confidently; and, eventually, she
came; it was a night of miracles.

Miss Shimada looked like a schoolgirl; slim, boyish, rather shy.
She crouched beside me, speaking in slow, uncertain English,
groping for the correct metaphysical terms. . . . Strange noises
from behind the curtains prompted me to poke my head round to
see what was happening in the great hall: a clop-clop of *geta* at an
accelerated pace stopped abruptly every few seconds, was followed
by weird incantations, and then resumed by the invisible priest in
a devilish—or divine—hurry. Then, from the great door in the
centre of the hall, a priestly figure emerged brandishing an
immensely tall torch whose fiery head he banged on the ground
several times before running out again. Attendant priests with long
brooms moved quickly forward to extinguish the sparks. Why the
hurry, why the curious rapid, nervous pace of the 'fire dance'?

Miss Shimada explained that it was intended to re-enact the
origin of the ceremony when the beginner priest Zittu, going
through the dragon-cave in Mount Kasagi, reached the Heaven of
Tosotu, one of the Buddhist Elysiums and saw the heavenly
members assembled practising a splendid service. The priest
wished to introduce it to the world but one of the celestial beings
told him that it would be impossible for humans to imitate it
because a day and night in heaven are equal to four hundred years

in the human world. Also, it had to be performed in the presence of the living Kannon. The priest replied that he would practise the ceremony in a hurry, running at a great speed, and so it has been performed ever since. It must be the only religious rite performed at an almost comically accelerated pace.

As for the living Kannon necessary for the ceremony, it is related that the priest Zittu went down to the shore near Osaka facing the elysium where Kannon dwells and prayed intensely until one day a boat appeared with a little figure of Kannon, about nine inches high, in the centre. This little figure had the warmth of human skin. The priest took it and enshrined it in the Nigatudo hall where it is said to have remained in a casket which nobody has opened since he died. This casket is brought into the hall during the Omizutori ceremonies.

The little Kannon is solemnly transferred from the sanctuary at dawn on February 21st and carried to the back of the chancel again to be carried back at midnight on March 7th. The bell is rung, incantations pronounced. On March 11th the priests selected for the ceremony, accompanied by attendants blowing tritons, make a pilgrimage of the holy places within the Todaiji temple precincts. This announces to the devotees that the ceremony proper has begun. The priests then repair to the Bathing Hall for a ritual bath.

At this stage, the priests cut out paper vestments lined with cotton, mend the special wooden pattens called *sashikake* which will later resound in the Great Hall, make artificial flowers, and torches and ask members of the congregation to prepare two thousand rice offering cakes. On the last afternoon of this pre-liminary stage the eleven designated priests bid their fellows farewell 'in elegant, archaic language'.

During the second stage of the ceremony the eleven priests retire to the Kaidanin hall in the temple grounds for a period of prayer and purification; here they wear the paper clothes they made during the first stage, recite *sutras* and engage in manual work. There is no heating in the hall, and February is a very cold month in Japan. On the last day of February, a general purification takes place at night by the light of torches and a solemn confirmation ceremony begins at two in the morning.

Soon after they have retired to their cell, an announcement is proclaimed: 'To the Hall!'; quickly changing their clothes and led by attendants bearing torches, the priests hurry to the Nigatudo hall; at the door they stamp the floor with their wooden shoes then they rush in and round the hall three times, stopping for prayer in the intervals.

What we were witnessing was the *Dattan* or fire-dance when the long white curtain separating the sanctuary from the Nigatudo hall is rolled up and a priest, disguised as a water-god, springs into the centre of the hall and sprinkles incense water, then jumps back and runs into the sanctuary; next the Fire god runs in and scatters fire from a censer; the gods then appear in turn some scattering sticks, some swords, striking clustered bells.

At the conclusion of the service, a list of names is recited which include those of every deceased person who has ever had any connexion with the Todaiji temple. In the middle of the list figures the name of 'A Woman In Blue'. In the Kamakura period, when the priest in charge, Shukei, was reciting the necrology, a noble lady appeared before him and asked in a mournful voice: 'Why have you missed out my name in the necrology?' She was wearing blue clothes and she disappeared before the priest could ask her name so he hurriedly added the words 'A Woman in Blue' to the other names and it has figured there ever since.

The service, whose purpose is to atone for the sins of the State and of the world, finished at three o'clock in the morning. Worshippers and onlookers poured out of the great hall and down the steps like lava sliding down the slopes of a volcano. Francis King emerged, pale and blond, from the darkness of the worship hall inquiring languidly: 'Are you feeling as exhausted as I am?' We agreed that in spite of our exhaustion, the dramatic spectacle had been worth the effort.

The Dantesque images of that glittering, crackling night were still fresh in my mind when, six hours later, we drove into the forest of chimneys and factories of modern Osaka where appointments had been arranged for me with the Matsushita Electrical Company, who manufacture everything from tiny transistor radios and television sets to electric bed-warmers, and with Kanebo, the textile manufacturers. This is the other face of Japan—the forward-looking, efficient, stream-lined face that is assuring her present prosperity and her present rank as the fourth industrial country of the world.

I was conducted through long, well-lit halls in which rows of white-capped girls were working with nimble fingers in as great a hurry as the priests of the Nigatudo hall, engaged in the mystic processes of twentieth-century achievements. The products are first rate, the finish impeccable; gone are the days when Japanese goods were considered to be shoddy and produced by sweated labour. The workers live adequately on their salaries and bonuses although they have not yet reached the state where they can afford automobiles and summer vacations like western workers. The 'boss' is still paternal in Japan. The welfare officer of a large concern like Matsushita will take presents to the workers on the occasion of their wedding, the birth of a baby, the graduation of their children. Higher grade employees spend a few days every summer in the company's splendid hot springs hotel at Atami, free of charge. The President of the company is a self-made man who started life as an errand-boy; the engineers and high-grade personnel spoke with pride of him and of their company.

Round the
kotatsu

This morning I spent a long time round the *kotatsu* talking with Yoshiko and her family. It is surprising how quickly barriers of reserve break down when one sits round the sociable *kotatsu* warming one's knees at a common source of heat—electric nowadays—one rarely sees the old-fashioned type of charcoal heater under a *kotatsu*.

Breakfasts continue to be enormous and more or less like any other meal with no special dish, except seaweed, to distinguish them from each other. I am offered meat, vegetables, salad with mayonnaise (from a tube) and it is considered a slight to eat only one bowl of rice. Yoshiko's mother has a large lacquer bowl of rice by her side, and a flat wooden rice spoon, with which she refills our small china bowls the moment they are empty.

It is considered a delicacy to dilute one's rice with tea towards the end of a meal and eat—or lap—this up with one's chopsticks. This is achieved with a slobbering noise which nearly makes me sick, for I must admit I am squeamish about eating habits. The use of chopsticks is all very well for solids, but when liquids or semi-liquids are involved the operation is more elegantly performed with a spoon. I know that it is 'done' to sip one's tea loudly and appreciatively, but this is the one point of etiquette which I abhor, cannot bring myself to follow, and never will.

Yoshiko's mother presides over breakfast. Grandmother sits beside her daughter in the role of chief supervisor. Father leaves early to go to work and the younger children follow soon after for school. The cousins from Tokyo sit around and ask questions about England. In the evenings, when we once again gathered round the *kotatsu*, father talked about H-bomb tests and peace. It is an understandable obsession with the Japanese.

People have more leisure these days, and the word 'hobby'—*shumi* in Japanese—has become fashionable. Most Japanese have a *shumi*; it is the 'done' thing and the Japanese, like the English, like to conform with the 'done' thing. Apart from the traditional arts, some of which are going through a revival, there has been a post-war 'boom' in choral singing, sponsored by middle-aged ladies; I am constantly meeting mothers in their forties who can join me in singing 'Coming through the Rye' in Japanese. This song, in the original translation, which I am told approximated the Scottish, was forbidden during the Second World War as an obnoxious enemy property, but it was acceptable in a Japanese version. Few people in Japan remember the original words and one of the more unusual requests I get from time to time is to write down the words of this song in English.

Yoshiko's mother goes to a choral society once a week where she learns Russian folk songs as well as 'Auld Lang Syne' and 'Coming through the Rye'; she has a pretty voice. The Japanese have already proved with their operatic Madame Butterfly that they can sing extremely well, in the western manner, when trained to do so. I must say that I prefer our full-resonated way of singing to the strangled, classical Japanese modes like *utai*, in which grand-mother is a virtuoso. She sang a song in *utai* style this morning, in honour of my departure, the farewell song of a Samurai; it went on for a long, long time in a kind of Gregorian monotone, slow as the gestures of a Kabuki performance. Yoshiko listened respect-fully, but without noticeable enthusiasm. She is a very modern young lady.

I asked Yoshiko a few abstract questions this morning, the sort of questions which the Japanese find so hard to answer, because they are not accustomed to thinking in abstract terms. I wanted to know something about her purpose in life, and what qualities she admires most in human beings. I am trying to find out what kind of an image the Japanese have of themselves, or would like to have of themselves, their people and their country, particularly the younger generation. I want to find out how far it differs from the image of the older generation. One hears that the young lack directives, moral instruction, and that parents have lost their disciplinary powers. All this sounds very familiar to one coming from the West where we have similar problems, but I would like to know what the young Japanese think about it all. But it is always so difficult to find out what the young Japanese think about anything!

First of all I tackle Yoshiko about friendship. She tilts her head and half closes her eyes, a gesture indicating profound reflection, and asks me to wait until grandmother has left the room, as if I had put a slightly disreputable question unfit for the old lady's ears, even though she cannot understand English. The real reason, I suspect, is that the mere presence of grandmother effectively prevents personal thought and expression. Wherever she is she brings with her an aura of *utai* and all that it stands for: the Samurai tradition, ancestor-worship, Buddhist rites and the stern virtues of obedience and respect for elders.

When grandmother had left us, Yoshiko put my question to her young cousin and they both argued for a while in Japanese. 'You see,' explained Yoshiko, 'we are not used to talking about such matters. At home we only discuss everyday things, probably because my mother and grandmother are so busy in the house; there is no time or occasion. But it is interesting—we shall think about your question.'

After some thought, Yoshiko tells me that she looks first for intelligence and understanding in friendship, and frankness. Her cousin agrees about frankness. I have observed that this quality is more in evidence among the younger generation. Old people still tend to conceal their inner feelings behind the impenetrable spirit-screen of form and convention.

Yoshiko's ambitions in life are intellectual, tied up with her studies. Few of the young people I have questioned on the subject look further ahead than a year or two. I am often asked whether our young people at home are different and I find it difficult to give an answer. I should say that on the whole our *girls* are more ambitious. They also giggle less and are not so tied to their homes—but this is the result of the different social set-up. It is dangerous to generalize. Girls in their late teens and twenties, like Yoshiko, are more naïve here; foreign teachers all agree that both boys and girls are more immature than young westerners.

I presume it is because so much ventilation is required for the immense quantities of steam let off by Japanese baths that their bathrooms—it would be more accurate to call them bath 'quarters' —are far removed from the main part of the house. In this house, for instance, a covered passage, open on the sides, slightly curved like a willow pattern bridge, separates the living-room from a separate building where the bathroom is located. The passage is a chilly one at night. . . .

Nobody attaches importance to where they sleep. Bedrooms are less personal than with us. Yoshiko told me this morning that she had slept downstairs; she usually sleeps in the room next to mine. There seem to be a number of rooms in the house which serve several purposes, a space-saving habit which the younger generation is abandoning in favour of our more rigid western system. There is never any possibility of having a nap in the middle of the day in a Japanese house; the siesta of which I am so fond is unknown and would probably be considered effete. Once your *futon* has been neatly folded and put away, the day begins in earnest and off you go to work, work, work, non-stop until bed-time when you are entitled to relax, but not a moment before.

Japanese Sunday

How do the Japanese spend their Sundays? Many young people have taken up mountain walking, which they call 'climbing', a pastime for which they dress as if they were about to scale Everest, when most of the hills round Kyoto are pretty, wooded cones whose summit can be reached in a couple of hours.

This Sunday Noboru took me to Atago, a hill situated to the north-east of Kyoto upon which is a shrine dedicated to a fire-spirit. There is a shrine or temple upon every hill and this lends an added interest to a walk. There is always something to see besides the view, some man-made aesthetic shape, some legend to ponder about or smile at according to one's temperament.

Noboru turned up at the bus station, transformed from a neat week-day Japanese into a Sunday climber, in heavy walking shoes, baggy trousers, leather jacket and navy-blue cap. All the young people in our bus were carrying weighty haversacks and slim plastic cases for maps. Noboru, needless to mention, also had a map—an impressively large one upon which he had marked our circular itinerary in blue ink.

We bought a picnic lunch from one of the many little shops that are open on Sundays: fruit, bread, butter, cheese, eggs, and tins of fruit juice. These are fairly expensive items, bananas are a luxury, but everything is expensive in Japan once you look for something beyond the indigenous rice, noodle and soy bean fare. The typical Japanese picnic fare consists of enormous rice balls into which, in the reverse order of our nursery rhyme about Jack Horner, you stick a pickled plum; these rice-balls are wrapped between two paper-fine sheets of seaweed. One feels as stuffed, after eating them, as if one had consumed one of those cotton-wool sandwiches said to be effective first-aid treatment for people who have swallowed pieces of glass.

The bus stopped under a cherry-blossom tree at the foot of a range of hills beside a dark gorge through which a silvery-mauve stream tossed and sparkled. We stopped on the bridge leading to the mountains to watch the foam-patterns round the boulders. The first lavender-coloured azaleas are in bloom between magnolia trees still in sticky bud. Thick carpets of violets spread beside the mountain path that runs upwards very steeply indeed. The hills are low, but the gradient takes my untrained breath away.

Some of the lazier members of our bus party pause for refreshments at one of the wooden inns clustered like toadstools near the bridge. Crimson paper lanterns swing on the verandas above the stream; it is tempting to tarry and daydream or—if one is Japanese—compose *haikus*.

The higher we climb, the more white paper prayers we find tied to the branches of bushes, wooden tablets with inscriptions to the gods, and formless stone images of Jizo, the god who protects children and who is so often dressed in a grotesque apron or a bib; he is a paunchy fellow with a smiling, pudding face who looks like the owner of a tuck shop.

Half-way up the hill we come across a very small temple and, being thirsty, we stop to ask for a drink of tea at the pavilion opposite the sanctuary. A woman nods and invites us to remove our shoes and sit on the veranda overlooking the valley, where a mist still lurks between the pine trees, leaving the peaks on the opposite side faintly visible. The scene is almost too Japanese to be true. We are brought tea and coloured rice-crackers with a nutty flavour.

After a few minutes, an ecclesiastical figure in black robes with shaven head appeared and sat down to talk with us. It was difficult to tell whether it was a man or woman. The broad, plump face, the shrewd, sunken eyes, the wrinkled hands, could have belonged to either sex. Noboru thought 'it' was a priestess. I thought 'it' was a monk. Confusion only became greater when a photograph album was brought out and a picture of a lovely girl in wig and kimono shown to us. 'That was me,' said 'it'. 'Good Lord!' I exclaimed to Noboru, 'has she changed sex?' My amazement caused the nun— for it was a nun—to laugh heartily.

It was too dark to attempt a colour picture, but I wanted to try; sometimes the miracle happens and a picture taken in the worst conditions turns out well. (One picture in this category, taken against all odds one late evening in Morocco, was subsequently reproduced on the dust jacket of my book.)

The nun had enough feminine vanity left to wish to be photographed in her priestly robes and she disappeared to put them on, requesting us to walk up to the little temple tucked away in a hollow behind a huge tree. An old man was bowing and mumbling *sutras* at the foot of the wooden steps; when we arrived he pottered off to a smaller pavilion to the right of the temple, like a bumble bee in search of spiritual honey from as many temple flowers as he could find; a group of young hikers in hobnailed boots passed along the road, glanced at us and went on their way.

The nun came over, gathering her voluminous skirts, a gorgeous ample figure in crimson and gold, wearing the benign expression of a potentate about to bestow a special favour on subordinates. Slowly ascending the steps, she slid open the temple door, disclosing a heavily gilded alcove flanked by flowers and ornaments in which a little image was seated with modestly downcast eyes as in a sacred boudoir.

The nun lit two candles with hieratic gestures, bowed before the Buddha image, seated herself on a red and white leather cushion, unrolled a scroll and proceeded to chant a long *sutra*.

In the middle of the performance, the old man shuffled back from his visit to the other pavilions, and stood once more at the foot of the steps, mumbling loud enough to interfere with the nun's chant; the duet went on for some time, the nun never raising her eyes or showing any sign of annoyance, the old man completely ignoring her.

The nun finally rolled up the scroll, bowed, snuffed out the candles, and beckoned us to accompany her into the next pavilion which contained 'national treasures'. It was very dark inside, but once the sliding doors had been opened we discerned the fearsome figures of the mighty guardians who are supposed to ward off evil influences from the precincts of the gods; they are even scowling enough to ward off would-be devotees. The image of the Buddha in this pavilion, meditating in the shadows of a plain recess, is truly magnificent, radiating majestic serenity and conveying, as few images can, the conviction of an inner vision. It is worth climbing Atago for this Buddha alone.

The nun repeated the process of lighting candles, unrolling a scroll and chanting a *sutra*. When she had finished, she turned round to face Noboru and began talking to him in low, confidential tones. I wondered whether she was delivering a sermon, or whether the chanting of the *sutra* had given her a sudden prophetic inspiration and I was impatient to hear what it was all about.

'Well,' I said to Noboru after we had all bowed to each other until our foreheads touched the *tatami* with its fresh, rustic smell of newly cut hayfields, 'Well? What words of wisdom fell from her lips?' Noboru smiled and shook his head. 'She was only telling me her life-story,' he replied. 'She has six children. Her husband deserted her when she was forty-five and then she took to religion. She says she is only a poor, ignorant old woman but she has found peace and happiness through the Buddha, who has taken away all the hate that was in her heart.'

The old nun plucked me by the sleeve and pointed to a side altar where two faded yellow photographs were unsteadily propped up beneath the flowers and the vases and the sacred ornaments. 'It is a photograph of my husband and of us all when we were happy together,' she explained. 'I have offered them to the Buddha.'

A cold, damp wind was blowing when we reached the summit and climbed the stone steps leading to the shrine of the Fire-God where, appropriately, a large log fire was burning in a pavilion beside the entrance; a band of pilgrims were huddled together on a bench eating rice-balls. A Shinto service had just finished in the main pavilion and a couple of priests in shiny black hats, taller but not unlike the headgear of Spanish Civil guards, were leaving the altar with its esoteric symbols of the mirror, the necklace and the sword.

A stone lantern silhouetted between pine branches against a cold cloudless sky leaned forward in an attitude of profound melancholy. I had seen many stone lanterns planted between pine trees, but this one was in some unaccountable way different. I stopped and it stabbed at my heart like a long-forgotten memory of a past life; it evoked no precise images, no special event, only a nostalgic emotion of a once achieved oneness in those particular surroundings. It was a long time before I could tear myself away. I took a picture, which to me is full of significance, but which others pass by; to them it is banal: just another stone lantern, another couple of Japanese pines.

It was twilight when we reached the bottom of the hill, and the crimson lanterns of the riverside inn were bobbing up and down like fireflies in the gathering darkness. We paused again on the bridge and listened to the now nearly invisible water. The crinkly range of hills in the background formed a solid inky black mass against a pearly sky faintly tinged with lemon yellow. A young mother in a blue kimono crossed the bridge with a doll-like infant strapped to her frail bent back, its tiny waxen face staring as fixedly as a Haniwa figure.

It was of course much too early to see real fireflies. June is the firefly month, when thousands are let loose in the Chinzanso gardens of Tokyo when, as I read in a newspaper report later, 'the tiny light of the fireflies creates a dreamy scene over the ponds and in the woods'. That summer, the Fujita Kanko Travel service held a month-long Firefly Festival in the Chinzanso gardens, which opened with an evening's entertainment for 'five hundred mothers and their children from Tokyo's homes for underprivileged families ... among the entertainments were performances by noted dancers and singers, and the descent of thousands of fireflies from a Cessna aircraft. The aircraft flying from Kochi Prefecture will drop over 300,000 fireflies, using small parachutes'. This item of news conjured up a delightful, wholly Japanese, picture of dainty girls exercising their nimble fingers on the manufacture of fairy-size parachutes for fireflies; were these attached to the fireflies by spider-fine threads? The ingenious technicalities involved baffle the imagination of a prosaic westerner.

In retrospect, I thought it was odd that a Buddhist temple and a Shinto shrine should have been built in such close proximity upon Atago, but Noboru assured me that this is quite common. 'It is the same on "Goblin-mountain", Kurama,' he told me.

'Goblins?' I repeated. I have always had a penchant for goblins. 'Yes,' said Noboru. 'Long-nosed goblins. They are supposed to have brought up a medieval prince whom they protected while a usurper was on the throne. They instructed him in many arts, including warfare and, when he was old enough, they escorted him back to the palace; I believe there is an esoteric sect of Buddhists at the summit of Kurama who go in for magic.'

Goblin-Mountain

I did not have time to find out more about Kurama until the month of May and this, surely must have been arranged by the goblins because, unknown to me at the time, it is during this month that the important moon festival takes place on the summit. Believers would say that I was 'led' there at the right time. . . .

Spiritual and spirit considerations apart, May is certainly the right time to visit Kurama, for nature is then at her Japanese best.

I stayed for a couple of days at the Fujiyama inn at Kifune, or 'noble boat', a village consisting of three inns, about the same number of houses and a shrine, nestling on one side of a stream at the foot of steep, dark wooded Mount Kurama; this is reached by taking an electric train that passes through some fairylike scenery and a taxi for the last two miles up the mountain gorge to Kifune.

The Fujiyama inn is built in two parts on both sides of a mountain road: the main part, containing suites of living-room and bedrooms, is modern enough to have a small bar on the ground floor; an open flight of stairs leads to the first floor, where two immensely long white lanterns are suspended from the ceiling; they reach half-way down the stairs, so that one has the impression of ascending to a shrine instead of a hotel bedroom. An open balustrade of rope and wrought-iron cordons off the carpeted corridors and a veranda looking on to the road. At the back, half screened off by a wooden partition, is a hand-basin and mirror in front of which the hotel guests wash their face and teeth night and morning. Tiny narrow hand-towels, and a toothbrush and paste, are provided for every guest and appear on the handrail every evening and morning the instant one requires them, Japanese innkeepers being endowed with prophetic insight and sense of timing.

To the left of the hand-basin was one of the most attractive Japanese toilets I have ever seen; but it involved the use of three pairs of footwear. One left the first pair outside as an 'engaged' signal; immediately inside the toilet, resting lightly on a flagstone, were a second pair of outsize slippers in which one tripped up a path of flagstones separated by large flat pebbles to the toilet for ladies on the left; here one found a third pair of slippers. The toilet is divided into two: on the left, is a *tatami* mat, a scroll and a vase of flowers; on the right, the tiled flush toilet on a raised step. It was all so perfect, so neat, so scrupulously clean that one hardly dared to use it. Outside the toilet is a hand-basin with a large flat rock below upon which to place one's feet.

There are pebbles everywhere, even in the bedrooms—cunningly arranged into a path running round the outer edge of the room, separated from the *tatami* by a polished ledge of bamboo. The hotel *yukata* for guests is navy blue and white (rather too stiffly starched for night comfort) with a motif of entwined arrows and a slate-grey *happi*, or three-quarter jacket. In this attire, which is changed every two days, guests are to be seen walking across the road to the bathroom in *geta*, escorted by a maid who, when it rains, holds a large umbrella over them.

The principal bathroom, the pride of the inn, for it is truly luxurious, is located in the annexe overlooking the stream, provided with private rooms and a long veranda upon which guests, escaping from the humid summer heat of Kyoto, dine to the cooling murmur of clear mountain water. There are wooden platforms on the edge of the stream for those who wish to be near enough to plunge their hands and feet in the rushing water, and round eel baskets attached to poles.

The bathroom is below, at the end of a long passage leading to an undressing-room containing clothes baskets, a mirror and wash-basin; to the right of the bathroom, windows overlook the stream and the wooded slopes of Mount Kurama; to the left is a wall of cleverly arranged rocks between which sprout ferns and aquatic plants; the pool, lined with green mosaics and long enough for at least three breast-strokes, is shaped like a half *sake* bottle; the floor is a design of flat, firmly stuck rocks and pebbles. Gentle indirect lighting behind the rocks makes the room glow with the dim softness of an aquarium. Water drips into the pool from a bamboo tube—chromium taps to regulate the flow are half-concealed on the left so as not to spoil the illusion that one is bathing in a mountain grotto.

The narrow mountain road outside the hotel leads first to a shrine upon a slope, to which the Fujiyama inn has donated a large lantern, then up a narrow valley which gradually broadens out to disclose peak after peak of thickly wooded hills covered with pines, maple trees, Japanese oaks, cypresses, cedars, and a multitude of streams and waterfalls tumbling down in cascades of jade-green froth between immense boulders, bordered by flowering shrubs.

In the month of May, the banks that fringed the paths were covered by pale mauve irises with a violet stripe upon each petal and a spotted yellow calyx; pink and red weigelas were in full bloom, lace-cap hydrangeas spread paper-thin petals which were borne away like confetti by the swirling current. Above the water-falls, long tremulous bridges of slats upon rickety poles were provided for slender Japanese hikers; they sagged alarmingly when I stepped upon them.

High up in the hills I saw a man carefully carrying a covered cage in which a captured *noricho* bird was singing unaware that he was a prisoner. (I was told that the *noricho* is a Japanese cuckoo, but its song is quite unlike that of our western cuckoo.)

Another man was prowling along the bank of a stream with a canvas kite-like contraption which turned out to be a trap for singing frogs. I could hear a frog's pretty, high-pitched tune, like a phrase from a musical box; if he wasn't careful he would be caught and kept in a little bamboo cage beside a pond in a private garden but, like the *noricho*, he would go on singing even when captive.

Opposite the Fujiyama inn a narrow path led up the mountain to the Kurama temple, with small pavilions on the way where pilgrims pause to clap hands and recite *sutras*, not in the rhythmic leisurely way of the nun on Atago, but at the hysterical pace of the wild litanies sung by the religious brotherhoods of North Africa and Pakistan. Every few minutes I came across a doll's-house sized shrine beside a waterfall in which invisible toads croaked rudely until I poured a bamboo ladleful of water over the stones which hid them. The water is no doubt considered to be holy by the pilgrims who stop on their way up and down to sip it with devotion.

Higher still, where roots of giant trees protrude in a writhing goblinesque mass, a fence surrounds the stone which marks the spot where the medieval prince had been released by the goblins; a stout rope adorned with tassels, Shinto-fashion, has been slung across the branches of a tree. The entire route to the temple is punctuated by holy spots, an eastern equivalent of the Way of the Cross which one finds in the mountains of Europe; but here the shrines are dark and sinister, the food offerings strange; the gods have other appetites than ours.

From the summit, a path winds between the trees to a wide clearing and the sunlit temple compound. A canopy of trees forms a dense background, a perfect foil for the bright red and green pavilions from which lanterns decorated with a stylized chrysanthemum swing with a gravely festive air.

In a small pavilion on the edge of the compound, two playful toy tigers snarl at passers-by like peevish cats; Japanese tigers are unconvincing; it is obvious that none has ever lived in Japan. The Buddhist bell under the wooden roof overlooks a wide expanse of valley and wooded hills. A long flight of steps flanked by stone lanterns and flowering shrubs leads down to the valley and the village of Kurama, the terminus of the electric railway line from Kyoto.

The serious young woman sitting in the office where one can buy talismans said to ensure rejuvenation turned out to be the Abbot's daughter. I asked her if I could see her father, Abbot Shigaraki, and she readily agreed.

Had it not been for her ankle-length, wide divided skirts, whose deep violet shade and swishing sound suggested the hieratic mysteries of temple processions, the Abbot's daughter, with her composed gestures, bright, efficient eyes behind glasses, neat little bun at the nape of her slender neck, could have passed for the competent secretary of a women's organization; in fact, as I learned later, she is the President of the Women's Club of the Kurama sun, moon and earth cult.

She ushered me into a light, modern drawing-room looking on to a terrace and retreated silently to fetch her father. A few minutes later, the Abbot made an effortless entrance from a side door, an impressive figure with flowing white hair and a fresh complexion, in wide lavender and grey silk trousers and a loose white jacket. Like many other Japanese religious leaders, he combines the dignified picturesqueness of a medieval prelate with the unaffected affability of a parish priest.

The Abbot was pleased to see a foreign visitor and he told me that he was in contact with an English organization whose ideas are very close to his. And what, I asked, are these ideas?

Noboru had been wrong about the esoteric sect on this mountain top; at least, he was out of date. I gathered that since the war the Abbot has 'modernized' the Kurama temple and creed which now sounds like a modified form of Shinto with stress laid on the sun, earth, moon-worship and a few ideas borrowed from Mrs Annie Besant. The Abbot is progressive. 'I am the only private individual in Japan who owns a cable-car,' he informed me. He has had this installed from the village of Kurama up to the temple, to facilitate the ascent of aged and indolent pilgrims.

The May moon ceremony takes the form of a communion through holy water sipped from minute silver ladles served from large silver urns by priestesses in white kimono and gauze masks, and it ends with prayers directed to the full moon by devotees holding lighted candles.

While the form of the ceremony may be new, the idea behind it is almost as old as Neolithic man. Water 'blessed' by the moon has long been considered capable of rejuvenating the old and of conferring longevity. The ceremony of water-drawing at Nara is a variation of this theme to which allusion is made in the *Manyoshu*, a Japanese anthology compiled in the seventh or eighth century, where it refers to 'the water of rejuvenescence in the hands of Tsukiyomi', the latter signifying the moon, or moon-man.

Most Japanese are, if not moon-worshippers, at least moon-viewers and it is customary to organize moon-viewing parties in the autumn from selected points of vantage. In the Katsura Imperial Palace of Kyoto, the seventeenth-century Prince Toshi-hito, who was particularly interested in the moon, built a platform overlooking a lake for this specific purpose, designed for the contemplation of the rising moon; from the tea pavilion built on the edge of another lake he watched the shadow of the moon reflected on the water. Moon-viewing, like its spring counterpart cherry-blossom viewing, is part of the naturalistic calendar which takes the place of religion for so many Japanese; these aesthetic ceremonies remind men with gentle obliqueness of the imperma-nence of life and beauty, the melancholy of age and approaching death, without the tortures of western analytical introspection.

April 30th   It is time for me to leave Kyoto and the wealth of new images I have collected here. Which of them, I wonder, will float to the conscious surface of my memory in the months and years to come? At the moment, I can think of the Golden Pavilion, light as a fairy ship above its reflection in the lake, the felted moss-garden of Kokedera, the architectural subtleties of Katsura palace, the thousand golden images of the Kannon, disturbing as a mad-man's dream, the alluring lights of Pontocho on the River Kamo, the flower and temple-covered hills.

Then there are the people who have enveloped me with their warmth and welcomed me round their *kotatsu*: Shizue has been the most affectionate and demonstrative of them all, but Yoshiko has proved, in many thoughtful ways, that she can forget her bookish pursuits and become human; she has been a devoted hostess. As for Noboru—dear, kind, devoted Noboru—he seems to have found a congenial niche at last; next month he is going to take up social work at an institution for the mentally retarded. This work should suit his idealistic, gentle and helpful nature. He may have left the Zen monastery but he does not belong to the acquisitive world. He tells me that his salary will be a little less than four pounds a week. Fortunately his needs are few.

En route:
Hiroshima and
Miyajima

I have stopped at Hiroshima on my way to Dazaifu and Kuma-moto. It is a Sunday afternoon during cherry-blossom time. A student wrote to me before I left home, proudly informing me that he was born in Hiroshima, 'the first A-bombed city'. A fountain is playing in front of the Peace Memorial Museum, a long modern building on piles built at the end of Peace Avenue; a group of young people are reclining on the lawns lazily watching the coach loads of tourists being deposited at the foot of the steps.

Inside the Peace Museum a grave procession of Japanese and Americans walk slowly past the gruesome exhibits, the burnt rags, the petrified objects rescued from this man-made Pompei of the twentieth century. An immense caption in English and Japanese assures visitors that the doctors of the Atomic Bomb Casualty Commission, a joint American–Japanese institution, have found that the bomb has *not* produced genetic disturbances in the offspring of parents subjected to A-bomb radiation.

The American doctor I met at the centre, who eats *sushi* and is learning calligraphy, confirmed this, adding: 'There are people who want to play up the effects of the bomb. They weren't as bad as they are made out to be.'

'But you are still treating the victims—they come up here every day!' I exclaimed.

'Sure,' he nodded casually. 'But most of them come up for examination. We're keeping a check. They don't all need treat-ment.'

'What about the people who have died from the effects, who continue to die—their names are inscribed on the Memorial Ceno-taph, in the "Book of the Past", some of them are quite recent, I have seen them. . . .'

'They would have died anyway. After all, it happened seventeen years ago; some people were bound to die from purely natural causes.'

The doctor likes the Japanese. Their way of life especially. He has a flat in town, with *tatami* and 'all the rest'. He also likes Japanese women. How does he get on with the Japanese doctors, I asked him. 'All right. But their approach to medical problems is all haywire.'

Do the Japanese think differently from us even when they have had a scientific education? I put the question to many people and their answers varied. Dr Koga, the curator of the Ueno Zoo in Tokyo believes that basically our thinking is the same; Professor Ishida, who lectures on cultural anthropology at Tokyo University, did not wish to commit himself; he said he was not sure; the head of a large chemical concern in the north believes that the Japanese are dualists: they attack a scientific problem along western lines and solve their personal problems 'on a different, Japanese wavelength'; a large group of people were of the opinion that the Japanese mentality *is* different in every sphere, less analytical than ours, less prone to see things in black and white, apt to 'go off at a weird tangent'.

I am inclined to concede that the latter view may be true of artists, of the tea-ceremony and calligraphy experts who follow ancient aesthetic traditions, but those responsible for Japan's industrial development obviously possess very clear logical faculties; there is nothing 'weirdly oriental' about their down-to-earth discoveries. The United States is adopting Japanese inventions, such as Dr Shuji Umano's process for the de-salting of sea water which has been in commercial use in Japan for two years; new processes and devices, from electronic brains to spray-on furnace linings, are being produced at an increasingly rapid rate. . . .

It is strange to reflect that if it had not been for Hiroshima, much of this might not have happened. . . . If it had not been for Hiroshima and the ensuing American Occupation—and five hundred million American dollars—the arrival of American technicians, the stimulus of American machines, the new Constitution forbidding the Japanese from building up an army and spending money on defence. The Buddhist precept invoked by those Japanese to whom I expressed my surprise at the general lack of resentment about Hiroshima contains an element of truth: evil is not permanently evil, good is not permanently good, everything changes, nothing is permanent.

On the wall of the stone chest in the saddle-shaped vault of the Memorial Cenotaph, containing the 'Book of the Past' which records the names of those who were killed by the Atomic Bomb of 1945 is an inscription which reads: 'Repose ye in peace, for the error shall not be repeated.' Close by stands the 'Statue of the Children of the A-Bomb', a modern monolithic structure, hollowed out like an empty womb, topped by the figure of a child on whose head rests a crane, the emblem of peace; this was built in memory of a girl whose premature death was traced to the effects of the A-bomb in her childhood.

There are no signs of a militarist revival, no ex-militarists in key positions as there are ex-Nazis in Western Germany. And yet, not all the professional army and navy officers of the last war, or the fanatical *kamikaze* suicide pilots imbued with Samurai traditions, lie buried beneath the memorials dedicated to them by . . . whom? By the same Rightist associations who raised a monument to the wartime premier Hideki Tojo, executed as a war criminal? Is it true that nationalistic dreams of power have been obliterated?

The Director of the Public Security Division of the Tokyo Metropolitan Police estimated recently that there are approximately 25,000 organized Rightists in Japan, and about the same number of unofficial sympathizers and supporters. Some of these are business men and manufacturers who are worried about Leftist labour groups.

These are the organizations in which ex-officers are to be found, in the company of old-time Rightists like Yoshiaki Sagoya, who spent twelve years in prison for killing a prime minister in 1930, and young fanatics like twenty-five-year-old Isao Kato, who directs the clandestine training of new recruits to the Youth Action Corps, a military group of the Greater Japan Patriotic Society. Kato wears high black boots, a military-style uniform, and he has enshrined in his house altar the black-framed photograph of the seventeen-year-old ex-member of the Corps, Otoya Yamaguchi, who murdered Socialist Party Secretary Inejiro Asanuma two years ago. These young toughs are dedicated to violent methods. It was they who arranged to kill former Prime Minister Nobusuke Kishi and the wife of a publisher who had printed a work in which the Imperial Family was ridiculed.

Groups like the Fatherland Protection Association, the Anti-Communist Volunteer Corps, the Rising Sun Youth Corps and the Japan Martyr's Party do not have many members—some associations have less than a dozen apiece, and they are being carefully watched by the police. Moreover, there is little public support for them. Most people are in favour of democracy and, above all, they are satisfied with their present economic prosperity. Far more concern is shown about Left-Wing activities. The Rightist movement is a lurking danger, the emaciated ghost of old militaristic Japan; but it is just conceivable that an economic slump, coupled with an increase of Communist activities, could trigger off a nationalist revival.

These are the extremists, but there are others who, though not so extreme, nevertheless express regret at the absence of any reference to patriotism, national defence, and the national flag in school text-books, and one wonders whether this is the thin end of a dangerous wedge. It all depends on what is meant by 'patriotism'— this was defined by the director of the Defence agency's Education Bureau, Mr Hisao Obata, as 'love for one's neighbour broadened to the scope of love for one's nation'.

Until recently the Self-Defence forces had existed in obscurity but they have been spending more money on public relations in an endeavour to stimulate public interest. In 1962 they staged a National Defence Fair in Tokyo which was sponsored by a private railway company, at which tanks and field artillery were displayed. The Prime Minister's Office, on the basis of a public opinion survey conducted in 1961, has estimated that half of the nation has no interest whatsoever in the Self-Defence forces, except as regards their duties in times of disaster and their co-operation in welfare activities. 'Behind all this,' wrote the *Asahi Journal*, 'lie major problems whose solution will require time, such as the revision of the Constitution and the elevation of the Defence Agency to a ministerial status.' I would add that behind this lies the absence of a public image of present-day Japan.

The wave of defeatism and abject admiration of the victor that followed the end of the Second World War is being replaced by a growing self-confidence and feeling of independence coupled with a lack of sense of direction. Where do the Japanese fit in? They do not seem to be quite sure. At the moment they are pleased and conscious of being the leading industrial country of the Far East; they export produce and technical personnel to other Asian countries and occasionally the attitude expressed in private towards these countries reflects the old-time Japanese arrogance and superiority complex; some Asian countries, Indonesia, Burma, Manchuria, retain bitter memories of the Japanese occupation, far more bitter than the memories left in Japan by the members of the American occupation, despite Hiroshima.

The brochure which the Japan Travel Bureau offers visitors to Hiroshima is a superb production; the cover represents a 'national treasure'; a scroll kept in Itsukushima shrine in muted colours of old gold and jade on which a devotee is represented kneeling upon a wave and offering a golden chalice to a Buddha seated upon clouds against a blue-roofed temple. The scroll is reproduced on a silver background. Inside are pictures of Miyajima island and modern Hiroshima city, described as 'again an important centre in Western Japan of politics, economy, education and communications; tourists will find here good hotel accommodation, delicious foods and many interesting sightseeings'.

Gaily decorated boats were gliding up and down the river on that peaceful Sunday afternoon; there was a landing-stage, festooned with artificial blossom and flesh-pink lanterns, below the hollow shell of the burnt-out town centre, the only architectural survival of the bomb damage, but nobody looked up at the rusty, naked girders as they passed.

The river reflected the clear opal blue of the sky; a tiny child in one of the boats stood up to try and catch the falling petals of cherry-blossom as they fell from the grassy banks and floated upon the gently flowing water. Quietly contented families were daintily picking colourful titbits from shiny lacquered boxes, streams of school children lined up beside the Memorial statue to be photographed; some of them had brought long streamers of coloured paper cranes to hang beside the countless others inside the Memorial—adding their little symbols of peace to the thousands waving in the breeze—propitiatory garlands to the God of Peace.

Two girls sidled up to me interrupting my reverie; before they opened their mouths I knew exactly what they were going to say: the tallest and boldest of the two touched my sleeve and murmured in my ear: 'May we speak English with you?' This meant that they would remain silent, their eyes riveted upon my face, while I did the talking. I guided them to an empty bench and asked them, in Dale Carnegie fashion, to tell me about themselves. The bold girl had relapsed into a state of Japanese passivity and all I could gather was that she belonged to a farming family outside Hiroshima, that she worked in an office in the city and shared a flat with her monosyllabic girl friend. She was one of the scores of office girls I met all over Japan, with whom communication is difficult. Maybe they believe they are behaving in a modest and seemly manner by refusing to expand, but it makes conversation difficult. Utter passivity, an occasional giggle and hand-before-face gesture, a few banal phrases, is all that one can extract from them during a first encounter.

After a lengthy half-hour, I begged to be excused from the ordeal and rose to leave. The two girls rose obediently, like well-trained schoolgirls, and bowed a smiling good-bye. They had not asked me any questions, they had merely basked in my presence, apparently believing that by some phenomenon of mental osmosis, mere proximity to an English woman was sufficient to enable them to acquire a better knowledge of English.

I do not wish to see any more of Hiroshima, but I do want to visit the shrine of Itsukushima on the famous island of Miyajima, which is publicized as 'one of the scenic trio' of Japan.

The local train is full of sightseers, the windows are wide open and a pleasant breeze floats in from the Inland Sea. In the distance, the powder-blue outline of hilly islands punctuates the blurred horizon; on the shore, hills are ablaze with multi-coloured azaleas, gay as a bridal kimono. Unfortunately, they are scarred by billboards. Does the excellence of Japanese beer and whisky have to be extolled so crudely? Traditional Japanese modesty and sense of time and place dissolve before the pressures of modern publicity and business methods. There are complaints in the Press, but people are apathetic. They only see what they want to see and they have an extraordinary facility for closing their minds to the unpleasant facts of life outside their front door. Will there be billboards on Miyajima, I begin to wonder, giant billboards erected with the connivance of priests in exchange for fat donations? Fortunately, there is enough sense of the sacred, enough reverence left for the three daughters of the Sun Goddess to spare the island from such a violation.

Scores of people pour out from the train and down to the jetty where a variety of craft will take us over to the cone-shaped island covered with soft, bouclé verdure, from neat efficient-looking little steamers to festival-type boats with dragon figureheads, like small versions of Up Helly A vessels. The red and green dragon craft is picturesque and lively, especially when it bounces through the waves, but the more conservative steamers look smoother, and I buy a ticket for one of these.

The island gradually comes into focus, disclosing long narrow valleys stuffed with a variety of trees and soft, sunlit blossom. Outside a little bay, its sturdy vermilion-lacquered legs lapped by the turquoise blue of the incoming tide, stands the famous seaborne *torii* of Miyajima, heralding our approach to the isle of the goddesses. An open-air theatre on piles stands half-way out to sea; on the stage, with outstretched arms and masked faces, figures who look like the incarnation of gods perform Noh plays for an audience well provided with picnic baskets and bottles of *sake*, who will sit and watch and listen for most of the day, with occasional intervals during which they put on their shoes—neatly placed in rows at the back of the theatre—and go for a meditative stroll under the cherry-blossom along the lantern-studded shore.

Before one reaches this idyllic spot, however, an arcade of money-makers has to be traversed, a double row of restaurants displaying colourful samples of food, shops full of *kokeshi* dolls and varnished trays surrounded by crowds of eager school children —always excellent customers—clutching purses filled with pocket-money provided by parents who are as anxious to 'keep up with the Matsuos as we are to keep up with the Joneses.'

When the arcade ends the five-storeyed pagoda, shrine pavilions and stone lanterns begin. Shrines and temples, unlike cathedrals, are scattered, separate entities, and Itsukushima is more haphazard than most. The entire island is sacred and places of worship are dotted about under trees, upon rocks, in secluded bays, on the summit of the hills. I climb half-way up a hill, find a pleasant café provided with *tatami*-covered platforms upon which several families are taking refreshments, and I pause to order lemon tea and enjoy the view of the *torii* between the cedars, stuck upon a solid sea, as minute from this height as a toy from one of the souvenir shops down below. The family on the platform next to mine are curled up like ferns in kimonos of varying shades of green. They are tenuously enmeshed in a network of elliptical shadows from the cherry trees behind us. I ask for permission to take their picture, 'a typical Japanese family on a day's outing at Miyajima', I shall describe them later to audiences at home, some of whom will ask me: 'Do the Japanese have only one wife?' or exclaim: 'But they look quite civilized!'

The picture is taken, smiles are exchanged, and the 'civilized' family resume their beer-drinking and quiet conversation: mother, father, grandmother surrounding a rosy-cheeked little boy in a gay pullover.

Under the boughs of pale pink blossom, over a small arched vermilion bridge, along the banks of a stream strewn with moss-covered boulders, into the darkness of the cypress woods: all is enchantment, all is serene discovery. I walk and walk and, upon my return, select one of the little restaurants overlooking the stream in which to eat a curry. The owner brings me a saucerful of peanuts with my bottle of beer and I offer some to a two-year-old boy seated with his young parents on the *tatami* next to mine. He clutches a fistful and his parents make him say 'thank you'. This he accomplishes by solemnly facing me, plumping himself on the *tatami* and bowing till his plump forehead touches the floor between his short outstretched legs.

On the steamer back, we trippers sit laden with parcels—flat boxes of cakes—the eternal bean jam disguised in a wafer wrapping, said to be peculiar to Miyajima, and round parcels of simpering *kokeshi*. Some of the young men have evidently been drinking too much and they lope round the deck like gibbon monkeys, holding out half-empty bottles of beer and *sake*. One of them pats a middle-aged matron on her well-groomed head but she takes no notice and he eventually passes on to be sick over the rails. Even one elderly lady has drunk too much, but she is aware of the fact and pathetically repentant. Her two daughters support her while she places her hand on her forehead, rocks to and fro and wails unceasingly: 'I am so sorry, so very, very sorry.'

There is a long wait before the train and I sit on a bench outside the station. A demure girl in a helmet hat, nylon gloves and high-heeled shoes, sits beside me and, after a while, offers me a piece of chewing-gum with an engaging smile. I accept it as graciously as I am able, for I loathe the stuff, and prepare myself for the inevitable 'May I speak English with you?' She is, as I guessed, an office girl from Hiroshima and she has spent the day by herself on Miyajima.

Has she no boy-friend, I ask her, and she blushes slightly as she shakes her head and replies, 'No, but I hope.' Did she hope to find one on Miyajima, or did she pray to the gods? She talks readily and joins me in the train, asking me what I think about Japan, the Japanese, cherry-blossom and raw fish. Tonight she is going to a western-style concert with a girl-friend. She likes classical music.

She is also fond of cooking and takes classes in domestic science, no doubt preparing for the day when a boy-friend will come into her quiet little life. Like the girls I met in Hiroshima, she shares a flat with another girl. She was very polite and proper and she never removed her gloves; she would be attractive in a kimono, without the helmet hat. As it was she looked as if she were ready to pose for a picture of 'the Perfect Office Girl of the Year', Japanese version; demure, diligent, punctual and dewy with virginity.

PART III

Southern Japan:

Kyushu

Dazaifu.
Modern Shinto

The farther south I travelled towards the island of Kyushu the more azaleas I saw in bloom. Flowers in Japan are all eye-appeal, they do not stimulate the nose; this may explain why the Japanese sense of taste is so deficient and their cuisine so insipid. The country as a whole is unsmelly and the voluptuous side of life connected with the olfactory sense undeveloped and ignored. Some parts of Europe may be too odorous for the frigidly fastidious; third-class railway compartments in Spain, for instance, with their exhalations of sweat, garlic, and stale rough wine, but these smells are *vital*, they belong to the very fibres of the people, they are essential if one is to understand them; this healthy stink is a badge of virility. Flowers, having to compete with such violent odours, produce intoxicating scents; all of them from carnations to heady jasmine, have a potency unimaginable to their fellows in Japan.

As we approached the Kammon Strait between Honshu and Kyushu all trace of flowers and bamboo slopes disappeared to make way for the stern, smoky signs of industrial civilization. Giant chimneys rose on either side of the railway track, pouring out sinister orange fumes; great mounds of coal glistened in the rain; long goods trains dragged past interminably. This is a well-known mining district and peering out of the window at the scene of unrelieved gloom, I began to understand why Soka Gakkai is making such headway among the miners and others who live in this depressing atmosphere.

For the first and only time during my stay in Japan the limited express arrived in Fukuoka half an hour behind schedule. To my surprise I was met by a delegation of three: Mr Morita, Councillor of Dazaifu and publicity manager of the Tenmangu shrine, the modern Head priest of Tenmangu shrine, Mr Nishitakasuji, and an internationally minded gentleman called Sugiyama, founder of a cultural association, now a hundred strong, on behalf of which he presented me with an immense bouquet gift-wrapped in gay streamers and cellophane. The Press had been invited, flash-bulbs clicked, and I was whisked off for an interview followed by a tour of the city before proceeding to the shrine.

The head priest of Tenmangu shrine was different from the others I had met hitherto—those of the picturesque, flowing-robe variety of Kyoto. Mr Nishitakasuji is closer in flesh and spirit to the modern, industrial city of Fukuoka and its contemporary aspirations. The main devotees of Tenmangu shrine are wealthy business men and industrialists.

Outwardly, nothing betrays the fact that Mr Nishitakasuji is a head priest. He dresses in western style, has studied comparative religion in an American university, and looks what he always intended to be but could not since he inherited a shrine, i.e. a journalist. In these disestablished days when shrine priests have to work hard to pay their way, Mr Nishitakasuji's journalistic gifts have proved useful, and Mr Morita, with his extensive knowledge of the Press and politics, is a capable ally.

Mr Sugiyama kept up a spirited running commentary as we drove along the busy streets and up to the West Park to look at the harbour. Fukuoka, he explained, has always been the gateway for trade with China, and it was through here that Buddhist culture was brought to Japan over a thousand years ago. There is now a population of over 700,000 and the industrial future is very promising. In the West Park, I was just too late to admire the beauties of the four thousand cherry-trees in full bloom when 'a multitude of people viewing the flowers gather in their vernal merriments'.

We were scheduled to lunch at the Kaidan-in Zen Buddhist temple near Tenmangu. The Abbot, a close friend of Mr Nishitakasuji, is renowned for his expertise at *shojin-ryori*. This delicious vegetarian Buddhist cuisine is infinitely more subtle than the vegetarian dishes devised in the West. It is no use asking the Abbots of the various temples for recipes, because these are closely guarded secrets.

A young monk served us while our host supervised the processional entry of numerous dishes presented like ritual offerings—scanty in quantity but precious in quality, muted harmonies of walnut and sweet sauce, sesame seeds, tender bamboo shoots, rosy raw ginger and grasses gathered from the nearby hills, delicate to the palate and attractive to look at; the very thought of meat was repellent at such a meal for which one felt unworthy; it was surely intended for a celestial or at least a purified being. I am convinced that before sampling *shojin-ryori* one should undergo a period of initiation, including a fast.

Both this temple and another one near it, where we paused to look at a museum of giant Buddhas displayed to us by a frail monk with a shaven head and the big-toed feet one notices in so many of Hiroshige's prints, looked poor and neglected. There were not more than half a dozen monks in each. By contrast, the Tenmangu shrine is highly prosperous. The head priest showed me round with modest pride; few people among the many visitors must have realized who he was.

This shrine is dedicated to the tenth-century scholar Sugawara Michizane, otherwise known as Kanko, a great scholar born to a noble family of Kyoto who occupied a high position at court but was later banished to Kyushu through the instigation of jealous rivals. After his death the repentant Emperor sent an amnesty to Dazaifu and ordered a shrine to be built over his grave. Kanko is believed to be an incarnation of the Kannon, the Goddess of Mercy . . . and his poems are thought to be divinely inspired. This explains the presence of so many school children at the shrine, especially before examinations, when they come to petition the saintly scholar for success.

There are no images in Shinto shrines, but Mr Nishitakasuji has made Kanko appear more real and human to his devotees by means of panoramic scenes from his life displayed round one of the smaller pavilions; these show the cardboard figure of little Kanko walking in the gardens of Kyoto composing his famous poem 'Plum Blossoms in the Moonlight', the Emperor bestowing one of his silked robes on his scholarly courtier, the exiled Kanko arriving on the shores of Kyushu with his servant and small son, his meditations, his death, the ox-drawn hearse which is the origin of a legend similar to those connected with the burial of European saints like St James of Compostela. In both cases, the oxen who carried the coffin are alleged to have stopped at a spot divinely appointed to be the site of their grave and subsequent shrine.

In addition to the life of Kanko, which attracts so many young devotees, there are revolving effigies of Maiko priestesses in glass cabinets, and a large playground for infants provided with a miniature railway. The engine, like the one at Mr Matsuo's 'Dreamland' in Nara, is a replica of one of the first locomotives to be used in Japan. The charming little railway looked so inviting that Mr Nishitakasuji asked me to join him in a ride. Off we went, the only adults on the train, gravely observed by a couple of sloe-eyed infants who were evidently wondering whether we would be able to squeeze ourselves into the narrow seats. We enjoyed the ride with youthful gaiety, but the infants eyed us reproachfully in the not unnatural belief that we were poaching on their preserves. The head priest is doing all he can to attract the young and bring them closer to the shrine, so that it becomes part of their life now and later. In one of the shrine pavilions, the Meiji Restoration of 1865 was planned; the present head priest is helping to plan another restoration—the restoration of Shinto in a new, non-political form.

Life in a
Nichiren temple

$\mathscr{S}$outh to Kumamoto, through lush paddy-fields and not very densely populated country. Where do the ninety-five million Japanese live? The country is said to be over-populated but it does not *look* like it, away from the main urban centres.

The people of Kyushu have rounder, pinker faces than their fellow-countrymen of Honshu; they are also more demonstrative, and their love-songs are pre-Confucian in their frankness. This island has always had more contact with the West—Nagasaki lies on its outward-looking coast, and this is the point from which western commerce and religion penetrated into Japan. There are said to be about 20,000 descendants of the 'secret Christians' who continued to practise their religion during the centuries of persecution in the small islands dotted along the coasts; a group of one hundred and fifty have recently been converted *en bloc* to the 'new' religion of Oomoto. There was little Christianity left among them: a few vague ideas about the Virgin Mary and the Crucifixion, a few payers, some in Latin but written in Japanese ideographs, a rough image of Mary on an abalone shell, two christening dresses, a shroud, three ancient calendars—heirlooms which have now been handed over to the Oomoto authorities of Kyoto. The younger generation could make nothing out of the garbled Latin; they are attracted towards native ancestor worship and critical of Catholic Confession; these, say the Oomoto missionaries are the main reasons for their conversion to the 'new' religion.

Kumamoto station. The frail-looking ladies in my coach, bent over their *obis* like dislocated puppets, steel themselves for the Great Squeeze Past; it is always a case of everybody for himself in Japan; only very rarely does a Japanese male passenger offer to bring a lady's luggage down from the rack; when he does so it is for a foreigner, and with the self-conscious air of a man who knows he is conniving to spread false national propaganda.

On the platform, an excited little man brandishing a large purple banner groups a semi-circle of beaming, well-polished gentlemen round him in a reverent brood; someone advances with a bouquet —a camera flashes—this time it is not for me but for a male party on my train, employees out on a binge from a neighbouring town, who are being welcomed by colleagues before being whisked off on a coach tour to Mount Aso; 'the largest volcano in the world', followed by an interminable meal, *sake*, songs, and giggling exchanges with waitresses. But the ice has not yet been broken by *sake* and smiles are restrained, measured out by the millimetre, and bows are very low.

There are hundreds of people on the platform, gesticulating frenziedly; if this were in the West there would be pandemonium; fortunately, the Japanese do not shout, children are well behaved, babies seldom yell, nobody spits or chews betel-nuts as in other parts of Asia and many of the germ-conscious citizens wear gauze masks—they cannot shout with those on—as if they had just come from attending an operation.

In spite of the dense crowd, I am fairly conspicuous, being the only foreigner to alight. A tall Japanese girl with hennaed hair falling to her shoulders thrusts herself forward with extended hands, followed by a pleasant, loose-limbed young man with an American gait: Noriko, my new hostess, and Al—her

Hawaian-born, English teacher—the gayest, freest, most refreshingly unselfconscious couple I met in Japan. With them there was never any barrier, not the thinnest sheet of ice to have to break through from the start.

Noriko has a frank, open face, rather long and broad for a Japanese, with well-defined features and a light complexion. Were it not for her eyes, she could pass for a European but even her eyes are not noticeably slanting. She has good, straight teeth, which is unusual for a Japanese.

Al is more typically Japanese in appearance, with the exception of his easy *démarche*, and he speaks American-English which he teaches at the local YMCA and to the employees of several firms who do business with the United States. He hopes that I am willing to address all these people; they have never seen or heard anybody from England, so I have great curiosity value.

Al seized my suitcase and Noriko led me to her car. Her English is poor but Al made up for it; whenever, later, we ran into language difficulties in his absence, we said, in chorus, 'Let's ask Al'.

As we drove through the undistinguished streets towards the Myoeji temple which was to be my home, Al expressed the hope that I would not find it 'too spooky'. The temple and, of course, the priest in charge, belong to the Nichiren Buddhist sect. Neither Al nor Noriko can tell me much about it. They are too young to be temple-minded. Noriko is twenty-two; she tells me that she went to one of the best high schools for girls in Kumamoto, where she met and made friends with Yukiko, the Nichiren priest's daughter. Although she does not have to do anything but arrange flowers, help in the home and wait for her parents to present her with a fiancé, Noriko prefers to be independent and she is training to become a hairdresser. Her father owns a chain of cinemas. These are sometimes called 'theatres' in Japan and I am constantly having to explain the difference between the screen and the live theatre. Theatre as such is known as Noh or Kabuki and modern experimental theatre is almost non-existent outside the largest cities. I fear that it is too late to compete with the tentacles of nine-channel television which I find everywhere, even in the temple.

We drive through a narrow street, over a narrow railway track, left by a row of wooden shacks and down an unpaved alley at the end of which the upturned tilt of a temple roof pierces the branches of a broad tree. A minute canal and a wide wooden gate separate the temple compound from the mundane rest of the world. In a flower vendor's shack on the corner of the boundary line a plump woman displays gladioli and gypsophila for the benefit of visitors to the cemetery.

We stop in front of the main pavilion, which is closed when no ceremony is in progress. A covered passage leads from the pavilion to the priest's house on the right; in front of the house, a small pavilion perched at the top of a flight of stone steps must be the abode of a sacred image; an old woman stands before it with bowed head and clasped hands from which a stick of incense sends up a slowly rising puff of perfumed smoke. The Nichiren sect use a distinctive brand of incense. I shall recognize it thereafter immediately I enter one of their temples.

A field of carefully tended tombstones, brightly decorated with marigolds and blossom, separates the compound from a neighbouring temple belonging to the Zen sect. Behind it, a narrow path leads to a *torii* and a shrine. The entire hill, from the foot to the summit, which is crowned by a memorial to the Buddhist war dead, is holy ground, amicably divided between tolerant, non-discriminating gods.

An empty cigarette carton mars the well-swept temple garden and I stoop to pick it up. Unknown to me my gesture does not pass unnoticed. The priest's brother has seen it and will comment later upon 'the mark of respect I paid to the temple from the moment I entered the grounds'. I have not the heart to tell him that I abhor litter wherever I find it—which is everywhere in Japan. Usually there is far too much of it for me to be able to remove.

Noriko advances jauntily on her high, sky-blue heels to slide open the front door and usher us into the spacious, unpaved hall; at the end of it, three wooden steps lead to a *tatami*-covered narrow ante-room and spirit-screen, from behind which our hosts appear soon after Noriko has cried: *Tadaima!* (here we are). Yukiko appears first, in kimono, because she has just returned from her *koto* lesson down the road and it is incongruous to play a classical Japanese instrument in western skirts; she is pretty, in a Japanese-doll way, with rosy cheeks, wavy hair, dark pupils accentuated by porcelain-shiny whites and heavy eyebrows; her features are more 'Japanese', i.e. flatter, than Noriko's, and she is much smaller. Myokoshi, her thirteen-year-old brother, is still at school.

The temple priest, Mr Arito, makes a short, shy appearance accompanied by his wife. I take to him at once and deeply regret the language barrier for, unlike the progressive head of the

Tenmangu shrine at Dazaifu, Mr Arito has not had any direct contact with the West. His background, his upbringing and his whole sheltered life have been essentially Japanese. Never before has a foreigner penetrated beyond the spirit-screen of his quiet dwelling.

Being Japanese, however, he understands the close bonds of friendship that unite his daughter to Noriko and I presume that this explains why he has so graciously accepted my alien presence. Nevertheless, I am a little embarrassed and ask Noriko to make quite sure that it will be all right for me to stay in the temple for ten days; if it is not, I shall make other arrangements. Al says he can 'fix me up' with a more modern family and he again murmurs something about the 'spooky temple atmosphere', which I call 'meditative'; I am enchanted by it and by the gentle Aritos, who appear to be a devoted and completely integrated couple.

Mr Arito bears himself with traditional Japanese modesty; he is short, sallow of complexion, has a shaven head and wears loose black robes traversed by a gold brocade stole over the right shoulder. He is grave but not ascetic and his face breaks readily into a kind smile.

His wife bustles round with typical Japanese housewifely effusion, and added nervosity, because of the foreign guest. I had always thought that the Japanese were a calm people, but this is not so. They are calm enough when you meet them in public, especially the 'top people' whose restrained code of behaviour keeps them so subdued at receptions and in first-class compartments, occasions when they surpass the phlegmatic British, but at home they are different, particularly the womenfolk, whose fluttering nervosity often amounts to a neurosis. The Japanese are great 'worriers'.

We shall have plenty of room in the temple. There is a double enfilade of six large rooms and we three musketeers, Noriko, Yukiko and I, are apparently going to have the run of the three on the left, which are separated from the enclosed garden by a wide veranda. The toilet is at the end of the veranda; a rock basin in the garden with a copper ladle on the side allows for handwashing. For the first time in a traditional Japanese house, I am provided with a wardrobe and a few hangers for my clothes in a dressing-room next to the larger room, empty except for a low table, where we shall sleep. Noriko tells me that she will spend the night with me at the temple.

Al is taking us to dine at a *sushi* restaurant.

I woke up to the sound of drums, and opened my eyes drowsily on the scowling face of Nichiren whose strong, broad face is reproduced on the *tokonoma* in our bedroom. Noriko is still sleeping soundly on the *futon* next to mine. The bedding here is different from other places, which makes for variety. The pillow is what I had always expected to find in Japan but never had so far: a small, sawdust-filled oblong encased in a one-sided linen cover, embroidered at the corners with a bright western-style motif, and tied to the back with tapes. In lieu of a top sheet I make acquaintance with a *tanzen*, a heavy, quilted, velvet-sleeved kimono in which you roll yourself when it is cold. Two thick quilts on top of this give adequate cover in this fairly mild weather, several degrees warmer than in Honshu.

There are draughts, however. Noriko has now woken up and gone to the toilet, leaving the sliding-door open by half a foot which lets in a chilly breeze that wraps itself round my head like an iced poultice. It is dark because the veranda shutters are still closed but I hear them being patiently opened one by one from the far end: first a rattling of each tall frame—there are twelve of them—followed by a heavy rumble as it is slid along a wide groove to the toilet end of the veranda and stacked away in a small compartment. A long shaft of light enters with the removal of each frame.

I should like to go for a walk round the garden, but I am housebound by lack of shoes. Eventually, I decide to go in search of them; they lie, dusty and abandoned, at the foot of the steps below the spirit-screen; I carry them to the sarcophagus-shaped step beneath the veranda, sit down, slip my feet into the shoes and stroll past the camellia bushes and Japanese topiary to the other side of the house, where I come across a tall, spectacled youth in a schoolboy's uniform digging up potatoes. He stops, startled, when he sees me, and smiles uncertainly in response to my greeting. I wonder who he is—perhaps some poor relation? He has evidently not heard about me and is full of discreet Japanese curiosity. I must look odd, in a white nylon and lace negligée and walking shoes. . . . Bowing with as much dignity as I can muster, I rapidly retreat.

Yukiko must have got up very early to prepare such a large breakfast, which is a kind of synopsis of the day's meals, including omelette, salad and mayonnaise, soup, rice and of course—seaweed. The three of us sit round the electric *kotatsu* in the dining-room. Noriko is thoroughly enjoying herself and says she will stay another night in the temple. I believe that she intends to abandon

her domicile for the duration of my stay and I fear that I shall end
by upsetting both pairs of parents.

While we are having breakfast, the lanky youth I had seen working in the vegetable garden lopes past the veranda and darts a rapid,
chameleon's tongue dart of a glance into the dining-room. Yukiko
reveals his identity: he is Isamu, a seventeen-year-old assistant
priest who is being trained by Mr Arito until he has finished high
school and can be sent to the Nichiren seminary in Tokyo. All these
expenses are being borne by Mr Arito who apparently finds novices
scarce in these materialistic days. Isamu comes from a poor family;
he has no father, and his mother is a hotel maid. His days are full:
in the morning he works in the garden and helps to clean the house
with a long-handled, gentle rice-straw broom; after this he may
have to assist Mr Arito or a neighbouring Nichiren priest with a
religious ceremony. In the afternoon, he may be clad in ecclesiastical robes or in schoolboy's uniform pedalling off on his bicycle to
a temple or to school as the case may be. He looks meek enough to
fit the Beatitudes and not particularly intelligent. Looking at him,
I am reminded of those large Spanish families in which the least
intellectually endowed male child was—perhaps still is—singled
out for the priesthood.

I ask to see the temple proper, and Mr Arito takes me in and
shows me what many Japanese books on religion refer to as 'the
sacred paraphernalia': a gilded image of Nichiren ensconced in the
recess of an oriental rococo altar, large suspended cymbals, a low
lacquered table bearing various scrolls, the *mokuggo*, a wooden drum
placed on a cushion shaped rather like a human head. Before a side
altar on the left, a wreath and a box of human bones had been
placed upon a temporary altar between two lighted candles. They
belonged to a deceased devotee whose family come to the temple
every day to pray until the bones are finally buried.

Buddhism, as I have seen it practised in Japan, intimately connected with ancestor-worship, is a religion of deaths and dirges. I
begin to understand why the younger generation leaves temple-
visiting until they are old enough to be preoccupied with their
approaching demise and why the break-away 'new' religions lay
such stress on happiness here and now, by way of contrast; the
dead, in the old religion, play a more important role than the living;
they are prayed for daily, before the memorial tablets and with
special emphasis, in the presence of a priest, every month on the
funeral date of the last deceased, and annually during the *Bon*

festival which is similar to our All Souls. No wonder the Japanese
have added our jolly Christmas festivities to their calendar.

There do not appear to be many devotees at the Myoeji temple.
I never see more than one or two old ladies at a time, fidgeting in
the cemetery (I observe that flower-arranging is not strictly
observed here—flowers are merely stuffed into a vase) or hob-
nobbing with the Aritos over a bowl of tea, but in the absence of a
properly constituted parish as we have in the West it is difficult to
ascertain the exact number of faithful. At festival time, I am told,
many people turn up. I should like to know more about the temple
finances, but how can I ask? I appeal to Al, who is western and
practical in his blunt approach to these matters, but he is as
ignorant as I am. The Aritos live well and we wonder, in our vulgar
western way, where the money comes from.

'I guess you don't want to see any more old temples,' says Al
hopefully, since he has no time for them himself. He is right. I am
living in a temple—and liking it more and more every day—but I
do not want to see any others. Al admits that he was wrong about
the spookiness of the Aritos's temple and he is beginning to
appreciate the atmosphere. He calls for us in the morning after
breakfast when we sit out in the garden and take scores of pictures
of one another. 'It sure is calm here,' says Al reflectively. Isamu
passes by barefoot, clanking his pail and grinning with pleasure to
see us taking time off. Wherever I go, families have had to interrupt
their regular routine to look after me and talk but once they
become accustomed to this relaxation they begin to enjoy it. It is a
mild form of shock treatment. The Japanese relax so rarely.

This morning Al took me to the local Press to be interviewed. I
was questioned by a pleasant young reporter who expressed surprise at my desire to live with Japanese families, and even greater
surprise when he heard that I was living in a temple. He wants to
come round with a photographer and take pictures of 'my day',
from breakfast time—to see how dexterous I am with chopsticks—
to a visit to the public baths. We will have to visit the castle,
because it is the only outstanding monument in Kumamoto,
although it is nineteenth century and has no artistic merit, and
eat in a *sushi* restaurant, to prove that *some* foreigners like raw fish.
Could he take a photograph of the temple priest? We shall ask Mr
Arito. 'Maybe he won't like to have photographers at the temple,'
I suggest, but fortunately I am wrong; the Aritos seem quite

pleased. They are beginning to enter into the spirit of my visit and they are extremely kind. I have asked Yukiko to cut down our breakfasts, but it is no use; she seems to be practising all she has learned at cooking classes.

We have become quite friendly with the young Press reporter, who has invited us to his home in the green hilly outskirts of the city. 'You will see the inside of yet another Japanese house,' he tells me with a smile, 'the modest home of a struggling reporter. And if you like I shall take you round to a farming couple who live nearby so you may see how the country people live.'

We drive up in Al's car and spend a long time locating the reporter's semi-detached wooden house. It is his day off and he is devoting it to us. He is waiting at the door, and when we are all safely inside on the *tatami*, he introduces us to his elderly mother and aunt, who share the house, and are busy preparing a lunch which will be served at 11 a.m. The reporter's small son crawls on to his knees. Like all Japanese infants, he is cheerful and uninhibited.

The reporter has another child, a little girl, who goes to a kindergarten. His wife is a teacher. The mother-in-law and aunt look after the domestic chores. In this instance, the arrangement appears to work well, but the reporter tells me what I already know, that tension between the generations is acute in present-day Japan and young couples do not find life easy when the mother-in-law lives with them. He questions me about marital problems in my country, about reading habits and education and standards of living. He is a quiet, philosophical young man, not at all like an aggressive reporter. He is anxious to know what I think about Japanese families and how their life compares with ours. He shows me a few of his books—translations from English, Russian and French novels. He has dabbled into existentialism, like so many of the post-war generation. The little house is drab; paint is peeling off the walls, and childish fingers have made so many holes in the paper frames of the sliding-doors that the ragged pieces of paper rustle in the breeze like scarecrows.

We even have a grandmother in our temple. I only made this discovery yesterday. I was kneeling in front of the dressing-table when the sliding-door to my right opened suddenly to reveal the pale, wrinkled face and dishevelled white head of an old woman who, after staring at me wonderingly, bowed very low and smiled faintly. I started back as if I had seen an apparition and for a moment I thought that the Aritos must be harbouring a lunatic in the temple who had escaped their vigilance. Why have I not seen her before? It is true that there are so many rooms in the temple, so many sliding-doors, mysterious recesses and dark corners, that a ward of lunatics could be concealed here for days without one knowing. Noriko informs me later that the pale face belongs to an invalid grandmother, who usually keeps to her *futon* in her own room, but curiosity had no doubt got the better of her.

It is time I paid my respects to Noriko's mother, and Al agrees with me that Noriko should sleep at home once in a while, but she only shakes her head and laughs at us. Finally, she drives me to her home and rushes indoors crying: 'Good morning, mamma-*san*!' to the amusement of the servant. I hope that I shall not be blamed for kidnapping.

Mamma-*san* appears, smiling politely, and bids me be seated in a wicker armchair in the western-style room overlooking the tiny garden. She is dressed in a skirt and pullover and does not look much older than Noriko, but her manner is entirely different. There is a tightness, an inner tenseness about her that one finds in so many Japanese wives in their forties. I must of course make allowances for the fact that she is self-conscious in the presence of a foreigner whose language she does not know. I present her with a mounted coloured print from England and ask Noriko to thank her for 'lending' me her daughter. I am quite sure that Noriko conveys nothing of this to her mother. She goes upstairs to her room to fetch some more clothes. I suggest that we should invite her mother to join us in an expedition to Mount Aso. We agree upon this and part amiably—at least I hope so.

We lunch in the local department store which plays such a pretty tune at closing-time. There is little variety but the food is cheap and many country people, shopping in town for the day, eat here with their children.

One of Noriko's ex-schoolfriends works in the gown depart- ment and we ask her to join us, but she is too busy. Masae is a tiny creature with a rosebud mouth and a beehive coiffure; she looks so exactly like a Japanese doll that I cannot take my eyes off her. She promises to meet us for coffee and cakes in the late afternoon, after work, at one of the dimly lit coffee bars frequented by the youth of

Kumamoto. Sweethearts meet there to whisper earnestly but they are too decorous to hold hands. How do young people behave when they go dancing? Al and Noriko promise to take me to one of the 'best' dance-halls this evening. The others, frequented by the wilder elements of the town, can be dangerous. Even Kumamoto has its gangs of 'Thunder Boys'.

The 'best' dance hall consists of a fairly large room with revolving lights which go dim every so often, and a toilet at the far end which caters for both 'ladies' and 'gents'; ladies have to pass through the open gents and it is not unusual to see totally unself-conscious young ladies powdering their noses behind urinating young gentlemen. The Japanese, as far as I know, do not make lavatory jokes. It would not occur to them. They are clinical about all natural functions.

Al and Noriko dance to the three-piece band—it is quite a good one—while I watch the couples on the floor. The average age seems to be about twenty. Many girls and boys dance with members of their own sex. The pace is slower than at home—but of course, this is not Tokyo, and it is the 'best' dance hall.

A neat young man comes up and asks me to dance. I explain that I am not dancing, only watching. He goes off a little regretfully, which I find amusing for I am almost old enough to be his mother. He returns after the next dance and asks: 'Why do you not want to dance with me?' Oh dear, this is terrible, maybe he thinks I am racially prejudiced; I ask him to sit beside me while I explain, slowly and in detail, why I have come to the dance-hall, hoping that the pleasures of 'English conversation' will make up for my refusal to take the floor. The young man listens attentively. He is about half my size, he has a square face and a shock of thick black hair. He informs me that he is twenty-two years old and that he is a dance-teacher in his spare time. He has twelve pupils, mostly under twenty, but some are 'quite old—nearly thirty'. He can teach six dances: the tango, the foxtrot, the waltz, the Blues, the Twist and the jitterbug. It is difficult to imagine him jiving—he is such a composed, elegant young man. Before he bows himself away, he gives me his visiting-card, which I add to the scores I have already collected. I thought that Spain was the greatest consumer of visiting-cards in the world until I came to Japan. My own box of cards was emptied weeks ago.

It is raining today, so we decide to go to the pictures. There is nothing bleaker than a Japanese house when it rains and the damp comes oozing up through the *tatami*, and under the sliding-doors; the cold water in the bathroom feels colder (there is never any hot water through the day to wash hands in, only a boiling bath every other night) and the exquisite bowls of tasteless Japanese tea served by one's hostess do not comfort like a good strong English brew. There is no cocktail cabinet, so that one cannot even take to drink in desperation. (I have only been offered one drink in a Japanese house since I arrived and that was in Tokyo. Yesterday I took Noriko to the Castle Hotel where she tasted her first Dubonnet. I do not think it would be wise to repeat the experience.) I am not a smoker, so it does not irk me that smoking is forbidden in the temple, but Noriko lights a cigarette the moment we leave the sacred precincts.

Yukiko joins us at the cinema in the main shopping street, where we pay our respects to Noriko's father, another Japanese who is embarrassed in the presence of a foreigner. He is a broad bald man with a sallow face and bad teeth; business is his life and he works late every day. We sit upstairs in front of two schoolboys with their arms entwined round each other's necks. The film, a contemporary Japanese love story, is easy to follow for the plot is of the simplest: girl student falls in love with boy student in Tokyo, invites him to meet her mother, who owns a Japanese inn in the north of Japan, but the latter wishes her to marry a rich old man. The young people arrive in a snowstorm—the boy is discouraged and finally decides to take the train back to Tokyo. There is a domestic scene, in which the meek inn manager who is secretly in love with the owner, pleads for the cause of true love. The daughter hastens off in the snow and recalls the student just in time before his train comes in. They return home, and a final scene shows the boy playing the piano, while his girl-friend bends over his shoulder, and mother, *toute attendrie*, walks slowly out to the veranda to watch the falling snowflakes, while tears roll down her cheeks and the meek manager watches her in the background.

There were, of course, plenty of other scenes: a family council, a fight between rival youths, a realistic *sake* cum geisha party at the inn, etc. Told like this it sounds like corn, but it wasn't. For one thing, the film was beautifully acted, the colours were muted, the scenes splendidly photographed, especially one of the candle-lit snow igloos made by children in northern Japan, in which they hold parties, leaving their snow-boots outside; the details of the interiors were perfect and gave an accurate picture of Japanese home life such as we rarely see in Europe—all those Samurai type of films they send us perpetuate a false image of the Japanese—and the banal story was uplifted by a quality of innocence, of almost medieval naiveté, like the tale of *Aucassin and Nicolette*. Noriko and Yukiko wept copiously and were quite red-eyed when the lights went up.

When we got back to the temple and called out the home-coming password: *Tadaima*! Mrs Arito came shuffling round the spirit-screen and whispered apologetically to Noriko: 'They will probably disturb Nina-*san*, but I could not send them away, two teachers want to speak to her. They had been waiting for some time. They had seen the article in the Press. . . .'

More bidders for English conversation!

Mrs Arito cast herself at our feet to impart this information; this sounds dramatically Victorian, but it is the traditional Japanese approach and the Aritos preserve these customs; all announcements, whether it be to deliver a telephone message or tell us that the bath is ready, are made on bended knee. It is catching and not to be outdone or appear uncouth, I find myself responding in the same manner. (I must remember to rub my knees with cold cream at night, in case they become calloused.)

Mrs Arito disappears while Noriko and I walk into the dining-room. The two teachers, one male and one female, whom Mrs Arito has served with tea and cakes wrapped in silver paper, are kneeling on the same side of the low table. They rise to greet me and introduce themselves, the man doing most of the talking in a loud voice accompanied by broad gestures. He is a teacher of English at a junior high school and she is his companion. They would like me to tell them about education in England and they simultaneously open a couple of copybooks to make notes 'and write down any unusual words I may happen to use'. There is not the slightest hint of an apology for intruding on my presence or taking up my time. When the Japanese are not being overbearingly polite, they are downright rude.

The man is repulsively ugly: lean, sallow, half bald, with decayed teeth and lecherous little eyes lit up by too much *sake* drinking. His companion, plump and fortyish, is dressed in western style and wears one of the popular helmet hats which I have hitherto always associated with demure maidens; her face is broad, very yellow, and her manner unctuous.

'How is it in England?' the man inquires, leaning confidentially across the table, 'Can teachers go to bars? Here it is very bad for us to be seen in one.' The woman nodded and sighed, 'If we do, we are not considered pure.'

I get rid of them as soon as I can. The Aritos appear and salute the departing guests; we all kneel in a graceful semi-circle in front of the spirit-screen to bow them out. 'You have a strong body,' says the male teacher irrelevantly before he goes. 'I know. I can see.' Mr Arito shakes his head reproachfully. He has not understood the words but he has smelled the *sake*.

There is to be a *koto* playing party at the temple this afternoon. Yukiko has invited her blind teacher and his wife. Our friend the reporter is also coming, with a Press photographer. There is a lot of running backwards and forwards and Isamu gives an extra energetic sweep to the *tatami*. The doors of our bedroom and the dining-room are opened to make more space. Yukiko brings six yellow flowers and a branch of blossom from her *ikebana* class and proceeds to arrange them in the manner prescribed by her teacher, under the Nichiren scroll. I have heard that Nichiren was a dogmatic and uncompromising reformer and that his devotees possess none of the tolerance associated with Buddhism, but Mr Arito is not like that at all: he performs his religious duties almost surreptitiously with the exception of the early morning drum performance. Sometimes, when I cross the room leading to the bathroom, I find him quietly chanting a *sutra* before a low table, with his back to the television set.

It is a warm, sunny morning and I lie upon the lawn, lazily following the flight of two large black butterflies, like levitating velvet bows, between the rose-red azaleas.

'Good morning!' says a bright, unfamiliar voice. I turn my head and see two pairs of black stockinged legs and, as my eyes travel up, two small pleated navy-blue skirts, two navy-blue blouses and sailor collars, and two round grinning faces. 'We have come for English conversation and to tell you about Japan,' said one of the schoolgirls. 'Not now,' I said firmly, 'can you not see that I am resting?' 'Resting?' repeated the second schoolgirl. They exchanged puzzled glances. 'To rest—rested—resting,' I murmured

weakly. The girls shook their shiny black heads and the eldest
drew a dictionary out of her pocket.

'I do wish you would go away,' I sighed. They looked at me and
smiled delightedly, as if I had paid them a great compliment. They
seemed unable to find the word 'rest' in their dictionary and as it
was a Japanese-English one, I could not help. By this time, I was
sitting up and more indignant than ever. I tried another word. 'I
want to sleep,' I said, with the appropriate mimicry. The schoolgirls looked at me unbelievingly. No, of course they wouldn't
believe me. No Japanese ever takes time off for a nap in the middle
of the morning. Perhaps they had walked a long way to come and
see me. Their idea of privacy is not the same as ours. . . .

'Sit down,' I said weakly, 'and we shall have some "English
conversation".' They sat on a flat stone and gurgled happily while
I went through the routine of asking them their names, ages,
addresses, their favourite subjects, their hobbies. At this point
'English conversation' always tends to flag. 'Ask *me* questions,' I
exhort them, hoping they will not ask me for my age, which they
often do.

Fortunately, Al appeared after ten minutes and liberated me. He
had come to take me to the sewing-school run by his wife and
parents. These seem to be popular. Kumamoto has several sewing-
schools and an unending supply of industrious brides-to-be who
wish to become good, diligent wives and mothers. I have seen row
upon row of them, always solemn, always earnest, in sewing-
schools and cooking-schools in every city I go to. They also learn
how to knit and embroider. I think of all those bright flowers on
those small pillow-slips.

A famous bacteriologist, seventy-eight-year-old Kiyoshi Komi-
nami, and his doctor-wife, have founded a school in Fujisawa to
train the future wives of Japanese emigrants to South America, and
they act as *nakodos* to their pupils. The curriculum includes Spanish
language lessons, flower culture, South American cooking, embroidery, tea ceremony, first-aid for fractured bones or snake bites,
and judo.

South American woods are used in the manufacture of the
Japanese *samisen*; so Yukiko's music teacher informs me this afternoon. He is surprisingly awkward for a blind person; his wife has
to guide his hands to the various dishes put before him, and to his
glass of Asahi beer. Mr Arito is in festive mood like the rest of us;
he too drinks beer and even smokes a 'Peace' cigarette. Noriko's

mother arrives in a beautiful violet-coloured kimono and silvery *obi;* at the entrance by the spirit-screen, she exchanges low, *tatami-*touching bows with the Aritos. The priest knows that this custom amuses me and he looks up at me with a knowing smile, aware that I am watching the scene with fascinated interest.

Al's wife arrives in a fashionable black and white kimono; she is tall, slender, delicate-featured, rather severe. A couple of neighbours, including the flower-vendor at the corner, have come in to help. Several lacquered tables have been put together and laden with dishes like a china exhibition. I thought we were only going to have a snack, but a series of snacks are produced; kebabs, fruit salad, cakes, beer and lemonade and, of course, Japanese tea.

It is time for the recital; the teacher, his wife and Yukiko, who has tied a blue pleated ankle-length apron over her kimono, take up their positions at the end of the room, kneeling upon cushions, heads bent over the long stringed *koto* before them. Their figures are silhouetted against a horizontal strip of vivid green and pink shrubs, a stone lantern, a patch of blue sky between the angular branches of pine trees. The music starts, a careful, plucking of slow plaintive minor phrases: tea-house music, full of vague regrets and fastidious nostalgia, music that never penetrates any further than the skin, precious, formal, the perfect accompaniment for Haiku, or moon-viewing parties—remote, floating on the edge of reality, too slight to stir the heart or soul, capable only of tickling aesthetic sensibilities.

When the guests have gone I find myself an apron, plant myself firmly behind the stone sink in the immense scullery and, despite the shocked protests of the Aritos, proceed to wash up. There is only cold water, a rag instead of a mop, and little room in which to organize the never-ending stream of bowls, cups, dishes, plates and glasses; there is scope for Taylorization here and much time must be wasted in preparing and clearing up meals.

Miyokoshi gets back home after eleven at night. He has been to 'extra classes', private lessons to help him pass those dreadful examinations. He is still rosy cheeked and bright eyed. Science and mathematics are his favourite subjects and he asks me to send him a big book on science from England. He is learning English but is much too shy to have 'English conversation' with me. We do not see much of him during the day. When he comes back from school he either settles down to his homework or retreats to his workshop at the back of the temple, where he indulges in wood-carving.

There is to be a *segaki* ceremony this morning in a neighbouring temple and Mr Arito asks me whether I would like to attend. As I expect, it has something to do with the dead; it is a monthly memorial service. 'You won't want to stay all the time,' says Al when he arrives, 'you won't be able to sit through all the ceremonial fuss.' 'But I *like* ceremonial fuss,' I tell him; 'ritual gestures fascinate me, a good religious service can be as effective as drama.'

The temple in which the *segaki* ceremony is taking place is only just round the corner; it is larger than ours and even the chief priest is outsize for a Japanese, with the commanding presence of a distinguished actor. He is splendidly attired in robes of purple, orange and gold and the tall black headgear one sees in Kabuki.

The ceremony had begun when we tip-toed in escorted by the priest's wife. Twelve ladies in dark kimonos were kneeling on cushions at the left-hand side of the temple, beating racquet-shaped drums held by a short handle in their left hand and struck by a curved drumstick in their right, under the leadership of an assistant priest. These priests, lined up in a double row in the centre facing the altar, were almost as numerous as the congregation.

I observe the presence of Isamu who is beating a drum with conviction, but his attention is not so engrossed by spiritual matters that he cannot find time to glance in our direction every so often. Mr Arito is gravely playing cymbals, in a peculiar manner: he first revolves them separately in opposite directions and then bends them towards each other so that the rims touch, emitting a curious disturbing sound. From time to time Mr Arito deserts the cymbals to read aloud from a yellow book placed upon a vermilion lacquered table. A little in front of him, an energetic young priest plays a large gong which echoes through the temple until it dwindles to the whisper of an incantation. Behind me, Al whispers that the large banners floating from the altar are inscribed with the words for 'love' and 'happiness'.

Our presence has been observed by the small congregation and a middle-aged lady in the front row turns round and beckons me to sit on a cushion next to her. 'If you move up there, you'll never be able to get out,' whispers Al urgently. 'I like it and I'm staying,' I reply. 'Okay—we'll come back for you later,' he says, and he and Noriko slip away. The service continues smoothly, rhythmically, soothingly, like the rise and fall of waves, interrupted occasionally by the whipping of the drums with erotic overtones which evoke memories of African brotherhoods.

When all is over, the yellow book enclosed in the vermilion box-table, the last genuflexions made by the multi-coloured high priest, the ecclesiastical procession files out solemn-faced and the elderly ladies foregather in a room next door for lunch. Yukiko is there, helping the temple priest's wife, and I am invited to the large room overlooking the garden where a banquet has been laid out for the VIP priests and one plump, shaven nun.

The high priest removes his impressive headgear, puts on his everyday expression, which is a jovial one, and quaffs a large glass of beer. He is a loquacious extrovert and Al is summoned to interpret our conversation. The priest wants to know about religious life in my country, what young people think and do. He is anxious, like many another priest in Japan and elsewhere, to attract the younger generation and he does not know how to go about it. Nobody knows how to pour the old wine into new bottles. I ask him whether he does any social work and he replies that the temple does not have enough money for such purposes.

I have expressed the desire to see how humble people live, and Mr Arito suggests that I might like to visit a remote relative of his, who is married to a tramcar driver and lives in a small working-class estate on the fringe of the city. Yukiko directs us there after the temple banquet.

The cluster of small wooden houses surrounded by fences, or in some cases a box hedge, looks neat enough in spite of the unmade roads between them. The tramcar driver's family live on a corner and their back garden is larger than most. There is room in it for a few vegetables—onions and spinach—two cherry-blossom trees, a goldfish pond and a long-tailed puppy. The average Japanese private garden strikes an English visitor as untidy and lacking in flowers; the Japanese are lost once they depart from the classical mould of a landscape garden with tamed trees, pools and stones arranged by an esoteric philosopher.

The little two-roomed house was small for a couple with three children, but it was as neat as it could be in the circumstances and in the usual absence of adequate cupboard space which means that so many things must be kept in boxes and tins piled up in corners.

The tramcar driver's wife is a large, capable-looking woman; I cannot imagine how she can squeeze herself into her minute kitchen to prepare the family meals; the bath cubicle, too, is only big enough for dwarfs. She is lucky, she says. Some of the houses have no bath cubicles at all and the inmates rely on their neighbours' goodwill. There is a certain amount of resentment between the 'have bathrooms' and the 'have nots'.

The living-room is full of fishing trophies won by her husband who, incidentally, earns approximately £30 a month. They pay £8 a month for the rent of their little house. There is a small television set in the room and a recorder. The youngest boy puts on a record of Kyushu folk-songs and the eldest, who is thirteen, brings out a camera to take a picture of us and then makes me sign my name under a picture of London in his geography book.

The eldest boy wants to teach mathematics when he grows up; the eleven year-old is only interested in sport at the moment; he has just returned from a game of baseball.

Their mother pours us out a glass of orangeade while the kettle boils for tea, sets down a plate of peanuts and wrapped cakes, and begins to peel a large orange and an equally large apple. We are also offered a bowl of hard-boiled eggs.

Like most modern Japanese wives of all classes the tramcar driver's wife has outside activities. She is a 'Green Auntie', i.e. she leads children across the busy roads on their way to school every day—a job for which she earns roughly £9 a month. She is also an active member of the local Parent–Teachers association.

At last we take our leave, stomachs rumbling uneasily as they cope with the mixture of beer, lemonade, tea, hard-boiled eggs, nuts and fruit which our hospitable hostess has pressed upon us. She waves us good-bye with a broad smile, she is friendly, frank, and obviously contented.

We are now going to see a much more sophisticated type of person: Noriko's dancing teacher, a slim young woman in a tight-fitting mauve kimono that accentuates her delicious pear-shaped little bottom. This part of one's anatomy plays a prominent yet subtle role in Japanese dancing; it is not vulgarly *stuck* out, as in modern western-style ballet—it is *left* out, the curve in the many movements that correspond to an inverted 's'. All the gestures preceding this movement are smooth and gentle, there is no Iberian violence, African eroticism or European dynamism about these dances in which the legs are never raised, only bent at the knees forming angles like a Japanese tree, or twisted like a flower-arrangement. The kimono is never raised; only the feet are visible, wrapped in white *tabi*: occasionally the ankles are bent backwards and the feet stamped in a fleeting mood of peevishness. The face is upturned like a simpering *kokeshi*, or swivels round provocatively while the nimble hands manipulate a fan with a conjurer's art.

The dancing teacher lives with her mother, a cat and a canary. She is twenty-eight and unmarried but, says Noriko, 'she is looking'. Where can she look? Surely she will require the services of a *nakodo*. There is no mixed social life, no opportunity for her to meet members of the opposite sex. Her pupils are young girls, some of them geishas, who never invite her to their homes. Parties are unknown, except ceremonial occasions when banalities are exchanged over cups of tea. The teacher presents me with a hand-towel on which her professional name is inscribed, while Noriko changes into a kimono for her rehearsal of a spring dance, in the company of another pupil. The music is provided partly by a gramophone record and partly by the teacher playing the *samisen*. When the girls are ready they advance on to the raised platform in the dance-room and courteously bow to their teacher, their hands on the *tatami*, their foreheads touching the ground. They bow again, just as ceremoniously, when the lesson ends.

We have been invited to a tea-ceremony at the house of one of Al's English pupils, a middle-aged lady with deplorable teeth who is wealthy enough to possess two tea-houses in her garden. The approach is deceptively modest, up an unpaved track above clusters of slummy dwellings near the railway line; the track swerves abruptly and ends in front of a short but impressive drive. Inside there is a profusion of stone lanterns and Japanese maples. A vermilion carpet has been laid upon the veranda behind the house from where a path of cunningly placed flagstones leads to the invisible tea-houses.

The lady of the house appears to be a professional organizer of tea-ceremony parties for uninitiated foreigners; among the guests assembled in the living-room we find a hefty, pipe-smoking American professor from the local university who says little but observes much, his slim, blonde wife dressed in an exquisite kimono of embroidered peonies on a white background, and a large-boned Canadian female teacher. Al looks glum. He hates 'all this ceremonial stuff'. The Americans engage in a cautious conversation with me. All the Americans I meet in Japan seem to resent my intrusion, as if it were upon their private domain. After their fiasco with China, they are trying to 'adopt' Japan. I fear that they may be due for another disappointment, however much of a success the

Occupation has been. For it *has* been a success, as alien occupations go, stimulating changes in Japan that have pushed the country forward. One only has to imagine what would have happened if the Soviets had occupied Japan instead of the Americans. . . .

Our party was not in a mood for tea-ceremony. I should have liked some initial advice, as I had never taken part in one before, but Noriko giggled, Al remained sullen and the Canadian girl was as ignorant as I was. The American couple and two Japanese guests had already been initiated and they were going to take part in an hour-and-a-half-long ceremony in one of the tea-houses, whereas we were to attend a shortened version for neophytes.

It was an ordeal from the moment I tried to slip my stockinged feet into an immense pair of *zori* (straw sandals) that didn't fit and kept coming off, sending Noriko into a giggling fit. I felt like the Ugly Goose waddling up to the dainty tea-house set among the trees like a gnome's dwelling in a fairy tale. Once there, we bent our heads and crawled through a small aperture into a monkish cell.

After a few minutes, our hostess, a dainty young woman clad in a maple-leaf coloured kimono, appeared at a door in the centre, and welcomed us with a low bow. Quickly kneeling beside the tea utensils on the floor to her right, she began to execute the stylized gestures, half ritualistic, half-theatrical, which constitute the Japanese equivalent of a religious communion. One famous seventeenth-century exponent tried to make it a more sociable affair but he never succeeded. Japanese social life has always been stiffly close to religious ceremonial, while this, on the other hand, lacks the grandeur of the Mass with the sublime significance of the Elevation bell; our Communion is a mystic transmutation, the Japanese tea-ceremony an inducement to meditative calm in a select atmosphere which is neither divine nor entirely human. That is probably what makes it so difficult for the foreigner to comprehend.

But, I repeat, we were not in the right mood even for meditative calm. The Canadian girl knelt beside me with her pleated skirt folded round her like a tent; as she was the first to be served and did not know what to do she had to ask aloud every time. Al kept muttering that he was no longer used to sitting on *tatami* and was feeling d—— uncomfortable. Noriko sniggered and made unhelpful remarks about how gauche we all looked. Our dainty hostess carried on as sweetly as she could, bending, rising, whisking the green tea to a froth, presenting the bowl like a chalice to each one of us, rinsing it, turning it delicately round in her flexible fingers.

We shuffled forwards, then backwards, bowed over the cup after having turned it round before raising it to our lips—three inches forwards, six inches backwards—every movement is as carefully measured as on a stage.

Yukiko now sleeps in our room, and shares Noriko's *futon*. The two of them whisper and giggle in the dressing-room every night, spending hours over their toilet and hair; their flow of language is as endless as Japanese telephone conversations.

Noriko pulls at my *futon*, 'Now we shall be nice and close—the three of us together,' she says. As a result, I wake up at dawn to find myself half on the *tatami*, shivering with cold; a light hand is shaking my shoulder. I half-turn sleepily and see the outline of Mrs Arito's wavy hair against the pearly grey light. She retires silently and Noriko groans, 'Five o'clock—have you forgotten our visit to the fish market?'

What a crazy idea! I was stupid to agree. A fish market is a fish market all the world over, with the exception of a few different species of fish—certainly not worth the trouble of getting up at five on a cold, wet morning. I can hear the rain pattering into the stone basin by the toilet. One of the temple devotees is the head of the local fish market and it was he, in a conversation with Mr Arito, who suggested that I might like to go. Knowing how fond I am of raw fish, the kind priest thought that I would be delighted to accept the invitation. Admittedly, I was enthusiastic about it last night, but now that the time has come, I think it was a mistake.

We put on our warmest clothes and shuffle out to the entrance. My toes are cold. If I ever return to Japan I shall take bed-socks with me to wear on the *tatami*. Yukiko smilingly brings us a cup of tea. She is staying behind to prepare breakfast but we tell her that we shall go straight back to bed when we come back and that she is not to whisk away the *futons*. Bent and miserable like the figures in a Hiroshige print of a wet day, we file out and bundle ourselves into Noriko's car. Splash, splash, splash through the streets to the market. Dark, dismal lorries block our way. Back into a side street. Puddles as big as ponds everywhere. The market. Well, there is nothing specifically Japanese about that. It is just a fish market. Well yes, perhaps it is different in one respect: the men are unusually quiet and even the auctions taking place urgently in odd corners are held in comparative silence. There are a few women about—of the sexless, *moujik* type one sees working on construction sites or in the rice-fields; women still do a lot of heavy work in Japan.

The head of the fish market comes up, bows and conducts us between the slithering masses of fish. I have seen most of them before: squid, bonito, flatfish, immense tunny-fish, silvery eels. Mr Arito remembers that tunny fish is my favourite and tells the head man. Immediately he orders two men to cut off a hunk for us. Two long, sharp knives are brought out and a couple of men deftly remove what looks like a six or seven-pound piece from the plump flanks—the colour of Japanese maples. It is worth a considerable amount of money.

'Would we like to see where the fish is stored?' the head man asks us. To be truthful, I wouldn't, but it is difficult to refuse. Unfortunately the storage plant is in another building and we have to climb several flights of stairs; on each floor, the head man throws open an ice-bound door and shows us identical masses of fish or, in other cases, fruit and meat, for he deals in many commodities. 'Come inside,' he urges, but it is freezing and this time I do refuse. Mr Arito is more polite; he steps inside and promptly catches a cold from which he will not recover until my departure.

We return to bed for a couple of hours. The tunny-fish is served for breakfast and also a piece of whale, whose identity I discover in time so as not to eat it. Few things make me sick, but whale-meat is one of them, as I had had occasion to discover in war time.

Noriko wants me to accompany her to see a 'famous Tokyo beautician', who makes up all the cinema stars, and who is at present in Kumamoto giving demonstrations at the leading department store. He is staying in a Japanese inn owned by Noriko's aunt and, judging by Noriko's excited descriptions of the young man, it is obvious that he has brought a whiff of the capital's sophistication to this provincial city. Noriko tells me that she has already met him in Tokyo, that she wishes to see him again and hopes to join forces with him, when she passes her hairdressing examination. So off she goes to see the young man and welcome him to Kumamoto, take him sight-seeing and generally make herself amiable. She does this naturally, without any affectation and it is brought home to me once again how persevering the Japanese are when they want something. Women, given the chance, are quite as ruthless as men.

The 'beautician', as Noriko calls him, occupies the star room in the little inn, overlooking a pool filled with goldfish and surrounded by rocks and miniature trees. He is still in his *yukata* when we are ushered in, and engaged in making up two of the maid-servants. He is young and slender, with a rosebud mouth and delicate, innocent face and features. His hands are as fine as a woman's. Noriko treats him like a brother and he reciprocates. We take him up the hill to see the Buddhist war memorial after he has dressed in a flamboyant red waistcoat and bow tie. I begin to believe that he is effeminate, he looks as delicate as a Japanese doll and I smile at him fraternally; evidently, I have misjudged the young man, my smile is misinterpreted and the most delightful eye-play begins which reminds me of adolescent encounters in Spain, another country where it is still difficult for young people to meet. The Japanese are very susceptible to eye-play and to the elusive romance of chance encounters which fit so well into their fantasy world.

In the afternoon, a young professor calls to take me to the university where I am to address a group of students who are studying English and American literature. Twenty of them are seated at a long table, the idea being that we should have a dialogue, but it is difficult to get them to open their mouths, with the exception of one intense young man with a prognathian jaw who is almost intelligible and asks strange, irrelevant questions about existentialism, communism, world peace and my opinion as to whether or not girls should wear cosmetics in college.

I ask them about their ambitions, their plans for the future. What do they want to do in life? The students remain tongue-tied. When I turn to the girls, the boys laugh cynically. It is a widespread notion that they only attend college to increase their value in the marriage market. The girls corroborate this by blushing and putting their hands in front of their faces. When they come to ask *me* questions, they are a curiously mixed bag, e.g.:

'Have you a husband and a son waiting for you at home?'
'Do you intend to remain celibate?'
'Do you drink alcohol?'
'What do you think of the reign of Elizabeth the first?'
'What is the best way to learn a foreign language?'
'What do you think of our pronunciation?'

'Can you tell us about the history of nineteenth-century England?'

On my way out, an earnest young man sidles up to me and asks me in a confidential whisper what I think about the Twist and do I dance it myself? A question I am repeatedly asked, all over Japan, is: 'Do you find us strange?' To this question I usually reply, 'The Japanese are normal human beings and I find nothing particularly "strange" about you. If you mean customs, of course you have your own, but this is natural, not strange. What is the use of travelling so far, just to find a sameness between foreign peoples and countries?' This puzzles, but does not satisfy them. I suspect that the word 'strange' is a euphemism for 'backward' or 'unprogressive', accusations which in underdeveloped countries sting even more than allusions to racial distinctions, but the Japanese have no justification for an inferiority complex.

I feel at home with people like the Aritos here in Kumamoto, Osaki-*san* in Shinkyo, or Hideto Mori in Tokyo, to quote a few examples, because they are content to be themselves; they imitate nobody; they are not static or backward, for each, in his own way, is striving towards perfection or improvement through religion or improved social conditions, but the striving comes from within and so they retain their Japanese individuality.

In the evening Al asks me to address another group of his pupils, employees of a manufacturing firm with a head office in the United States. They consist of young technicians, a couple of salesmen in their twenties and a girl secretary. I find them as tongue-tied and bashful as the students. They sit round a table with eyes lowered and only one of them, who occupies a managerial post, dares to talk and laugh and stir his colleagues out of their innate fear of losing face by making mistakes. I ask them what they want most from life. The girl wants 'to collect all the books in the world', one solemn young man wishes to become a first-rate technician in his speciality, another wants a 'fine sports car and a beautiful girl', the rest giggle, blush and remain silent.

After this exhausting session Al suggests that we go for a drink and we walk down to the main street into a bar kept by one of Noriko's cousins, a buxom, heavily made-up young woman who cultivates western sex-appeal while still retaining her Japanese unsophistication. Her two youthful assistants in beehive coiffures are admired by a couple of young men from the suburbs who have come into Kumamoto on business and are now rapidly getting drunk on cocktails.

One of them realizes despite his drunken haze that he has been presented with an opportunity for 'English conversation' and he asks me which part of the States I come from. The announcement that I am English provokes the same sort of pleased astonishment that an ornithologist derives from the discovery of a rare bird off its usual migratory course. 'How did you come here?' I tell my story and they nod with the slow emphasis of alcohol-fuddled minds. The conversation drifts on to the subject of Japanese wives. Noriko agrees that they are inclined to be jealous.

One of the young men from the country tells me that he has spent the afternoon in the library listening to records of his favourite clarinet player. Noriko's cousin asks us to choose from a pile of records and a sentimental American selection is played on the recorder. The young man confides to me that he would like to ask one of the bar-girls to go out with him, but he does not dare, because she is so beautiful. He is afraid she will refuse. I teach him the English proverb, 'Faint heart never won fair lady', to give him courage, which he repeats thoughtfully over and over again but he still does not dare to take the plunge and perhaps lose face.

Tadaima! Home at last, rather late—but not too late to avoid another 'English conversation'. Mrs Arito informs us that three small schoolgirls have been waiting for my return for over an hour. As usual she has given them tea and cakes. I have turned the temple into a tea-room since my arrival but Mrs Arito, tea-conscious as a vicar's wife, takes it all as a matter of course. The three gnome-like little girls kneeling in front of the low table rise quickly when I appear and their apple-pip eyes shine brightly. The eldest is fourteen—she looks about twelve—and her sisters are thirteen and eleven. I am surprised that their parents allow them out so late at night.

'Where do you live?' I ask them. 'On top of the hill,' replies the eldest. 'That is a long way for you to walk—aren't you afraid?' 'We are three strong girls,' says the eldest, flexing her small muscles. She wants to be a university professor of languages, she studies every night until midnight and rises at seven. She has no leisure now but once she enters university she hopes to find time for sport and drama. What does she do, what does she think about apart from her school subjects? She shakes her head vigorously. 'I think about my university entrance examination all the time.' 'And on Sundays?' 'My father takes us out to a restaurant for lunch. Then we go back home and he reads to us from the newspapers, usually about accidents—and then we discuss how they could have been avoided.'

Isamu brought out some magazines while I was sitting on the grass and showed me a picture of London. He seems to expect me to be pleased about this; he probably thinks, like many other people here, that I should be homesick. Isamu continues to sit beside me, grinning his friendship. I am never left alone for five minutes.

The Japanese are a gregarious people, like most orientals, yet they are also lonely, and a dark streak of pessimism runs through their character. They confide their secrets more readily to strangers than to their next of kin, or else to a trusted friend, although they do not always act upon a friend's advice. Family pressures are still strong. Even Al, who looks so modern and Americanized, has altered the whole course of his life, given up living in Hawaii where he had a good job, to come and be near his parents. He even allowed them to arrange his marriage for him. The so-called 'westernization' of Japan is still very much on the surface, it has not yet penetrated into the inner stream of consciousness; perhaps it never will—at least, not until there is a social revolution in the country comparable to the one which has shaken China out of similar beliefs.

Yukiko comes out to ask whether I would like to visit a carp-flag factory? The director of one has just rung up—he is a temple devotee—to invite us over.

It is the carp-flag season and gay streamers, swollen by passing winds, tug at slender poles like live fish at the end of a line. Some poles have five or six carp-flags dangling from them, one for every boy in the family; other houses display banners portraying historical characters. There are no banners for little girls who, when the custom was first invented, were not supposed to have to go out into the world and struggle like their brothers. (My belief is that Japanese boys do not struggle *enough*—against conventions, the boss system, parental tutelage.) The carp is a decorative symbol but, like so many things in Japan, it lacks substance, like the reflection of the moon in a temple pond.

The flag-factory is a family business conducted in a series of wooden shacks where perspiring men and women in white bonnets step daintily between brilliant pools of vegetable dyes—greens and reds and blues and yellows—bubbling like volcanoes in great black cauldrons. The workers step backwards and forwards with tiny cups of dye which they pour on to the long banners stretched out on a belt; each design is separated by a thick ridge of seaweed paste. When all the operations are completed the banners are taken out to dry in a tall covered outhouse.

Before we leave we are taken to the owner's house behind the factory to be introduced to his wife and to his old mother, who is lying ill on a *futon* in a darkened room. It occurs to me that this must be one of the most uncomfortable countries in the world to be ill in bed, immobilized like a dying fish at the bottom of a pond, with no possibility of being propped up.

After lunch we stop to watch girls practising judo at a judo temple; the head priest is a judo champion who has had a gymnasium built for the young people of his congregation. One of Al's friends introduces us to the burly priest who presents me with his visiting card; he calls himself a 'Reverend' like so many other modern priests. Al's friend is as large and broad as a *sumo* wrestler, pink-faced and rather sad-looking; perhaps this is because he cannot practise judo as often as he would like; he is a railway ticket-collector and works long hours at the station. He worked for the American Occupation Forces and keeps on saying 'Yes, Ma'am', 'No, Ma'am' to me, in respectfully nasal tones. He takes us to the gymnasium and watches impassively as three sturdy girls in white trousers are repeatedly thrown violently on to the ground by their instructor; valiantly, they rise, shake themselves like puppies and close in to take more punishment.

Noriko announces that she wants us to take our bath at her home (she may have had private information that the Aritos's water-heater system has gone wrong). We find her mother kneeling on the floor beside her calligraphy professor, a thoughtful man with long hair and a long, creased face. He gives me a demonstration of his art—an abstract interpretation of a poem on Mount Aso; his brush hovers over the paper before he starts, like a hawk about to swoop on its prey; but once the brush has touched the paper there is no hesitation, just a long continuous fluid movement. There are different brushes for different purposes. One is made of chicken's feathers and gives a delicate feathery effect; another is made of sheep's wool—'from under the armpits', I am told, and I wonder by what curious process of experimentation this art secret was originally discovered. . . .

Tadaima! Mr Arito is about to leave the temple to visit a house where he is expected to recite the monthly *sutra* for the dead; he says that we can go with him, if we like. 'Okay?' inquires Noriko, with one shoe on and one shoe off. 'Okay,' I reply and we go back to the car.

Mr Arito telephones in order to make sure that my alien presence will not be too much of a shock. The house is a tiny wooden one not unlike the tramcar driver's home, in an unlighted street on the fringe of the town. The family consists of an elderly mother (whose husband, an army officer, died six years ago; it is for the repose of his soul that the *sutra* is to be intoned) her daughter and her son, a young man about thirty who teaches English in a junior high school. He speaks English remarkably well and we talk together while Mr Arito disappears into a backroom, lights the candles in the Buddhist alcove, accompanied by the mother and sister and proceeds with the Saddharna Pundarika *sutra*. From time to time he interrupts his reading and rings a small handbell. The womenfolk kneel behind him with heads bowed. This ceremony is repeated every month; at the conclusion of it the priest is invited to drink tea and eat cakes in the living-room and the mother discreetly slips two or three hundred-yen notes into his hand. (Mr Arito had two more families to visit—so that the evening, I sordidly calculated, would profit him by about a pound. Well, that is *one* source of revenue, but admittedly it is a mere trickle.)

I express the hope that I am not preventing the son from attending the ceremony. He smiles and shakes his head. 'Oh no, not at all,' he replies, 'because, you see, I am a Christian. Some neighbours told me about it and I became interested. Now we go to the Lutheran church together. Not all my friends know that I have been converted. They are not interested in religion.'

'I was a little afraid when the priest rang up,' the young man confides to me now that we are on friendly terms, 'and asked if he could bring a foreigner to our house. We have never had one before. As you see, our house is very poor and there is nothing of interest in it.' I explained that I was interested in people and that I was grateful to him for letting me cross his threshold. He laughed happily; he had never spoken to a western Christian before and I regretted that on this occasion he had not met a more fervent upholder of the creed. Mr Arito looked at us quizzically and smiled as if he understood, without the need for words, what was passing in our minds. I tried to draw out the sister, a clerical worker in a town office but she was too bashful and modest in the presence of her mother. It was strange, and very Japanese, to be gathered together so amicably in the name of two such different prophets.

The last few days have passed all too quickly. It has been warm, and I have been too lazy to keep up my diary. We have been to Mount Aso and to a hot springs resort, we have attended a sixty-first birthday party, a celebration at which a man is supposed to be reborn—and a wedding, in an adjacent temple, for which Mr Arito turned up in a suit and felt hat, which he left behind, for he is not used to wearing one.

We have visited a boys' orphanage run by American missionaries and had lunch in a tea-house owned by one of Al's pupils, where we ate cold pale green and white noodles tastefully draped round blocks of ice like seaweed over an iceberg.

I have seen saddled cows in country lanes driven by women in starched white bonnets, and shoe-shine women in wide straw hats in the main town square; I have seen a geisha alight from an old-fashioned rickshaw (they are the only people who make use of them) and two lumps of salt placed at the entrance of a restaurant to chase away evil spirits. . . . Tonight I saw a lacquered tray, over a yard long, filled with succulent *sushi*, a gift from Noriko's mother, who came in a silvery grey kimono to attend the farewell party organized in my honour.

Presents are showered upon me: beautiful dolls, paper lanterns shaped like pagodas, a musical-box that plays a tune I heard at the *koto* party . . . even Isomo has brought a gift: a pair of lacquered chopsticks and miniature *geta*. After dinner Miyokoshi brings out the tape-recorder and we record songs . . . I am taught '*Sakura*', the cherry-blossom song, and join with the rest, in Japanese, with a peculiar accent. The Aritos bring out a large visitor's book and I write a few gushing but sincere phrases; Noriko is requested to translate but she breaks down in tears. We are all sad.

Beppu to Kobe

*M*y last morning. It is the anniversary of the day when Nichiren received his great inspiration as he contemplated the sunrise and so, every year, his devotees ascend a mountain and play their racquet-shaped drums before the rising sun.

We rose before five and Noriko drove us up the hill where a large statue of Nichiren was erected in 1958. About fifty people, dispersed in small groups, are already playing their drums, facing the golden rim of the quickly rising sun. The early morning mists hang like cobwebs between the pine trees obliterating the city below. A priest intones a *sutra*, the drums play faster and faster to assist the birth of the sun which bursts suddenly from the soft grey placenta of cloud, throwing out gigantic golden spokes, which transfigure our wan faces. This, I felt, is the Life-Giver, the only God that matters, and I joined whole-heartedly in the age-old worship.

Yukiko had stayed behind to make us a large chicken and onion omelette for breakfast. We were joined at this meal by Mr Arito's brother, who spoke lengthily and sententiously on the subject of world peace. Mr Arito busied himself packing my presents into a box. Yukiko discovered a tear in my skirt which was hurriedly mended before we raced to the station in Noriko's car. Al had already secured a place in the queue, for my train to Beppu had no reserved coaches. Noriko's mother was there, the yellow-toothed teacher with his female companion, and Isamu in his school uniform, murmuring '*bon voyage*' and shaking my hand in western style.

Japanese trains never stay long in a station and in the excitement of securing a seat, there was hardly any time for emotion. I take a picture of the group on the platform. My eyes pass over each one of them with varying depths of emotion; their eyes, too, are bright and trembling. I suddenly realize that the one important, precious thing our eyes have in common, in spite of their different shape, is the capacity to shed tears.

Spring is not a nostalgic season and soon the sadness of parting is effaced by a new sentiment: admiration for the beauty of the landscape from Kumamoto to Beppu.

Immense blue-grey boulders streaked with Gorgonzola-green patches of lichen precede the entrance to jet black caverns in which candles flicker like dragons' eyes in the awesome interior; a minute crimson *torii* in the valley below announces the imminent presence of gods. Tassels of wistaria festoon the hills. Sprightly rivers, translucent blue, green and pink, foam and eddy between tall cliffs. Villages of farm dwellings, before which trays of red and white beans are drying in the sun, flash past like toys on a conveyor belt; proud little men in cone-shaped straw hats drive motor ploughs through rills of chocolate mud while their less fortunate neighbours make do with the slow churning of impassive buffaloes; from time to time they meet and cross one another's path as so many other phases of old and new meet and run side by side in Japan.

Women in long rubber boots bend at right angles over silver rice-fields in which clouds are gently mirrored as they float by in the breeze, the only stable figures in a moving landscape. Nobody straightens up to wave when our train goes by as they would in Spain or Italy. Work is work and play is play. Only the carp flags respond to our festive mood, stretching and pulling on their flexible poles, now thin and starved, now puffed and pompous, according to the caprice of the wind. In the background layers of misty mountains bathe in a mother-of-pearl haze; like Japanese ghosts, they have no feet.

It is spring and everything looks young, even the passengers on the train, most of whom appear to be honeymoon couples; demure girls in white helmet hats and brand new dresses; elegant young men in new suits with new expressions on their faces. A few couples behave naturally, but most of them are self-conscious and have not yet settled down to their new state; all of them behave with the utmost decorum.

For a few minutes before we reach Beppu, enclosed between steep hills, our train zigzags along the edge of a deep blue sea upon which a fleet of tiny boats, each one provided with one triangular sail, like clipped butterflies, are neatly poised upon pointed waves. I have reserved a berth in a first-class cabin and I anticipate the pleasure of dining on board and writing a few letters overlooking a harbour of twinkling lights before we sail at 11 p.m.—a bright ending to my stay on Kyushu island.

Alas, such luxury is not to be. This is not a well-appointed Hellenic cruise in the Mediterranean but a utilitarian little voyage across the Inland Sea in the company of hundreds of school children. There is no question of dining on board—we shall not be allowed on until 10 p.m., one hour before the boat sails again for Kobe. I learn later that the boat has not yet *arrived* from Kobe and that the hard-worked crew will only have one hour in which to clean up and prepare for the new flow of passengers. I doubt whether such efficiency could be matched in the West!

I leave my luggage in the shipping company's office and, after a walk round the harbour, wander up one of the main streets to the arcades where shops will remain open and dazzling until after our boat sails. I buy a tiny nude *kokeshi*, without arms or breasts, eyes modestly lowered, a patch of towel between her legs and a tub of water by her side. '*Sento*' (bath-house), I murmur to the salesgirls; they squeal with laughter and put their little hands in front of their blushing faces. I also buy a lot of basketwork—it is as fine as filigree in Beppu, and postcards of people buried up to their necks in Beppu's curative sands.

Some of the people who come here for these peculiar sand-baths are roaming round the shops, dressed in identical khaki-coloured *tanzen*; I thought they were pilgrims until I noticed that there were many young couples among them. Pilgrims are usually elderly, single, and of the female sex. I then remembered that Japanese hotel guests are given a 'uniform' which facilitates shopping expeditions—they give their names to the shopkeepers who send the bills up later to the hotel. The souvenir-craze has caught on in Japan even more than in the West, because the Japanese always have been inclined to give presents on the slightest pretext. I pass for the second time before the shop where I bought my nude *kokeshi* and the salesgirls wave and smile broadly. When I feel hungry I part the strips of a blue curtain, walk into a small restaurant and sit on a stool at a long narrow table in the company of other visitors.

There are antique shops in the main streets, for American tourists, and mysterious 'Tea-rooms' for American Forces personnel. A boy hands me a piece of blue and white paper on which I read:

DE LUXE TEA ROOM D E N E N
W E L C O M E

Deluxe room . . . DENEN is home of soldiers. THE FIRST refresh Yourself WITH EXCELLENT MUSIC NICE DRINKS STATESIDE COCKTAILS AND BEER AND COMFORTABLE FEELINGS
The notice did not go on to say what was supposed to happen after 'THE FIRST' and the inculcation of 'COMFORTABLE FEELINGS', but the message was more discreet than the vulgar advertisements for lecherous tourists which one so often sees in Tokyo newspapers, but I have been told that the ambiguous advertisements for massage sound more promising than they are in fact, e.g.:

'Enjoy & refresh yourself! Will guarantee complete recovery from weariness after a hard day's work, travelling, over-coming normal fatigue or effects of preceding night's party. Experienced attractive masseuses are awaiting your visit!! Open from 2 p.m. daily'

'Complete massage given by pretty girls. See our luxurious private rooms'

'Turkish bath. Deluxe mood at modest charge. Romantic bath and charming masseuses will soothe your fatigue'.

Another Turkish bath advertises a 'decent bar and the beauties always await your patronage'.

When I get back to the shipping office by the quayside I find the place swarming with schoolboys and girls and adults, and rever-berating with canned music, laughter and chatter; the official with whom I left my luggage indicates by sign language that it has already been sent on board. There is a queue six deep on the left; the right-hand side, with its benches and fewer, more casual-looking passengers, has a more first-class air about it.

To make sure I ask a man in the queue: 'Is this the queue for the first-class cabins?' He replies without looking at me, 'Maybe.' I spy an intense-looking young bespectacled American in the com-pany of a Japanese seated on one of the benches and I renew my request. The young American puts me right—the queue is *not* for first-class passengers, who are to be allowed on board within a few minutes, and I must obtain a piece of paper in exchange for my ticket. He amiably obtains this for me as he speaks Japanese fluently. He is a Fulbright scholar, travelling with his Japanese teacher; they have been visiting potters in various parts of Kyushu and have bought some interesting specimens. The young American is the first and only person I met in Japan who actually *likes* Tokyo. 'The pace is just right for me,' he says.

After a walk on the small deck and a brief look at the disappearing lights of the harbour—all harbours look alike to me—with the exception of a select few like Hong Kong and Vigo—I find my cabin and begin to undress. What luck, I have the place to myself! The boat glides smoothly through the oily sea, the night is warm. I am in my nightdress, in the middle of washing, when a vigorous knock on the door announces that I shall not be alone after all. I hastily throw a dressing-gown over my shoulders and open to a steward armed with several pieces of luggage, followed by a honeymoon couple—a helmet-hatted girl and her husband wearing one of those impeccable suits that look as if they had just been pressed. I wave my arms in an inward gesture intended to convey hospitable feelings; for a split second the young couple stand at the door transfixed. They do not, or dare not, speak a word of English and they are obviously confused and embarrassed to have to share their cabin, and perhaps the first night of their honeymoon, with an alien.

I finish my toilet rapidly and climb up to my upper berth, leaving the cabin free for the newly-weds who hardly exchange a word. The young husband discreetly leaves the cabin while his wife undresses, an operation which takes place behind closed curtains. I resolve to rise before six, when the scenery is supposed to be at its best. I do not sleep, in spite of ear plugs.

The steward brings in a pot of tea and three little bowls just after 5.30 a.m. The young husband is already up and washing laboriously; it always seems to me that orientals take more time over their toilet than we do—they certainly take far more time than I do. I am immobilized in my upper berth while the young man brushes his teeth one by one, shaves meticulously, brushes his hair endlessly, looks into the mirror, all this silently, while his wife is still hidden behind curtains. Frantic with impatience I take a bold downward plunge and sit by the window, looking out to sea. This sends the young man out into the corridor. The wife peeps out then closes the curtains again. From the movements of the curtain I can see that she is dressing in her berth. Later, before going up on deck, I turn round and wish them: *Sayonara-otasshade!* (good-bye, good luck). They smile, bow, and look pleased.

The scenery is disappointing. We pass several small islands, several fleets of fishing boats and an American tanker. The islands are rather bare and the coast does not compare with the beauties of Miyajima. I had expected something more exciting, like the coral islands of the Moluccas or the gorgeous tropical coastline of Sumatra. The young Japanese around me are busy taking photographs of everything in sight and almost out of sight; surely those distant, hazy blobs of boats will never come out, not even with the best Japanese camera!

PART IV

Northern

Japan

Technicians in Niigata

O am on my way to Niigata, on the north-west coast of Japan, a city of 300,000 inhabitants, where I am to meet a different type of Japanese from those I have been staying with up to now: the scientifically bent younger generation.

My future host, Yoshiyuki, had replied to my letter in the *Asahi Evening News:* 'I am glad to inform you that you may be able to stay at our city in the Japanese style. . . . I am 26 years old and chemical engineer. I am not married but don't worry about your lodging, because I have many friends who are married and have a comfortable home. They could offer, with glad, their house for your lodging. I already appointed them for your lodging, adding this I could offer you our dormitory if you would like to, our rooms are strictly individual. . . . You can see the location of our city on the map, strictly longitude East of Greenwich 139° E and 38° N. . . . I am working at chemical factory where we produce many chemicals and chemical fertilizers. I fear I couldn't tell you my wishes enough, please come our beautiful country.'

I was intrigued by the idea of staying in a dormitory, even for one night, to see what living conditions are like in them. Yoshiyuki informed me in his next letter that this would be arranged, and that I could also stay on the company's housing estate, in the home of a married colleague who was studying French and eager to converse with me in this language. Would I like to stay on a farm? If so, we could go to Sado island where the French-speaking colleague had relatives. Sado island has the reputation of being very beautiful; it is rich in folk-songs and dances and many classical poems extol its charms. Altogether, my visit north promises to be interesting.

There was no limited express train to Niigata (I was informed that there would be one within three months) and so I was faced by a ten-hour journey in a full compartment, with no dining-car to resort to, food being available in luncheon boxes bought for a couple of hundred *yen* at the main stations; gaily wrapped two-tiered boxes containing tit-bits of fish and pickles in the upper compartment, rice and a plastic tube of soy sauce in the lower one.

I took the train at Ueno station, which does not cater for foreigners like the Central station (the north has fewer advertised attractions than the south of Japan—above all, it has nothing that compares with Kyoto) and there is no pretence at propaganda. I was, for the first time, dumped unceremoniously at the station by a taxi-driver who did not find me a porter, and when I did find one, he ambled along unconcernedly, very unlike the smart-stepping 'Red Caps' of Central station. There are less elegant kimonos to be seen on the platform and in the train, and the passengers appear to be either less informed about family planning than those of the stream-lined expresses or more inclined to take their progeny with them when they travel; there are many infants who climb on the seats and pass sticky hands through my hair until they get their first glimpse of snow when, with delighted cries of: '*Yuki!*' they stick their hands on to the window-panes instead.

Spring has not yet arrived in the north where nature is sterner and more majestic. The Japan Alps with their snow-capped peaks and ranges soar above desolate valleys where all is grey and brown and weary-looking, untouched by the youth of the new year. It is raining hard and the peasants in the fields are concealed in straw pokes and cloaks. They used to wear straw boots but now they can afford rubber ones which are less picturesque for tourists; the straw specimens are finding their way into folk-museums where they will no doubt soon be followed by the straw hoods and capes. Young people with skis get out at various stations on the way. My travelling companions are very 'traditional Japanese' and we cannot converse; they eye me stealthily when I open my luncheon box and are surprised to see me enjoy the contents with chopsticks and a knowledgeable air.

It is still raining when I reach Niigata station. Once again, I am the only westerner on the train and my host identifies me easily. He is accompanied by Mr Morito, his French-speaking colleague, and together they escort me to the station cafeteria for a preliminary talk. Yoshiyuki is a nice-looking young man with pleasant, easy manners; there is no old-fashioned reserve about him; he is consciously trying to be 'modern-style Japanese' with American inclinations, sartorial and otherwise.

Mr Morito, who is two or three years older, is less of an extrovert; he speaks more softly, smiles less broadly. He belongs to the 'intense' type of Japanese and he has had the merit to learn French all by himself, with the aid of records. I am the first person he has ever had the opportunity of speaking to in that language and I am surprised at his excellent pronunciation. He tells me that he hopes to win a scholarship offered by the French Government to Japanese technicians with a knowledge of French; he has already written to several firms in France and he shows me the polite but negative replies with their: 'If, in the future, etc.' which he pathetically finds 'not discouraging'.

Yoshiyuki hopes to go to the United States. He follows classes at the American Cultural Centre of Niigata and gets up at 6.20 every morning to listen to the daily English-by-radio class broadcast by NHK. He is so anxious to study and 'improve himself' that he has broken with a too demanding girl-friend, after consultation with his closest men friends, so that he may give more time to his after-work studies. (Another difficulty about the girl-friend situation, which he confides to me later when I have attained the rank of a confidante, is that he is afraid of making her pregnant; like many young Japanese, whom one had imagined would be clinically knowledgeable on the subject, he knows little about birth-control and is anxious to know what we do about it in the West.)

Mr Morito wishes me to spend a couple of nights in his house and so, after a coffee and a chat, we take a bus into town and then another one to the chemical company's housing estate on the outskirts.

Niigata is a clean, modern city; much of this is accounted for by a great fire which burned down the older part of the town eight years ago; there seems to be only one slummy part left, wooden shacks along an evil-smelling canal, similar to those I have seen in Tokyo.

The green-uniformed bus conductresses call out 'orrye, orrye', as in other parts of Japan; the passengers in neat, drab gabardines returning home from work look the same as their fellows in Tokyo. I mention this because several people in Tokyo—all of them Japanese—who had never been up north, talked about these regions as if they were backward and primitive. I was to find no trace of this, even in the villages outside the town. For a visiting tourist in search of vivid local colour, Niigata is definitely not primitive enough, not even 'typically Japanese'.

At the end of the bus journey, however, I *did* find something typically Japanese: a muddy lane leading up to the housing estate. This was, of course, a much smaller estate than the Tokyo show-piece I had been taken to by Miss Harada; it is divided into various classes of dwellings: four-storeyed blocks of flats marked with large black letters, individual bungalows for higher grade staff, and rows of terraced two-storeyed houses with pocket handkerchief gardens, for the others. Mr Morito, his wife and two-year-old son, live in one of the latter, at a nominal cost of about ten shillings a month. His salary is less than half what a British engineer would earn.

The house consists of a living-room and tiny kitchen separated by a divider on the ground floor, and two small *tatami*-covered rooms on the first floor. There is a public bath for the whole estate at the end of the unpaved road; 'ladies' hours' are from 6.30 to 8.30 p.m. There is no television set in this house, but a recorder which Mr Morito uses for his French lessons.

He shows me his books, which have probably cost him quite a lot of money, before his wife comes in with a young neighbour who will help her prepare the special supper planned in my hon-our. Mr Morito's wife is from Hokkaido; she is pretty, with a fair complexion and a bright, unsophisticated smile; they met when they were classmates; a typical 'young generation' romance.

As the space is so limited, Yoshiyuki and I are requested to go for a walk until supper time. It is raining hard and the roads are muddy; we trudge round and round and Yoshiyuki points out his factory in the distance; he evidently feels that he 'belongs'—that is where his future lies, and he is proud of his company's achievements. He is sorry that the new plant is not yet completed and that I shall therefore not be able to see it; as he is in the design department he is familiar with every detail of the new construction. Tomorrow, he tells me emphatically, as if he regretted that he could not do so today, he will introduce me to his section manager and I shall be shown round the factory. I anticipate this visit with slight fore-boding and hope that it will not be too technical.

Yoshiyuki's parents live in Kyushu and his elder brother looks after them, thus freeing the more fortunate younger sons. Yoshi-yuki has not seen his parents since he graduated from Tokyo University three years ago and joined this firm. He only gets four days' holiday a year and the fare is costly. . . .

I ask him how he obtained his present job and he explains that technicians are at a premium in Japan and that many large firms invite university students, even before they have actually graduated, to inspect their works and become interested in the possibility of joining them as soon as they have obtained their diploma or degree. The Niigata firm had paid Yoshiyuki's fare up from Tokyo and he had decided that there was a future in it. His present salary is about £30 a month but he manages to save as he lives in the firm's dormitory, takes most of his meals in the canteen, and uses a bicycle for transport to and from town and on his holidays. His hobbies are: English, playing the guitar and dancing. The study of English is of course useful to him in his career. Will his firm allow him to go to the United States? How will he go? He looked vague when I asked him these practical questions.

My host rises early and goes off to work on his bicycle, in the rain. I hear the factory sirens at 7.30 a.m. and peer out through the window on to the rapidly accumulating puddles in the road. An hour later my hostess runs upstairs to announce: 'Breakfast-ready.' She learned some English at school but is afraid to use the little she knows. Her mother has arrived, perhaps she lives near, and she helps to look after the crawling two-year-old while her daughter serves me with fried eggs, rice, and seaweed. I cannot stay on here, giving so much trouble, in such a cramped space, although, I daresay, Mr Morito would like to have more French conversation lessons. When he studies in the evening the wife goes to a next-door neighbour so as not to disturb him.

Conversation being difficult, I retire to my room and try to read on the flat *futon*. At ten o'clock, I hear the voice of a young man downstairs and, soon after, my hostess comes up with a paper bearing a message from the visitor, Mr Hiroyuki, a colleague of Yoshiyuki's who has kindly come to take me out sightseeing. But I cannot go sightseeing in the pouring rain—and what is there to see in Niigata anyway, except people—so I decline the offer on a return slip of paper. I do not feel in the mood for a prolonged 'English conversation' in some dim espresso bar in the city.

It clears up, in a half-hearted way, just before noon and I paddle through the mud, to queue up for the town bus along with a dozen people in mackintoshes and white rubber boots. We pay the little conductress before climbing into the bus. It is a single-decker and, like the passengers, spotlessly clean.

In town, I lunch at the department store, which has a large restaurant on the fourth floor divided into a western-style self-service room, a row of *tatami* rooms divided by wooden partitions, and a *sushi* counter where I order my favourite tunny-fish and halibut. From the roof-garden and children's playground there is a panoramic view of the city and distant sea, flat and uninteresting, without trees or noticeable landmarks. It gives me nothing to think about.

After my *sushi* lunch, I take a taxi to the chemical factory outside the town, built near the river and a railway track. It is modern, spacious, brightly polished. I am taken to an office on the first floor and soon Yoshiyuki and Morito appear in the rubber boots they wear on the job, to inform me that the section manager will come and see me and show me round the factory. A number of foreigners come to see the factory every year, but I must be one of the first non-technical ones to do so.

The section manager arrives and I am formally introduced. He is a lean man in his early fifties with greying hair, spectacles and the precise, Teutonic manner of middle-aged Japanese gentlemen who have a rank to uphold. The manager is a Rotarian and hospitably inclined towards foreigners; he speaks fairly good English and he prepares to take over from my young hosts in the paternalistic way common to so many Japanese bosses. Yoshiyuki asks him if it is all right for me to stay for a night in the dormitory, and his 'boss' nods gravely while I bluntly explain that it will be an added experience for me. To my surprise, the boss invites me to spend a night in his own home—presumably so that I shall have a taste of life in the upper as well as the lower spheres of the firm's personnel.

First I must endure a long lecture on the chemical processes which take place in the factory, given by the manager, and demonstrated by means of a device on the wall that lights up when certain buttons are pressed to show various letters and numbers; I make an effort to follow but soon my unscientific mind becomes blank, the necessary connexions are not being made in my brain which can only register human, not chemical relationships.

Now for a visit to the factory in a high wind. Undoubtedly there is a certain grandeur about these vast halls filled with throbbing machines from Germany, Great Britain and the United States, the high towers from where particles of chemical fertilizer drop in cascades of shiny white particles, fine as the sand used for *bonseki* pictures on lacquered trays. They symbolize the opposite poles of

Japanese achievement: the small-scale works of artists bent over brush and potter's wheel, and the large-scale products of industry being turned out by Japan's chemists, scientists and technicians. In the packaging department, a group of women workers in white caps and jeans are sorting out bales of fertilizer destined for various Asian countries; Japan is helping to develop her neighbours. Soon her steel may help to develop Siberia. In the industrial sectors of the nation one detects the sense of purpose, the desire for compensation, after her military defeat, that has made Japan the fourth largest industrial country in the world and the equal of the industrialized West. It is evident that to have reached this point, the qualities I have observed in the engineers of this factory must be repeated in many others spread over the country: their sense of loyalty and pride, their diligence and sense of discipline.

I am introduced, over tea and cakes in the office, to two other engineers and the conversation becomes more general. The lives of the young men are very much absorbed in their work and no doubt this single-mindedness accounts for much of the country's present prosperity. I am told, however, that pure scientific research is sometimes hampered by too individualistic an approach; the average Japanese scientist is not willing to share his discoveries and co-operate with his colleagues.

The manager's shiny black car glides up to the front door. I am borne off in triumph and my young hosts of yesterday and tomorrow wave with a disappointed smile; they will have no 'English conversation' tonight; that pleasure is reserved for their boss, whose chauffeur drives us first to my humble home on the estate to pick up some clothes and enable me to change into something more appropriate to my rise in social status.

While I am upstairs changing, the manager sits on the *tatami* with Mrs Morito and fondles the little boy, to whom apparently he is the equivalent of a godfather. He was the *nakodo* for the Morito's wedding arrangements. Now I begin to understand why he feels he should entertain me—a boss-cum-*nakodo* has obligations towards his protégés, and he is supposed to take a personal interest in their lives. Mrs Morito talks and laughs with him easily, without any trace of obsequiousness.

The manager lives in a newly built, modern-style house in which we sit upon chairs but sleep upon *futons*. Since his wife has not been warned of my arrival I shall be taken out to dinner at the new

western-style hotel opposite the station. In the meantime, strawberry and cream sponge cakes and tea are served in the drawing-
room overlooking a garden full of rose-bushes, ordered via a Tokyo
nurseryman from abroad. Roses and angling are the manager's
hobbies; his wife makes dolls; she is of the old-fashioned, polite,
bending-from-the-waist type of Japanese housewife, a little flustered by my visit, embarrassed not to be able to speak any English.
The son from Tokyo is glued to the television. The atmosphere is
'old-style Japanese'; father firmly in command, wife in background,
and no demonstrativeness shown between the members of the
family.

After the western-style meal, with which we drink *sake*, we take
coffee in a lounge filled with wedding guests, the men in tails, the
ladies in kimono with a black background and five large dots
symbolic of the felicities of married life. Are there no geishas in
Niigata, I ask my host; his expression softens immediately. Am I
interested? In that case, he will take me to see some local dancing
by the *maiko* at a tea-house to which he often escorts foreign
guests.

At the tea-house, the manager is treated like an old friend. A
middle-aged 'geisha controller' sits and talks to us over tea, beer
and cakes, while the *maiko* are summoned. The manager becomes
friendly and relaxed in this congenial atmosphere, far more so than
at home. He removes his jacket, squats on the *tatami*, smokes,
drinks and laughs—all the starch has gone out of him.

Three delicious little *maiko* arrive at last; I look forward to the
discreet knock, the slow pushing back of the sliding-door, the first
glimpse of glittering ornaments on the shiny black wigs as they
tilt their pretty little heads, kneel on the *tatami* and, fan in delicate
hand, await the signal to come in and entertain us. The two elder
girls are sixteen years old, pale and demure, the third one is fifteen,
round-faced and schoolgirlish—she has only been training for a
month. They wear gorgeous, sophisticted kimonos and *obis* but
they still look like little girls in fancy-dress. We treat them like
children, and ply them with cakes until it is time for them to show
me three dances from Sado. The older woman plays the *samisen* and
rebukes the youngest for a mistake she makes in one of the dances;
the little girl blushes underneath her make-up; they still have a long
way to go before they become accomplished dancers but they show
promise and are as pretty as an oriental dream.

Sunday morning. The manager has been up since 6 a.m. working in the garden. I take a Japanese bath before an immense breakfast and a visit to the city by car. The gardens round a shrine attract many visitors, it is the only green patch in Niigata. It is sunny and it would be nice to sit on a café terrace and watch people passing by, but Japan has not adopted Continental-style outdoor cafés and there is nowhere to sit except in gloomy coffee bars. There is a small aviary in the gardens and three little schoolgirls are sitting in front of it, painting a peacock. I admire their bold use of colour and sense of form. A few yards away I am astonished to see a statue of a dog on a pedestal, a typical Japanese breed, like a plebeian chow. A long inscription on a tablet relates how the original, Tamako, saved his master's life on no less than three occasions when he was climbing the Japan Alps. The Mayor of Niigata very rightly thought that these exploits justified the raising of a memorial.

Before lunch, we drive the manager's son, who is returning to Tokyo, to the airport. Father and son do not speak during the drive, and they nod a casual good-bye before parting. Yoshiyuki has been invited to lunch, which the manager's wife has evidently spent the entire morning preparing. During lunch all heads are turned towards the television set, to watch the progress of an amateur singing contest. I offer to help clear up, but this is refused. I indicate by gestures that there is a lot of work involved and I place an arm round my hostess's frail shoulders; my gesture has a surprising effect. My hostess almost crumples up, tears come to her eyes, and she pats my arm. I realize from her response that although she is not accustomed to such treatment, she is not averse to signs of affection and probably could do with more from her husband. In her intuitive Japanese way, she has understood what I am thinking and her eyes are bright with gratitude.

Even Yoshiyuki is observant in such matters; as we walk along the banks of the river, after picking up a colleague who wishes to join in the 'English conversation', he remarks that there are still many 'old-style' Japanese husbands about. He wants to marry a modern girl, he says, with outside interests, with whom he can go walking and hiking. But before that, he wants to have 'many adventures'. . . .

There is more sharing of domestic tasks among the young of the lower-income groups. In the course of our walk we come across a young couple, their heads wrapped in a towel, beating *tatami* mats out in the street. In this spring-cleaning operation the husband was taking as active a part as his wife.

I have never been to a Japanese strip-tease show; I thought that these were confined to Tokyo and foreign visitors but there is one in Niigata and curiosity prompts me to look inside. My escorts have never seen one either and they are more self-conscious than I am.

The all-male audience is definitely low-class—a sprinkling of workmen, perhaps a few small tradesmen and a group of country louts. They are too absorbed to notice the entrance of a foreign female. The strip-tease girls—five of them altogether—are more bosomy than the average Japanese. Two of them look like wet-nurses. As I have never been to a similar show before, I have no basis of comparison, but I thought that the bosomy girls with their fixed smile and occasional pale imitation of an Arabian belly-dance were not particularly sexy. One hand was modestly maintained between their legs. At one point, a plump girl bent over the footlights to offer a cigarette to the simian-looking males in the front row. All except one were too bashful to accept it; the girl smiled and spoke to them coaxingly, more like a sister than a sex symbol.

Four of the girls were dressed in western style but the fifth wore a kimono and Japanese wig. My reaction, which had been neutral during the preceding performances, suddenly changed; I felt repelled and nauseated, so firmly has the kimono become associated in my mind with a mythical *princesse lointaine*. In subsequent conversations with western males, I discovered that their reaction was similar to mine.

Still pursuing my sociological explorations, Yoshiyuki escorts me to a dance-hall on the floor above the American Cultural Centre. It is very similar to the one in Kumamoto. At the entrance, I leave my handbag with the cloakroom attendants, who look about fifteen years old, and they wrap it ceremoniously in a plastic *furoshiki* to which they pin a number. The toilets are mixed, as in every other Japanese public place. The room is packed with informally dressed adolescents. Some couples dance cheek to cheek. There is little air and I make for a window. The dance-hall is in the street next to the narrow one in which I watched the *maiko* dance last night in their traditional style tea-house. Here, only a few yards away, their modern sisters in skirts and sweaters are jiving with youthful partners while they, no doubt, are performing before sallow-faced gentlemen old enough to be their fathers and grand-fathers.

I did not wish to stay too long in the suffocating dance-hall, as tomorrow we are leaving for Sado by the early morning boat. A young woman, Miss Tanabe, is accompanying us, with her mother, to introduce us to our farm-hosts and help with the domestic arrangements. As far as I can gather, Miss Tanabe is an ex-school-mate of Mrs Morito's and related to the Sado people.

We board a bus and stop at the factory gates; from here a five-minutes walk up the road takes us to the dormitory, or hostel, set back from the road in three connecting wings housing eighty employees.

We leave our shoes at the entrance and place them in a bunker marked with the individual names of each employee; Yoshiyuki hands me a new pair of slippers which he has inscribed with my name. Several young men are playing ping-pong in the central wing; to the right, on the ground floor, are the bathrooms (ladies' hour has long passed so that I have to wash in an adjacent room provided with wash-bashins over which Yoshiyuki stands guard). Beyond this is a laundry with three small washing and drying machines and ironing-boards, and a tiled toilet divided into several compartments.

I find that I have been allocated a room between Yoshiyuki and Hiroyuki, who is on night shift. The rooms are all the same, and look on to a courtyard. On the opposite side of the courtyard are the canteen and the kitchen. 'I have asked the servant girls not to make a noise and wake you up. They start work very early,' said Yoshiyuki. I was touched by his solicitude just as I was touched next morning to see that his instructions were being carried out; from my window I could see a little army of female domestic staff moving about on tiptoe in the kitchen, speaking in whispers.

Each room in the hostel consists of a microscopic 'hall' only just big enough for one person to stand in and remove his shoes before stepping on to the *tatami*; a shelf is provided in this hall for a plastic wash basin and towels. The only piece of furniture in the room was a low table upon which Yoshiyuki had placed a bowl of goldfish borrowed from an absent colleague, to provide 'an artistic touch', as he put it. I was afraid I should knock them over during the night, if not before; there was not enough space for a human being *and* goldfish in that doll's house room. 'Put them out in the corridor if they are in the way,' suggested Yoshiyuki.

The paper-covered partition on the corridor side of the room had a cunning one foot high sliding door at the base through which the servants pass milk, newspapers, etc., in the morning. A similar sliding door on the window side of the room concealed a built-in 'larder' in which the thoughtful Yoshiyuki had placed a loaf of sliced bread, a packet of butter, a bottle of milk and a pot of marmalade for my breakfast, as he realized I would probably not wish to rise as early as the factory employees and would prefer the privacy of my little room.

The *futon*—an extremely thin one—is kept with the rest of the bedding in one of two built-in cupboards, the second serves as a wardrobe. 'It gets so hot in the summer that we sleep directly on the *tatami* without a *futon*,' Yoshiyuki told me.

Hiroyuki popped his head round the door to ask me whether I could do with an extra cushion. This was the young man who had offered to take me sightseeing the day before. Yoshiyuki asked him into his room for a glass of canned beer. He is tall, gentle, rather shy, a graduate of Niigata University and only twenty-two years old; his parents live in a village about an hour from town and he suggests that we pay them a visit upon my return from Sado, so that I may 'meet some rural people'.

Sado island

Our little steamer, camouflaged under a gay canopy of red and white streamers, looks as though it had been chartered by a group of wedding parties but this must be an everyday Japanese excursion custom, because postcards are on sale everywhere illustrating a departure similar to ours, under the same weight of bunting. Friends on shore continue to throw out more and more streamers until they reach us no longer but fall into the river where they float like the entrails of some fantastic creature from a science-fiction film. The people on the quayside wave us off as if we were bound for a long voyage of discovery instead of a three-hour passage to one of the most famous islands of Japan.

Yoshiyuki and I were the last passengers to get on board—the steamer was actually waiting for us, Miss Tanabe and her mother having alerted the shipping office authorities. I wonder whether they would have waited if I had been just another Japanese traveller?

Miss Tanabe is a plump amiable young lady dressed in a two-piece linen suit, a helmet hat and high-heeled shoes; she is voluble, but only in Japanese. Her mother, an elderly lady in sombre kimono, has settled on the *tatami* which one finds even here, on the deck of an excursion steamer. Miss Tanabe is one of the stay-at-home and look-after-mother Japanese girls, of whom I seem to come across so many. Only half the female population over the age of fifteen goes to work, according to the 1960 figures, or 39.1 per cent of the total working population. Three million more women are at work now than ten years ago (the population has remained fairly steady) and the trend is towards a still greater increase. There are approximately two million more women than men so that one is bound to find spinsters. This must be a great hardship for the Japanese, who are so fond of children.

The sea is as calm as a pond in a Zen garden and the great mass of Sado island a hazy dream on the horizon. The deck is crowded with groups of sight-seers, mostly middle-aged—no school children for once—seated in circles like discussion groups at an open-air seminar. Two or three old ladies are wearing gauze masks, their fear of germs extending even to sea breezes. Everybody has a *furoshiki* by his side, but these are being rapidly untied—the sea breeze is stimulating an appetite in some and a thirst in others.

A group of people seated aft look particularly gay and I watch with interest as they unpack their belongings amid peals of laughter. One of the men, a grey-haired, distinguished-looking person holding a bottle in one hand and a *sake* cup in the other, looks up and beckons me to join them. I turn to Yoshiyuki: 'Look, they are calling us.' 'Do you want to go?' 'Of course—I want to meet as many people as I can. Besides, they might be offended if I refuse.'

We pick our way between the 'discussion groups' and introduce ourselves. The members of the group do likewise. They come from Shiga prefecture and are on a three-day holiday. The 'leader' of the group, the man who invited me over, is a school-teacher; the large, florid man sitting beside him is a farmer, two others are civil servants. They have brought their wives, attractive, full-faced ladies in bright kimonos who are obviously as ready to enjoy themselves as their husbands.

Room is made for us on their *tatami*, cups are placed in our hands, *sake* and Japanese whisky poured into them alternately until we burst into song. I know before I start that the ladies will join me in 'Coming through the Rye', which they do at Japanese pace until I spur them to a rhythm more appropriate to bagpipes; finally, to their great delight, I give a demonstration of a Highland fling and a country reel. 'Why, she is as light as a fly!' exclaims the teacher. Our western dances, with their skipping and hopping, give an impression of take-off, in striking contrast to the firmly rooted Japanese dances; even in male dances, where legs are raised this is accomplished by means of slow ponderous movements, with frequent pauses in between. Dancing is the least ethereal of all the Japanese arts.

The slopes of Sado island have become clearer and we sail round the southern tip towards the flat waist in the centre; the northern end rises to heights still covered with snow. We are bound for the extreme north, off the tourist track, but first we must take an excursion bus to a point on the coast where we change into a motor-boat and then, on the last lap, a bumpy local bus to the village at the end of the road. The last two villages marked on the map are up in the hills. We hope to visit them tomorrow.

There are three excursion buses waiting for us of the type one sees all over Japan: they are painted either in cream or in green, they are comfortably and freshly upholstered, they are provided with the most talkative guides in the world and the most vocal drivers. Ours is no exception. As soon as we are settled, the green-uniformed guide begins to lecture us on the history of Sado island and to inform us that the cultural level of the islanders is particularly high thanks to the great numbers of distinguished political prisoners who have been sent here in exile throughout the centuries. Nichiren, too, was exiled here for a time and we shall visit the temple in which he stayed.

By way of relief from historical details, the guide breaks into the well-known Sado folk-song with its haunting chorus: 'Sa-Sa-Sado-Sa', syllables that mean nothing but are stressed with a playful lilt, in contrast to the otherwise sad, slow verses. The driver joins in and then a microphone is passed round to the passengers and solo pieces requested from us. I oblige in English and in Spanish, after

which an avalanche of questions pours in: Where do I come from?
Why have I come to Japan? How do I like it?

A man in the front seat gets up, announces that he is the head of a
local travel agency and that, if I have no objection, he will interview
me on behalf of everybody in the bus. 'But I want to look at the
scenery,' I murmur plaintively to Yoshiyuki. Not only is the interview prolonged but it is followed by queries from some of the
male passengers; they are farmers and want to know about farming
in England. Some of these provincial people do not know that we
cannot grow rice. I tell them that I miss cows in the landscape—
they are astonished to hear that we keep ours in the open. Japanese
cows are sedentary creatures, kept in sheds, for there is little
pasture.

At last I am free to look at the scenery. We are being taken up a
hill to see some gold mines, although very little ore is extracted
nowadays. The outside of the mine looks like a deserted ant-heap,
bare slopes upon which holes have been burrowed and flimsy
scaffolding erected. There are few people about. We get out to
visit a tiny 'gold mine museum' with models of what the mines
look like inside and specimens of minerals including samples of the
beautiful five coloured Sado marble, in the rich tones of ochre and
burnt sienna used by prehistoric artists. Outside I watch women
labourers at work on a building site, passing bricks to one another,
having baskets of cement on their backs.

There are a couple of temples on our schedule, another museum
whose speciality is model houses, and a shrine where some emperor
is buried. Our fellow-passengers crowd round them with the avid
yet blank expression peculiar to sightseers the world over.

The azaleas are in full bloom here, but they do not grow so high
as in the south. After a while, we desert the lush interior with its
thickly wooded slopes and handsome houses for the poorer villages
along the narrow strip of coast, where the houses are built together
as closely as limpets and winds are so strong that the outer walls
must be protected by thick thatched fences about ten feet tall; they
look as inadequate as woad-stained warriors lined up against steel-
helmeted and armed Roman invaders.

Limestone rocks and snow-covered mountains tower above
villages whose inhabitants cannot live by fishing because of lack of
transport, so they have scratched out paddy-fields up to the edge of
the sea—it is surprising that the salt-water does not flood them.
This is the most rugged, windswept landscape I have seen since I

arrived in Japan, where nature is generally less chaotic than in the West—an ally rather than an enemy to be placated. (Upheavals such as earthquakes and typhoons come from either below or above the earth, not from its gentle serene surface.)

Farther north, as we see from the motor-boat that bounces like a dolphin along the edge of the coast, the island defends itself against the elements by sharp red teeth of rocks bared as grimacingly as Kabuki masks; in the blue-black pools at their feet, shot through with sudden specks of vermilion, are rowing-boats from which solitary men in coolie hats probe with long poles ending in a hook for the black Sado seaweed, pronounced by connoisseurs to be particularly delectable, which fetches high prices on the Niigata market.

The motor-boat leaves us on a rocky ledge; we are the only passengers to alight, and we grope through a natural tunnel and up a steep flight of stone steps to the hill-top where we find a fishing-pool, and a marine museum full of strange creatures whose names are written in Japanese; the fish are interesting, especially the all-black ones with turned-up snouts (perhaps these black fish conceal themselves in the black seaweed) specimens of which we shall eat later on for supper, but the most fascinating objects are the gliding, viscous *murasaki-uni* that look like a cross between sea-anemones and baby octopuses, gorgeously purple and pink, chalice-shaped, sprouting a Baroque headdress of feathery tentacles like an urn of aloes in some abandoned Italian garden.

In a cafeteria beyond the museum three girls are roasting prawns and prising out the contents of large, twisted shells. They inform us that there will not be a bus for our destination before another hour, so we have time to wander along the marshy upland and watch a farmer planting soy beans in holes neatly dibbed round the edge of his rice-field. A stunted pine leans over a corner of the field, the setting sun melts into its reflection on the watery surface and, to the right, evening clouds advance to snatch the snowy peaks from view.

We shiver in the breeze, waiting for the local bus which lumbers up with a mixed load of mud-caked farming folk and round-faced schoolgirls in dark blue trousers. One of the old farmers is wearing leather shoes with a separate compartment for the big toe. The bus weaves in and out of tunnels, high above the coast where Buddhist tombstones grow like petrified forests on stony patches which cannot be used by the living, and down again to the scalloped shore dotted with fantastic rocks in cruel twisted shapes that stretch far out to sea; upon their summit a lonely pine stands out like the artist's signature.

Our host and his wife are waiting for us at the bus stop. Both they and their house are less rustic than I had expected. Our host is an ex-farmer, now a forestry officer, with an extensive knowledge of trees and plants. His wife has prepared us a large supper of the black fish we had seen swimming about in the marine museum. We eat in the room where the four of us are going to sleep because, although the rooms are large, there are not many of them. The bath is formidable and rudimentary, with an approach of insecure planks upon which I tread warily. Yoshiyuki, who is an admirable host (my male hosts are as thoughtful, if not more so, than the female ones), went on a reconnaissance tour of inspection in order to be able to warn me of possible snags. 'Don't take out the planks at the bottom of the bath,' he tells me, 'they cover the heating apparatus and you might get badly burned.' 'Don't worry,' I reply, 'my curiosity doesn't go to such lengths.'

There is no light in the bathroom (closet would be a more suitable word) and there seem to be no ledges upon which to place soap or towels, so that the operation must be conducted in steamy darkness with a great deal of groping and slithering over planks. The water is so hot that I cannot possibly get into it; I end by washing myself down progressively in two basinfuls of water.

Donning a *yukata* provided by our hosts, I slink under the heavy quilts of my *futon* between Yoshiyuki and Miss Tanabe, who refuses to come to bed with us until all the lights are out. 'I did not think that Japanese girls were like that,' I observe to Yoshiyuki, who replies, 'She is unmarried and shy.' Perhaps for the same reasons she has nightmares through the night and I am woken up several times; when Miss Tanabe is not having a nightmare, her mother on the *futon* opposite begins to talk in her sleep. Yoshiyuki, who is youthful and uncomplicated, sleeps like a submerged crocodile.

It is a warm, brilliantly sunny morning and we make off for the hills, guided by our host, who is unsuitably dressed in a dark suit, collar, tie and wide felt hat. Rice balls are provided for our picnic and we set out gaily after a breakfast of rice, eggs and Sado seaweed.

We make frequent stops on our way through the village, to greet our host's acquaintances: a man making a *tatami* mat inside his little workshop overlooking the one and only road, bent old women with faces as sharp and cracked as the rocks that guard the coast. A man invites us to see his pigsty; he is the only person in the village who possesses pigs. I admire their pink rotundities and above all the absence of unpleasant smells in the beautifully kept sty.

Beyond the pitifully small paddy-fields at the end of the village, marked by a semi-circle of towering rocks veined in cream, green and Vandyke brown, we came upon the 'sacred zone': Buddhist steles at the foot of a gnarled tree, archaic figures of the Buddha at the entrance to a grotto and, in front of it, the village crematorium, a fenced-in enclosure black with smoke and ashes; on top of the small pyre in the centre was a bowl of rice from which a pair of chopsticks protruded, signifying that a memorial service had been held there for a recently deceased person. The upright chopsticks indicated the sacred nature of the rice and was also supposed to ward off evil spirits who might wish to disturb the peace of the dead.

We padded softly along a wide stretch of fine, lion-coloured sand to where a path led upwards with the breathtaking abruptness of all Japanese hill-paths, into a scented undergrowth of wild flowers and shrubs, round the hill and up again, round another hill and down to a mountain stream, over the stream and up beside a waterfall, round and round and up and round one of the most exciting coasts I have ever seen. It was like walking through the Garden of Eden— we even met a snake—the variety of plants was endless.

Among them was a profusion of honeysuckle and rhododendron, blue flowers that resembled Anchusa but were sweetly perfumed, pink bells of Shortia, which I dug up on our return for my rockery at home, carpets of cyclamens, Japanese pepper with golden panicles of tiny, seed-like flowers and heady perfume. None of the contrived gardens of Japan can compare in richness and variety, in scent and colour, with this never-ending natural garden of Sado coast.

We found spirits again at the summit of the third hill, a small, rustic *torii* and a flight of steps leading to a Moses-like bush where the gods live and speak, and behind it a poor village whose inhabitants live by gathering seaweed along the rocky coast. We walked into a house where our host had friends; the men were out and an old crone, bent at right angles, ludicrously attired in wide knickerbockers, was watching over the tattered bits of bedding, the fly-covered tables, and an infant wrapped up in a dirty shawl under the table. She offered us tea, we ate our rice-balls, and our host bought two large bundles of black seaweed; then we turned back, to reach the village in time to catch the last bus. We are spending the night with relatives of the Tanabes.

Our new host is a farmer, who was once a mathematics teacher— 'a very severe one,' Miss Tanabe informs us, 'who often used the stick on his pupils.' Now fate has used the stick on him. He was one of the absentee landlords whom the new farm reform laws have obliged to cultivate a portion of the land he possessed before the war. The rest of the land now belongs to former tenants. Many landlords in a similar position are banding together to claim compensation from the Government; they protest that they had to sell out at ridiculously low prices.

This is a six-roomed bungalow; the bathroom is even darker and the floor more wobbly than in our former residence. Our host, a grave, earnest, bald man is interested in botany and zoology, on which subjects he possesses a number of books. Although the Japanese are said to be over 99 per cent literate, and I have no reason to doubt it, one rarely sees many books in their homes; at least, I never do. I have yet to see a library in a private home. The few books I have been shown by hosts are brought out with solemnity, like their artistic heirlooms.

We are offered a bowl of hot water before our supper. Upon inquiry we find that this is a Sado custom, intended to prepare the stomach for the meal. There are many medicinal herbs in the hills and our host is very knowledgeable on this fascinating subject. I hope that the Japanese will one day compile a book on their folk-medicine as the Chinese are doing.

The ninety-five year-old grandmother, our host's mother, sups with us before retiring to her room. She caused a sensation in her young days by eloping—in a boat—with the young man of her choice. It was one of the greatest scandals on Sado island. When the couple eventually returned they were forgiven and few people now remember the romance. Our host's wife looks less attractive, in spite of her comparative youth, than the old lady. We learn afterwards that she was a family maid, whom our host married after his first wife's death.

The sleeping arrangements here are even odder than at the first village. I share a room with Yoshiyuki. 'Is this a Sado custom?' I ask him, preparing to enter a statement to this effect in my diary.

'Not at all,' replies Yoshiyuki blandly, 'Our host believes it is a western custom. I did not say anything because I know they are short of space. It would only have complicated matters.'

Hiroyuki's village

It is Hiroyuki's day off and he is all dressed up ready to escort me to his village. His sister, who works in an office in Niigata, has also taken the day off, I learn later, to help her mother prepare an extra special lunch which is to be 'one of the great floral occasions'; Japanese meals always strike me as being more in the nature of horticultural displays than gastronomic treats.

There is a lack of initiative in Japanese kitchens—as in other aspects of their life. You never hear a Japanese housewife say, like one of her western counterparts, 'do you know, the other day I put a bit of this and a bit of that together just to see what it would taste like; Jim thought it was terrific and we've decided to call it. . . .' In Japan you cannot cook, you cannot place a flower in a vase, you cannot pour out tea, without belonging to a 'school', and following rules laid down by a teacher.

We do not go to the main station to take the train to Eguchi, but to a small toy-like station provided with long, plush-covered sofas for passengers to sit or curl up on. They are more comfortable than many a Japanese bed. One wonders whether they were made specially for this station or whether they were bought from a Japanese eccentric with a penchant for the Third Empire; there is a definite Louis-Philippe look about these unusual pieces of furniture. At home, I reflect, hooligans would long ago have ripped open the plush or chipped the carved arms, but here, in a station that caters for the peasantry, they are unstained and intact.

Passengers relax in these small trains. A peasant woman on the seat beside me puts up a dirty foot on the bench opposite. It is the first and last dirty foot I saw in Japan. Two women who have not secured a seat crouch on their heels in the gangway, as if they were on a Japanese toilet; they find this attitude relaxing. I remember what I was told some weeks ago about the possibilities of meditation in the *benjo*. . . .

Hiroyuki tells me about his family, the old uncle who dominated them until his death, his mother who was a school-teacher in Niigata and has high blood pressure, his father, an ex-civil servant, who now cultivates a plot of land in the village and advises the villagers on tax and financial matters. Hiroyuki is delightfully candid and as innocent as the virgin I am sure he is.

We get out at a country station, walk down a country lane between paddy-fields, taking a round-about route so as to pass through the village before Hiroyuki's. There seems to be a village every quarter of a mile in this wide plain. They all have one great advantage, discovered only a few years ago; natural gas, which provides every household with fuel, light and heat.

The houses are protected by trees, the vegetable plots are neatly laid out; tender plants are raised in thatched 'greenhouses' with lids raised during the day to catch the sunlight. There was nobody about, the villagers must have all been working in the rice-fields. Brightly coloured *futons* and quilts were hanging out to air on ropes outside each wooden house. It was very calm. There were no visible animals, no barking dogs.

The entrance to Hiroyuki's village was heralded by a crematorium—a more modern one than at Sado, made of concrete, with an outhouse at the back where images are kept. The village shrine, farther on, is neglected and has been turned into a playground Hiroyuki pointed this out proudly, implying that the villagers are progressive people who have outgrown the old superstitions.

We walked unceremoniously into Hiroyuki's parents' small house where I was made welcome with tea and cakes before a large meal served upon tiny lacquer trays. I discussed land reform with Hiroyuki's father, and women's clubs with his mother, an intelligent woman who asked me whether I would like to meet some farmers' wives; if so, she would summon three ladies from the local women's club to talk to me after lunch.

The three farmers' wives arrived in their working clothes and spoke freely in front of Hiroyuki's mother. They were pleased to meet a foreigner. As Hiroyuki told me, 'this is the first and probably the last time that they will have the opportunity of talking to one'. They wanted to know about the conditions of women in the West, about our children and whether they are as independent and anxious to leave the land as theirs are. One woman said that her eighteen-year-old daughter wanted to take a flat in Niigata, where she had secured a clerical job, and live alone. (Run-away children are a problem in Japan—nearly two thousand of them, from urban areas, were rounded up in Tokyo in 1961.)

Economic conditions on the farms are much better than they used to be before the war, the farmers' wives told me. Some of them have electric rice-cookers which deal rapidly with what used to be a long daily chore. Their husbands, however, expect a hot meal at home at midday and they were surprised when I told them about the women at home who take out cold meals to their men-folk at harvest-time.

They would not have the leisure to come out and talk to me in the old days, they said. Now it is better. But they rise at 4.30 a.m. and go to bed at 8.30 p.m., so they have little time for watching television. Sometimes they take the children shopping into Niigata. There are no entertainments in the village—no village hall, no parties. The members of the women's club meet to discuss the field they hold in common, whose produce they sell, distributing the proceeds among the members as pocket-money. When they attend club meetings they leave the children with the grandparents. It is 'not done' to leave them with neighbours.

I asked them about birth control (Hiroyuki blushed like a girl when he had to translate this); yes, they had had instructions from Ministry of Agriculture representatives; it was a good thing—they practised it.

Who decides the budget in their home? Do their husbands give them an allowance? It is very much a matter of individual practice. One wife said her husband was generous, another that hers was rather mean, a third that they discussed everything together. (Farm incomes in the village vary from £320 to £1,000 per annum, according to Hiroyuki's mother.) Strangely enough, when I asked them about their hobbies, they mentioned sewing, women's meetings and 'washing'! Presumably washing is so much easier than working in the fields that it is considered a pastime!

Like all Japanese, they have a highly developed artistic sense. When I suggested taking their picture in the main road before they left, they replied 'it will look nicer behind the peonies'. The peonies, too, hid the fact that they were wearing their workaday jeans.

Some weeks afterwards, Hiroyuki wrote to tell me that the rice had been transplanted and a celebration held to pray for a good harvest in the autumn; special rice cakes called *sasa-machi* had been prepared for the occasion, and wrapped in young bamboo leaves—the colour combination of green and white which symbolizes early summer—and many dishes were served to all who had helped in the work. These celebrations are tending to die out, he wrote, 'in these days of land reform and mass-communication, which have also altered the old relationships'; as he ate the cakes, he wondered how long the custom would survive. The rainy season had started and, he concluded, 'Blessings of God are rich, green fields of young reeds and willows bending to the wind. . . .'

Life in a
kindergarten

*Y*oshiyuki accompanies me to the station, a little sad that the great adventure of entertaining a foreigner is over. He cheers up, however, at the thought that hereafter he will feel less shy in a foreigner's presence. He asks me a few last searching questions about love-life in the West. From time to time he comes across expressions in western magazines which he cannot understand and his dictionary does not supply the answer. For instance, he would like to know what a 'French kiss' means. . . .

I prepare myself to face a very different group of people at my new destination: Kahoku, a small township in a rural area about one hour from Yamagata in north-eastern Honshu. My host, Mr Adachi, explained in his first letter to me, 'I am a high-school teacher teaching English and history and geography. I run Kahoku kindergarten, one of the first of its kind in my home town. About one hundred and fifty little children attend my kindergarten.

'And here is a wonderful episode about my kindergarten and England. Queen Elizabeth II gave the Christmas message in 1955 as follows: "We must adventure on if we are to make the world a better place." How inspirating her words were! At that time my home town had no kindergarten at all. I earnestly had been praying some good people would start kindergarten for not only my child but also all children of my home town. And as no one wanted to set to work in this noble project, I, school-teacher of very low salary, at last made up my mind to start the first kindergarten, however difficult the obstacles might be. And the Queen's message was always my guiding star through my efforts. Before the opening day of my kindergarten, I sent a letter of thanks for the Christmas message to the Queen directly. And the Queen sent her large-sized photograph to encourage us through the British Embassy in Tokyo. How thankful we were! Now my mother is the principal of the kindergarten and my wife teaches with four other women. If you can live with us, I think you'll have wonderful opportunities mingling with Japanese little children and primary and high school children. . . . Foreigners seldom visit northern Japan so you'll be able to collect wonderful materials not yet written by any foreigners before. . . .'

Since Mr Adachi had admitted that he was a 'school-teacher of very low salary', I wrote back suggesting that I would pay for my keep while I stayed with him and his family, but he would not hear of it.

The train journey across country from Niigata to Yamagata would take me all day, as cross-country train journeys generally do—not only in Japan—with a change at a little town called Fukushima, where I would have to wait for three hours for the limited express to Yamagata. There was nothing to see in Fukushima and nothing to do except buy *kokeshi* dolls. I asked Yushoyuki to write out a few sentences on cards so that I should know how to ask for the left-luggage, the correct platform for the train to Yamagata and an appropriate sentence to address to the porter when I wanted to get my luggage out again. I studied these phrases until I was able to repeat them with parrot fluency.

At Niigata station, passengers lined up dutifully like Balinese ducks at the edge of a rice-field; the loudspeaker relayed a slow tempo record of 'Auld Lang Syne' requested by the friends of a stout business man who stood in the centre of a bowing swarm buzzing with Japanese courtesies. Yoshiyuki put my suitcase on a rack by a window seat when the train arrived and hurried out again quickly, it is so easy to be trapped in a Japanese train's anxiety to get away on schedule. He was fighting back tears; 'modern-style' Japanese are not supposed to be sentimental.

It rained and rained and the rice-fields and muddy village lanes seemed to be peopled by armies of scarecrows in straw bonnets and cloaks; great knobbly fingers of snow still gripped the mountain-summits and ashen-grey torrents poured down their sides; the landscape is more masculine than in the south and the inhabitants are said to be less sensitive (the same north-south dichotomy exists here as in other countries although the Japanese are a fairly homogeneous race compared with those of western nations).

There was no dining-car on the train so I leaned out of the window when we stopped at a busy station where vendors were patrolling the platform with gaily wrapped luncheon boxes. There were two kinds of boxes and, not knowing the difference, I bought the one with the prettiest wrapper. Unfortunately it turned out to be a box of horrid soy-bean paste filled cakes, my particular *bête noire*. I was so hungry that I ate two of them, leaving the rest on a convenient ledge as there were no children to offer them to.

Fukushima, like most junction towns, is particularly unattractive and on that particular day its unpaved streets were full of large-sized puddles that made progress difficult for anyone but a kangaroo. One wonders how many people develop suicidal tendencies during a visit to a town like this, where even the *sushi* is third-rate and coffee bars bleak and cold. There is absolutely nothing to do. No museum, no art gallery, no public library to wander into. In the absence of any cultural attractions it would be merciful if the authorities were to abandon hypocritical pretence and allow involuntary visitors between trains to sink into the temporary oblivion provided by a gin-parlour, opium den or brothel, as (except for the second) were once found in Far-West frontier towns. As these are taboo, people prowl through the streets thinking up new and awful vices—so far as one can judge from their taut, brooding faces.

I stopped a man to ask him where I could find a coffee bar; but he fled like a wild thing and people looked at me reproachfully as if I had been importuning an innocent male. Few people speak English in these out-of-the-way places and they are terrified of losing face when one addresses them in their language. Eventually, however, I found an amiable shopkeeper who escorted me to an espresso where I read the translation of a Japanese novel over coffee and the chocolate-filled sponge cake which one finds all over Japan, a little staler than usual in Fukushima. I could have written letters but I did not dare to for fear that they might reflect my temporary depression. So far I have been fortunate. I have not had many rainy days in Japan. One of my friends came here in the summer and it rained every day; it has given her an ineradicably jaundiced view of this country to which she has vowed never to return.

I had reeled off the sentences inscribed on Yoshiyuki's cards with such ease that the porters and ticket-collectors at Fukushima were under the false impression that I could speak Japanese, and they replied in long, incomprehensible phrases to which I could only shake my head and sigh. There was no porter visible, but a laughing ticket-collector (a very rare bird) winkled one from his hide-out after about ten minutes—a dignified, sallow-faced, inscrutable little man who bore himself with the nobility of a Samurai retainer, and carried my Marks and Spencer suitcase as if it were a gold-embossed casket.

I do not know whether I have been particularly fortunate in my experiences with Japanese porters, but I have invariably found them of a gentle, almost paternalistic nature, too courteous to stare at the tips I give them before they say 'thank you' as western porters are rudely inclined to do.

English porters are fairly helpful as a rule, provided one treats them as equals; French porters, in wide blue baggy trousers and open-necked shirts, breathing fumes of *pinard* down one's neck, look more like dock-hands and they are liable to treat customers and their luggage with ill-disguised contempt; Spanish and Italian porters bear down upon one with ferocious intensity and the light of battle in their eyes, prepared to use your luggage as a weapon against clamouring rivals. They usually find time to tell you their always tragic life-history between platforms; with Japanese porters, however, one feels that they would rather commit old-fashioned *hara-kiri* than descend to such a personal level.

Yamagata is a pleasant, modern town surrounded by hills and ski slopes, the centre of a wide agricultural district famous for its fruit, especially cherries, well provided with hot springs, temples, *kokeshi* makers, potters, schools and Rotary clubs, most of whom have never had the opportunity to meet a foreigner.

Mr and Mrs Adachi were waiting for me at the station with a newspaper reporter who took a picture of us exchanging hand-shakes and toothy smiles for the benefit of the local Press, and began to interview me as we walked out of the station and into a cafeteria where Mr Adachi ordered bacon and eggs. (It is the

Japanese custom not to ask guests what they would like, but to order for them.)

Mr Adachi, a tall, lean, bespectacled, earnest-looking man in his thirties, is obviously accustomed to assume command and give orders. His wavy-haired, rosy-cheeked little wife, in western-style dress, fluttered round helpfully as the second-in-command. She is gay, friendly, and intelligent, an ex-graduate of Sendai University. The couple were married through a *nakodo*; northern Japan is conservative and traditions are adhered to more strictly than in the south. Mrs Adachi is the daughter of a confectioner. 'That is why,' said her husband blandly, 'she has such bad teeth. The *nakodo* said to me afterwards, when I told him that I had had to take her to the dentist, "you should have looked at her teeth during your first interview", but that would have been rather difficult—after all, I was interviewing a woman, not a horse.' It is not unusual for a Japanese husband to denigrate his wife in public—it is considered to be a proof of modesty.

There is not much room on our cafeteria table for three plates of bacon and eggs, so Mr Adachi leaves me with the reporter and moves to an adjacent table. His wife, who does not appear to be eating—she is not used to western-style food and cutlery—persuades him to return as his services are required to interpret questions and answers. The young reporter is so astounded that a foreigner should have chosen to visit Yamagata that he asks me over and over again: 'What made you come here?'

We drive to Kahoku in the Mayor's car, graciously lent for the occasion of the 'Arrival of the First Foreigner in Kahoku'; Mr Adachi thinks we should stop at the Mayor's house and pay our respects to him. 'Please thank him for the car,' he urges me peremptorily. We cross a well-cultivated plain of rice-fields in which fruit trees have been planted upon circular plots of land well above water-level. Fan-shaped bunches of rice straw are suspended from the outer walls of the farmhouses to dry in the sun. Piles of faggots, neatly wrapped in sheets of bark, are stacked in the corners of courtyards. A woman in a straw bonnet regulates the traffic beside a road-mending site. A wide river reflects snow-capped hills between two waving sheets of a rose madder-coloured aquatic plant. . . .

It is dark by the time we reach the Zen Buddhist temple where the Mayor of Kahoku lives with his family of willowy, bowing females who advance to greet us and usher us on to the *tatami*. The Mayor

is a jolly, chubby, broad-faced man of about fifty, who is so
popular with the local community that he has been re-elected
Mayor for sixteen years running. He is the President of various
associations and takes a lively interest in the people's welfare. Now
he is about to leave for Tokyo on business. I venture to ask him a
few questions about Zen and he informs me that he belongs to the
'non-thinking' school of meditation, which obviously suits him
for he looks refreshingly unperturbed. In return for my interest in
Zen he passes some flattering remarks about England and Christianity, and deplores that the Japanese are 'losing their good
qualities'. I tell him, to console him, that our priests at home are
making the same complaints about us and prevent myself from
adding, 'and they have been saying so since the Middle Ages'.

The Adachis' kindergarten is the last building in the town except
for a girls' junior high school, at the end of a stony road leading to a
village at the foot of the hills. The Adachis live in a two-storeyed
whitewashed wooden house which they wish to transfer to the
opposite side of the compound when they are ready with their
ambitious plans to build a swimming-pool and a properly laid out
garden. In the meantime there is a playing-ground with a couple
of swings in it and an L-shaped one-storeyed kindergarten, with a
large hall provided with a stage, cloakroom and toilets in the short
side of the L and classrooms in the long side. To my surprise, a
large Union Jack is flying from a pole in the playground—one of
two borrowed by Mr Adachi in my honour from the British
Embassy in Tokyo, who took the opportunity to send him an
illustrated pamphlet in Japanese about England. This caught Mr
Adachi's fancy so much that he asked for a hundred copies for
distribution among his various acquaintances. The Embassy, with
a typically English mistrust of enthusiasm, replied that they could
only spare sixty.

A stony path leads to the entrance of Mr Adachi's house where
his mother, a friendly, sprightly lady in her sixties, sportily dressed
in trousers and a pullover, is waiting to greet us; also his delightful
little daughters: eight year-old Isako with bright, observant eyes,
who will later paint a vivid portrait of me with special emphasis
upon my necklace and ear-rings, and four year-old Mariko, the
pampered 'baby', affectionate and cuddly as a teddy-bear, her hair
cut in a monkey-fur fringe like a Japanese doll; she, too, will paint
my portrait in a bold brilliant colour scheme, making my eyes very
big and blue; only one kindergarten child will notice that they are

green and be daring enough to paint them in what is for the Japanese an unusual colour.

Mr Adachi had warned me that there might be a 'small delegation' of junior high school children waiting for me to say a few, a very few words. . . . There they are, kneeling with folded hands, in a semi-circle on the *tatami*, reverent as a congregation. The first thing they want to know, like their fellows everywhere else, is 'what do I think of Japan?' They are the first of many contingents of all ages whom I shall see and speak to both here and at their schools in the surrounding countryside. Mr Adachi is determined that as many of the younger generation as possible shall hear an English accent for the first and perhaps last time in their lives. In the more progressive schools I shall be tape-recorded, and asked to read stories, which will probably be played back endlessly to goodness knows how many classes of Japanese children whose pronunciation is often clearer than a European's and more comprehensible.

'Please take your bath,' says Mr Adachi peremptorily; his wife leads me to a steam-filled little room in which I find a tall wooden barrel with a stool beside it.

My bedroom is upstairs; there is a tall lacquered clothes-horse in it upon which I can hang my clothes, a low table, and a dressing-table; grandmother thinks I might like an armchair, but I assure her that I am quite happy without one. I tell them that I eat very little breakfast, but I know they will refuse to believe me. I can see that Mrs Adachi junior is going to worry and be nervous wondering whether 'she is doing the right thing' and I entreat her, through her husband, to take my presence calmly; it is of no avail, she is too excited to be able to sleep.

I cannot get to sleep for a long time myself; a strong wind has arisen and the wooden house shakes to its foundations in the most alarming manner. 'It could blow down any moment,' I say to myself, 'I wonder what happens during a typhoon or an earthquake? It's quite dangerous. . . .' Two days later, when I casually ask Mr Adachi whether they have many earthquakes in Kahoku he replies: 'Why, didn't you feel the earthquake we had the first night you came?' They occur so frequently that nobody thought it worth mentioning.

Sunday morning. The sun is pouring through the thin cotton curtains. The whole house is astir and muffled sounds of hammering and nailing reach me on my *futon* where I wait, lazily, until I hear Mr Adachi's voice calling from outside: 'Miss Epton, please come to breakfast.' As I guessed, it is a large one. Two charming young kindergarten teachers help to serve me. One of them is a local girl who has recently returned from a month's experience of unhappy marriage in Tokyo. She was betrothed through a *nakodo* to a rich philanderer who made her so miserable that she asked for a divorce. 'He probably thought,' said Mr Adachi, 'that an innocent country girl would make less fuss about his escapades but he was wrong, because Yoshiko has a mind of her own and she refused to be treated with such a lack of dignity.'

After breakfast I go upstairs to put on a party dress for the 'official reception' in the kindergarten hall, to which the Press and the Yamagata television reporters have been invited. The occasion of my visit coincides with the school's third anniversary so it is a double fête. As I sit on the flat cushion in front of the dressing-table and bend forward to pull on my stockings I hear an ominous crack across my back followed by a flash of such acute pain that for five minutes I remain paralysed and unable to straighten myself. Lumbago—today of all days! After what seems like an eternity I succeed in putting on my stockings and raising myself, but every step I take is agony.

I *must* walk over to the reception hall, I *must* be present at a performance prepared and rehearsed for weeks! Sheer will-power propels me and I hope that my short, slow steps will be taken for a dignified sense of occasion.

The kindergarten hall is full of chubby, golden-skinned children who behave much better than similarly captive children at home; rows of mothers squat in the background, television cameras flash in our faces, reporters ask endless questions, the kindergarten's executive committee huddle together for a group photograph, Mr Adachi controls us all with superb poise, Mrs Adachi, her mother-in-law and the kindergarten teachers direct the children with admirable precision and good humour—all goes well, not a tear is shed, no child disgraces itself during the three-hour performance.

I am formally introduced and I stand on the platform a little stiffly to make a brief speech which is translated to three times its original length by Mr Adachi; the children sing a welcoming song specially composed for Nina-*san* in the course of which they bow till their round foreheads touch the *tatami*; and they conclude by waving little hand-made paper Union Jacks and Japanese flags—

crosses and rising suns mingle fraternally in their tiny hands but they are soon removed by prudent teachers who rightly fear that the game might get out of hand.

The show begins—each class will display its dancing and singing prowess. A row of three-year-olds in flowered hats and *happis* enjoy their own performance; one little girl removes her hat and pushes it playfully over to her boy-friend in the front row of the audience; shocked by her lack of discipline, he solemnly pushes it back to her, stretching across the stage to do so, but she will have none of it and kicks it back to him with a loud chuckle. A ballet teacher from Yamagata introduces a western item; she is followed by the four-year-olds dressed up as elves and rabbits.

I am presented with a magnificent gift parcel, which contains a round cradle with a Japanese baby doll comfortably snuggled between blankets like a bird in a nest. This kind of cradle was in use in this region until only a few years ago.

At noon, we walk back to the Adachis' house where a select group of adults connected with the administration of the kindergarten, and the ballet teacher from Yamagata, sit over a bowl of noodles and question me about my travels. They are particularly interested in my visit to Yalta and ask me many questions about conditions in Russia.

My host studied for a time in a Biblical seminar in Tokyo; he was a Christian, but he 'lapsed' after a disagreement with a Baptist minister, who prevented a Japanese colleague from attending his mother's Buddhist funeral rites. The Japanese, who are so easygoing about such things, cannot understand an intolerant attitude; rigidity does the Christians much harm in Japan.

When the guests have gone, Mr Adachi shows me several albums of Press cuttings and letters which he has sent to various newspapers over a period of years. He is evidently *un auteur manqué*, and a would-be world traveller condemned by economic conditions to remain in Kahoku. One of his first letters, written when he was fifteen years old, was a plea to be allowed to join General Franco's army; a few years later he wrote to Hitler to upbraid him for his treatment of the Jews; lately there had been some correspondence with a college in Rumania which offered free language courses to foreigners—but they did not offer to pay for the fare and this Mr Adachi could not afford. Mr Adachi is too lively for his humdrum life. 'Too much peace, too much routine,' he complained in a recent letter. 'I get up at the same hour, go to my school at the same hour, do the same school teaching, meet the same people, return home by the same bus. . . . While I am in the same environment, Algeria won independence on July 4th and yesterday was French National Day. Whenever I hear the calling voice of revolution my childish young heart burns for something new and adventurous and I want earnestly to shed my blood for something noble. I am always in *Westward Ho!*'

More guests arrived—a botanist, who has promised me some hill-plants to take home, an old gentleman who dabbles in historical records and wants to interest the authorities in a museum, a doctor who invites us to dinner at his home, a soy sauce manufacturer, and a *sake* blender who invite me to inspect their respective factories. . . .

At last I tell my hosts about my lumbago and inquire about a masseur; the doctor lends me his car and off I go, wrapped up in a *yukata* and wearing *geta*. A knot of people at the gate are waiting to have a look at the 'foreigner'; they will become a permanent fixture. In addition, I shall have a retinue of schoolgirls whenever I walk out of the house and most people will down tools during my progress, through Kahoku. There is nothing hostile or jeering about the way they stare; on the contrary, everybody smiles and the atmosphere could not be friendlier.

We drink a bowl of tea with the masseur and his family round the *kotatsu* before the massage session begins. Another patient, a sturdy labourer, joins us. The masseur looks very Japanese but—he has blue eyes! This is the first time I have seen such a phenomenon.

After we have drunk more tea, the masseur leads me to a side room where I stretch on a camp bed. He proceeds to massage me, very decorously, without asking me to remove my *yukata*; Japanese massage is extremely thorough; nothing is left out. Toes and fingers are wiggled and twisted and the session lasts a long time. Suddenly the masseur interrupted his massage of my spine, moved across to a side-table, and began to extract some chinky objects from a glass jar; as I was lying on my stomach I could not see what they were. Then, to my horror, he placed something cold on my spine and began to *hammer it in*.

What is the Japanese for 'What are you doing?' I *had* read the phrase somewhere. By the time I had puzzled and failed to remember, the masseur had hammered in a few more tacks—that is what they felt like—at other spots along my spine. Was this a form of acupuncture? Anyway, there was nothing I could do about it. Fortunately the masseur did not apply anything as drastic as *moxa*, a herb which is burned on the skin and leaves scars. I cannot truthfully report that the massage cured my pain, although I was eager to have faith in the 'tin-tack' treatment. I was informed later that a fine needle had been inserted into my flesh to stimulate the 'fatigue spots' on the spinal column. In the end a strip of medicated plaster and a rest on the *futon* cleared up my lumbago.

There is another party in the reception hall this evening, a 'mothers' do' at which I am asked to speak. What will interest them? I talk about women's activities at home, my impressions of Japan . . . but when it is over and I sit among them, they pluck up courage to ask me the sort of questions they did not dare voice when I was on the platform. What they want to know is: 'Do I perm my hair? Am I wearing evening dress? Do I always wear nail polish?' They laugh when I tell them I wear less nail polish than the ladies in Tokyo. A masculine type of woman with her hair pulled back into a tight bun dances a spirited Samurai dance, followed by a firefighter's dance, with *brio* and fine, sweeping gestures. Mr Asahi, the soy sauce manufacturer, who is an administrator of the kindergarten, shows a colour film of last year's outing into the hills.

I started the day by visiting the kindergarten after breakfast and, at Mr Adachi's request, teaching the children a few words of English, with gestures to help them remember. They pick them up at once. Then I watch them dancing a Japanese variant of 'Oranges and Lemons'.

Grandmother tells me over a cup of tea that she belongs to the New Religion called Risshokoseikai, or 'Association for Success' and she makes a mild attempt to interest me in it. As soon as I begin to ask precise questions, however, she becomes vague, says that 'it is difficult to explain' and suggests I visit the headquarters of the association when I am in Tokyo. I am told that this is one of the most vigorous of the New Religions, with one and a half million members, thousands of trained teachers and many branches. Its doctrine is based on the Lotus Sutra.

I have begun to make acquaintance with the neighbours in our road. Immediately opposite the Adochis' house is a farmhouse where the women make *zori*, or straw sandals, from rice straw. These are sent to a factory down the road to be pressed and finished. Many women make a few extra yen by this kind of

homework. In the factory, the *zori* are put into long tins shaped
like old-fashioned irons, which are piled up and put into an oven
to be heated and straightened out. A doctor lives opposite, in an
elegant modern villa. He and his wife have invited us to dinner;
one of the guests is to be the post-mistress, a Tokyo University
graduate who speaks English.

We stroll into the one and only bookshop which sells mostly
magazines (only ten copies a month of the more 'intellectual' type
of magazine like *Chuo-Koron*) and textbooks. There are also a few
Japanese translations of Russian, French, English and American
classics.

I pay my respects at the local Municipal office and meet a Mr
Hayashi, who is also the priest of the local Shinto shrine. Every
September, at the annual festival, he dances an ancient Dragon
dance which has been handed down from father to son since the
eighth century when it came to Japan—first to Kyoto—via China
and before that, India. Since I shall not be here in September he
very kindly offers to dress up in the fearsome mask and fine silk
garments preserved for the annual occasion, summon the musicians, and perform the dance in his own home beside the shrine;
he also shows me a national treasure of a scroll, dating from the
sixteenth century, representing different phases of the Dragon
dance.

Today we went into Yamagata. The 'authorities' sent a car, a
driver and the head of the local cultural centre with whom we
visited the temple of Yamadera, beautifully set among pines and
cypresses above a mountain stream, a *kokeshi* maker by the bridge,
and a potter who makes beautiful greenish-blue ware; each piece
comes out of the kiln in a different colour so that customers cannot
make repeat orders; the son shows us round as his father is at an
exhibition. 'Now that he is famous he goes out a lot and neglects
his pottery,' said the son sadly.

In Yamagata, we dined with the editor of the local newspaper,
Mr Ohira, in a western-style restaurant at the top of the newspaper
building which also contains an art school, a domestic science
school and a private radio station—all owned by the same pro-
prietor, all very modern and in good taste. Before this I saw the
Mayor, who gave me a bronze medal on a chain and with whom I
had a long conversation about *wabi* and *sabi*, those peculiar
Japanese characteristics which are said to enshrine the Japanese

heart and soul; nobody can define these terms. It is part of the mystery. Like the so-called 'eternal feminine', I strongly suspect that it is a myth behind which nationalists conceal themselves in a fog of hazy notions.

There was a Congress of kindergarten teachers on in town to which I was dragged to say 'a few words'. I spoke for five minutes flat to ten rows of solemn-looking young women in kimono, kneeling on *tatami*. Among the organizers was a mild-looking Japanese Anglican minister who came up to me afterwards and asked me in a soft voice if I would like to look at his church—it was only just down the street—'because it may remind you of your country,' he said. It *did* remind me of England. It was an exact replica, in miniature, of one of our less attractive types of Victorian parish churches. It had been built in 1910 by an English clergyman. 'Have you a large congregation?' I asked the Rev. Kataoka. 'About one hundred and fifty,' he replied with a wry smile, adding quickly, 'but they are very sincere.' As we drove back to Kahoku Mr Adachi said 'The Reverend Kataoka is a good man. During the occupation, when some of the American troops were very haughty and arrogant with us, he preached to them at their camp and their behaviour altered in consequence.' 'Perhaps you would have liked to talk with him a little longer, about Christianity in Japan,' suggested Mrs Adachi with friendly tolerance.

I have spoken to at least five hundred school children during the last two days, and given evening classes to a few scores more at the Kahoku kindergarten. I have also spoken to the local women's club. Their leaders asked more intelligent questions than the usual average. They are worried about young people, their delinquency, the violence shown on television. If they hoped to look to us for guidance they were sadly mistaken, as I had to tell them: We too would like to know the answers.

Tonight, we dined in the highly individualistic house of Dr Miyamoto, who has the striking physique of a Kabuki actor, with brilliant eyes and an expressive face. The doctor is a man of learning, taste and originality. The furniture in his dining-room has been made to his own design in a mellow, golden-coloured wood with a deep grain. It includes a swing-chair suspended from the ceiling, in which he and his patients can relax and meditate. Modern paintings on the walls alternate with ancient scrolls; he has a unique collection of talismans from various shrines. In my honour he burns a little New Year's incense and explains that at the end of every year poets send verses to the Emperor who selects the best; the winning poem serves as an inspirational basis for the manufacture of that New Year's incense, to be burned during the New Year celebrations; it is sold in shops with a copy of the poem.

The doctor is also a *gastronome*. We drove with him out to the country before dinner and walked down to a pool by the river where a man was ordered to catch rainbow trout for our supper. He dipped two fishing nets into the river and brought them up again full of wriggling pink and silver fish.

A couple of visitors were announced while we were having dinner. They turned out to be a schoolgirl, aged thirteen, accompanied by her father; she had heard about me and called at the Adachis' house before being directed to Doctor Miyamoto's. The object of her visit was to present me with a lantern-decoration, made of coloured paper fashioned into the shape of cranes—the bird of peace and happiness—as a token of goodwill. This *objet d'art et de patience* had taken her over two months to make.

After dinner the doctor took us to see one of his patients, a man who had recently had one lung removed and was still very weak. He had lost his job and was incapable of doing hard work so the doctor taught him how to make dolls. He has now become adept and has more orders from department stores all over the country than he can fill. The man did not seem to be at all well, but our visit cheered him. The doctor bought several dolls for me and I told his patient that I would show them to people in England and that his fame would spread overseas. It was thoughtful of the doctor to take me. Wherever I go in Japan, I come across similar gestures. Oddly enough they are less marked in the personal relationships between husbands and wives which vary from house to house, but the tendency is to follow the old traditional ways; husbands rarely take their wives out. Here in Kahoku I have been to two households of young married couples where the husband is tyrannical and domineering, and one where he is helpful and affectionate; I have seen one middle-aged husband who is charming to strangers but who ignores his wife and hardly ever replies when she speaks to him, while yet another educated middle-aged husband lets his wife do all the talking and remains, self-effaced, in the background.

Today we lunched and bathed at a charming little hot springs hotel at the foot of one of the many cone-shaped hills that surround Kahoku plain; the idea was to have a quiet day and a siesta after an exquisite lunch, but the advent of a boisterous singing party in the adjacent room made this impossible.

Mrs Adachi took me off for a bath before lunch; there were several bathrooms. Downstairs we were shown a glorious jade-green pool situated in the centre of a large tiled room; but there was some snag about our using this—for a reason which I could not follow, so the attendant took us upstairs and slid open a door, revealing a plump, naked gentleman of mature years sitting reflectively on the edge of a bean-shaped pool; he looked up inquiringly, without evincing the slightest embarrassment, and a few words were exchanged—Mrs Adachi was in a flutter, the gentleman perfectly calm. Mrs Adachi bowed and shut the sliding door firmly. Then she hurried back to our private room where Mr Adachi was talking with her father, the ex-confectioner now turned farmer—who was to lunch with us. 'Ah,' said Mr Adachi gravely after she had explained the situation in rapid Japanese, 'this is a mixed bathing-place. You will have to wait a little.' 'If your wife believes that I object to the old man in the pool,' I said, trying to be helpful and broad-minded, 'tell her that I do not mind at all. He could be our grandfather.' 'Maybe,' answered Mr Adachi, 'but Japanese grandfathers have bright eyes. No, no, you had better wait.'

Mrs Adachi's father, a sturdy, tough, sixty-three year-old little man with a weather-beaten face, drove us over to his farm in his lorry. He had turned to farming during the war when sugar was rationed and now, he said, nothing would ever persuade him to go back to an indoor life. He keeps abreast of the latest developments by attending an agricultural conference in Tokyo every summer.

My attention was drawn to a curious object protruding from the summit of the rockery in his azalea-filled garden. It looked like a tombstone. Could it be a tomb in memory of his first wife, Mrs Adachi's mother? 'It isn't a tomb at all,' it was explained to me, 'it is a memorial offered by successful employees of the confectioner's shop who have gone into business on their own account and are grateful for their ex-boss's help and tuition. They did not want to wait until he was dead to make a public tribute.'

The ex-confectioner smiled with affectionate pride as he contemplated this unique monument. 'Now come and look at my chickens,' he said, leading us along a little path to his latest interest: a multi-storeyed, self-revolving chicken apartment house (made in Japan) full of gleaming white Leghorns. 'See how good these are,' he said, 'the house revolves automatically—each chicken has an apartment to herself; as the house turns very slowly, the chicken enjoys a change of scenery which prevents her from becoming neurotic.'

Last night we had a splendid farewell party at the Adachis' house, one of the rare mixed parties I have been to in Japan—rare even for the Japanese. Each guest performed—a song or a dance— and Mr Asahi of the soy bean sauce factory gave an original ventriloquist turn, with a *kokeshi* doll painted on his knee and wrapped round with a scarf. *Sake* flowed freely and jokes became almost Rabelaisian. Little Mariko fell asleep and had to be carried up to bed. She was a picture in her diminutive kimono. Even I put on a kimono.

Some unknown person has chalked up on the board in the school ground, in large characters: 'Goodby (sic) Miss Epton, Please come again!' I only wish I could.

June 4th   This is my last day in Tokyo and I nearly had a heart attack. When I called for my air tickets at the office of Japan Airlines, the smiling little girl behind the desk remarked sweetly: 'I suppose you have had your Alien Registration card stamped?' 'My *what*?' I gasped, 'I have never heard of such a card.' 'You must have one, with three photographs—since you have been in Japan longer than sixty days,' she chirruped delightedly, 'and it must be stamped before you leave by the Municipal office of the ward in which you are residing.' 'I am leaving tomorrow—and I have no spare photographs,' I said weakly. 'You will not be allowed to leave unless your card is stamped,' said the little girl with Teutonic inexorability.

Fortunately the Foreign Office came to my rescue. They took photographs on the spot, and they sent me to the Municipal office with a courteous young travel agent who deals with their official guests. 'Why have you not come before?' asked the severe bespectacled official behind the Aliens Registration desk. 'Because I did not know I had to,' I replied. 'Then you must write down on this piece of paper why you did not come,' he insisted. 'Why?' I wanted to know. No explanation was deemed necessary. I supposed it

must be some form of penance. I read many months later that
defaulting aliens are often required to write abject confessions to
the authorities; this 'low posture' ensures instantaneous forgive-
ness. My own confession was illegible to the official who, after
scrutinizing it, asked me to write it over again in block letters.
'While I make out your card,' he said in a mollified tone of voice,
'please correct my English,' and he handed me a translation he had
made of an article in a Japanese newspaper, together with a red
pencil.

A queue began to form behind us as I pored over the official's
homework, a story about a boss, his subordinate and an invitation
to a classy golf club which the subordinate modestly refused while
appreciating the sentiments expressed by his employer. 'Here is
your card,' said the official with a smile and a bow. 'And here is
your corrected translation,' I said, returning the smile and the bow.
I left him poring over my corrections, while the queue of aliens
looked at me with murder in their cold, light eyes.

The adventure is over and with a heavy heart I say my last
sayonaras. I have begun to love the country and the people who
opened their doors and—I believe—their hearts to me with such
frankness and generosity. I live for the day when I shall be able to
return, stand before the *tatami* and cry out joyfully: *Tadaima*!

Index